Ethnic Minorities and Dutch as a Second Language

STUDIES ON LANGUAGE ACQUISITION

This series will focus on both first language acquisition and second/foreign language learning. It will include studies on language acquisition in educational settings, first/second/foreign language loss, and early bilingualism. High quality dissertations and other individual works will be considered for publication, and also collections of papers from international workshops and conferences. The primary goal of the series is to draw international attention to current research in the Netherlands on language acquisition.

Editors of SOLA:
Guus Extra, Tilburg University
Ton van der Geest, Groningen University
Peter Jordens, Nijmegen University

Guus Extra & Ton Vallen (Eds.)

Ethnic Minorities and Dutch as a Second Language

1985
Foris Publications
Dordrecht - Holland/Cinnaminson - U.S.A.

Published by:
Foris Publications Holland
P.O. Box 509
3300 AM Dordrecht, The Netherlands

Sole distributor for the U.S.A. and Canada:
Foris Publications U.S.A.
P.O. Box C-50
Cinnaminson N.J. 08077

CIP-DATA

Ethnic

Ethnic minorities and Dutch as a second language / Guus Extra and Ton Vallen
(eds.). – Dordrecht [etc.]: Foris. – (Studies on Language Acquisition; 1)
With ref.
ISBN 90-6765-114-1
SISO * 838.5 UDC 803.931-054.6
Subject heading: Dutch language for ethnic minorities;
research.

ISBN 90 6765 114 1 (Paper)

© 1984 Foris Publications - Dordrecht

Printed in the Netherlands

Table of Contents

VI

Acknowledgements

We want to thank Pieter Nieuwint and Marianne Sanders for their assistance in the translation of some of the manuscripts, and the Department of Language and Literature of Tilburg University for its financial support of editing this volume.

Guus Extra & Ton Vallen
Tilburg, March 1985

Language and Ethnic Minorities in The Netherlands: Current Issues and Research Areas

Guus Extra & Ton Vallen

0. INTRODUCTION

In the Netherlands Dutch may be characterized as the language with the highest social prestige; it has the largest number of speakers and the most official functions. However, for many people (children, adolescents and adults) Dutch is not the language of their primary socialization process: they learn and use Dutch as a *second* language. It is often erroneously suggested that this is a recent phenomenon. For a long time the Netherlands has been a multilingual society in which both indigenous and non-indigenous minority languages are spoken. The former are regional varieties (with or without a 'language' status: cf. Frisian as against the Limburg dialect) which lead a far livelier existence than is often supposed; the latter are language varieties which have been introduced into Dutch society from outside. Even before World War II Chinese, Italian and Polish were home languages in the Netherlands.

Language is a directly observable and crucial factor in the interaction between ethnic minorities and their Dutch surroundings: on the one hand, the chances of success of ethnic minorities in education and social participation depend to a large extent on their command of Dutch, and on the other hand the (re)valuation of ethnic minority languages within Dutch society runs up against opposition and limits. In schools there is a growing presence of a generation of pupils to whom the Dutch educational system with its preponderantly monolingual and normative tradition has hardly been geared as yet.

In this introductory contribution we shall pay attention to the composition and size of ethnic minorities in the Netherlands (1), to the main characteristics of research in this field in general (2), to linguistically-oriented research areas in particular (3), and, finally, to the contents of this Volume (4).

1. COMPOSITION AND SIZE OF ETHNIC MINORITIES IN THE NETHERLANDS

Like most other Western and Northern European nations the Netherlands has, over the last decades, been faced with a rapidly growing number of immigrants who, for whatever reason, have taken up temporary or permanent residence.

In the first place we refer to people whose origins lie in the ex-colonies, especially those who are natives of the former Dutch Indies (the present Republic of Indonesia), Surinam and the Dutch Antilles. Within the group that hails from the Dutch Indies, the Moluccans take up a special position, not only in ethnic, cultural and religious respects, but also because of their involuntary 'repatriation' to the Netherlands in 1951.

The second large group of immigrants hails from Mediterranean countries. Most of them are natives of Turkey and Morocco. Considerably smaller is the number of Spaniards, Italians, Yugoslavs, Portuguese, Greeks, Tunisians and Algerians.

A third group is formed by political refugees. These are mainly natives of Latin or Middle America, Vietnam or Eastern Europe.

The picture of the multi-ethnic Dutch society can only become complete if we further include the Chinese (originating from various countries) and the immigrants from other Western European countries and from North America.

In sum, of the more than 14 million inhabitants of the Netherlands about 7 per cent is of non-indigenous origin. In Table 1 a survey is given of the sizes of the most important ethnic (and cultural, as the case may be) minorities in the Netherlands, in January 1983. The data are mainly derived from Vermeer (1981), Schakel (1984; 1985), Van Praag (1984), Penninx (1984) and from various publications of the Central Bureau of Statistics, e.g. Statistisch Zakboek 1984. As constitutional criteria for Surinamers, Antilleans, Moluccans and, to a degree, Chinese are lacking, their numbers are based on estimates. The same goes for the number of people from the Dutch Indies, virtually all of whom are Dutch nationals.

In the following section some demographic data regarding participation of ethnic minorities within Dutch educational institutions are presented. We restrict ourselves to infant and primary school education (4 to 12-year-olds), since most of the contributions in this Volume are concerned with these initial educational levels. The most recent figures date from the schoolyear 1982–1983 (CBS 1984). In this schoolyear about 6% of the pupils in infant school (n=398,804) and about 5% of the pupils in primary education (n=1,201,512) had non-Dutch nationality. This does not comprise children of ex-colonial origin. Their numbers are not precisely known;

Table 1: Sizes of the most important (n > 1000) ethnic/cultural minorities in the Netherlands in January 1983.

Source country	Number January 1983
Ex-colonies	
Surinam	185,000
Dutch Antilles	42,200
Moluccan	35,000
Dutch Indies (excl. Moluccan)	250,000
Mediterranean countries:	
Turkey	154,200 (Jan. 1984: 156,000)
Morocco	101,500 (Jan. 1984: 107,000)
Spain	22,100
Italy	20,600
Yugoslavia	13,900
Portugal (incl. Cap Verdian Islands)	9,300
Greece	4,100
Tunesia	2,700
Refugees:	
Hungary	4,000
Czechoslovakia	2,000
Poland	1,500
Turkish and Armenian Christians	3,700 (Jan. 1984)
Chile	2,000
Vietnam	6,000
Other countries	4,800 (Jan. 1984)
Chinese (excl. Surinam and Vietnam)	
People's Republic of China	
Taiwan	
Malaysia	
Singapore	30,000
Hong-Kong	
Other countries:	
Federal Republic of Germany	42,900 (Jan. 1984: 45,000)
United Kingdom	39,300 (Jan. 1984: 42,000)
Belgium	23,600 (Jan. 1984: 24,000)
United States	11,000
France	6,500
Ireland	2,100
Denmark	1,200
Other American countries	8,000
Other Asian countries + Oceania	30,000
Other African countries	4,000
Caravan Dwellers	17,000

4   *Guus Extra & Ton Vallen*

they have either Dutch nationality or more than one nationality, or they are stateless, as, for instance, most Moluccans. In 1982-1983 the total number of children of ex-colonial origin was an estimated 2200 for infant education and 5600 for ordinary primary education, not including the children of Moluccan origin and those who hail from the Dutch Indies.

Table 2: Numbers of ethnic/cultural minorities in Dutch infant schools and ordinary primary schools during the school year 1982-1983.

Source country	Number of children in infant schools	Number of children in ordinary primary schools
Turkey	8,808	22,225
Morocco	6,790	14,929
Spain	748	2,344
Italy	500	1,903
Yugoslavia	661	1,249
Portugal (incl. Cap Verdian Islds)	637	1,493
Greece	141	552
Tunesia	148	128
Chile	76	261
Vietnam	317	928
People's Republic of China Taiwan Malaysia Singapore Hong-Kong	977	1,905
Federal Republic of Germany	649	2,261
United Kingdom	601	1,633
Belgium	219	655
United States	227	445
France	160	238
Ireland	15	56
Denmark	13	56
Other European countries	200	677
Other North American countries	46	166
Other South American countries	121	363
Other Asian countries	989	1,889
Other African countries	160	280
Australia	21	82

The number of schoolchildren born from ethnic minority groups varies per region and place, of course. Outside of the big cities and the industrial areas the percentage is often considerably lower than the national average. In a city like Rotterdam, however, 31% of the pupils in infant school and 27% of the pupils in primary schools during the schoolyear 1982–1983 were of non-Dutch origin.

In Table 2 numbers are given for pupils from the ethnic minority groups mentioned in Table 1 about which information is provided by CBS (1984).

As regards the increase in the sizes of ethnic minority groups in the Netherlands prognoses have only been made for four groups: Turks and Moroccans (Van Praag & Kool 1982), and Surinamers and Antilleans (Kool & Van Praag 1982). Table 3 provides information about the sizes expected for these groups in 1990.

Table 3: Numbers in January 1983 and prognosis of maximum/minimum numbers of four ethnic groups in the Netherlands in 1990.

Ethnic group	Number 1983	Maximum prognosis 1990	Minimum prognosis 1990
Turks	154,200	196,000	165,000
Moroccans	101,500	149,000	119,000
Surinamers	185,000	230,000	210,000
Antilleans	42,200	70,000	65,000

As regards the age category 4 – 12 the data provided by Van Praag & Kool (1982) allow us to make the following prognosis, exclusively for Turkish and Moroccan children (Table 4).

Table 4: Numbers for 1982–1983 and prognosis of maximum/minimum numbers of Turkish and Moroccan 4 to 12-year-old pupils in Dutch schools in 1990.

Ethnic group	Number 1982–1983	Maximum prognosis 1990	Minimum prognosis 1990
Turks	31,033	40,000	32,800
Moroccans	21,638	36,200	27,600

2. RESEARCH ON ETHNIC MINORITIES IN THE NETHERLANDS

In recent years research on ethnic minorities in the Netherlands has considerably increased for various reasons (see also Penninx 1984):
- in the 'seventies there was a marked increase in the size (and therefore the visibility) of ethnic minorities as a result of family migration and births in the Netherlands;
- the government had to acknowledge the fact that in the interaction between indigenous and non-indigenous inhabitants of the Netherlands (including verbal interaction) a problem had presented itself which required attention and state policy;
- for a diversity of reasons universities have shown increasing interest in research into concrete social issues.

In the Netherlands research on ethnic minorities is financed in three different ways: the first type of funding concerns 'free' academic research; the second type concerns research commissioned by the National Science Foundations ZWO and SVO which support fundamental and education-oriented research respectively; and the third concerns 'contract-research', commissioned by national, regional or local (governmental) bodies, especially ministries and large municipalities.

Within these three types of funding, however, the growth and the size of ethnic minority research have more systematically developed in reverse order. As a front runner there is contract research commissioned by various ministries. Secondly, at the instance of the minister of education ZWO has developed a special research programme by which also linguistically-inspired minority research may be able to profit (see ZWO Beleidsnota 1985). And, finally, research capacity at the universities is gradually being invested more systematically in this area, among other things by the institution of special professorial chairs and/or by research programmes that are carried out by groups of researchers.

Owing to the large share of (inter)ministerial contract-research in the total research effort, government policy exerts a clear influence on ethnic minority research. Especially short-term and policy-relevant (and in practice ever more often policy-supporting) research has been stimulated, whereas at universities, owing to the modest share of academic research, longer-term research programmes with more fundamental research questions are virtually lacking. However, without a theoretical framework empirical research will be fruitless both for policy-making and for the development of scientific knowledge. Moreover, there is the danger that in short-term projects too little use is made of the knowledge and experience acquired abroad in this field. In addition to this, research questions should not be unilaterally generated by government policy, but academic research should also generate questions related to policy.

Within the whole of socio-scientific research on ethnic minorities in the Netherlands linguistically-oriented research takes up a rather modest position, the main reason being the limited share of linguistically-oriented contract-research in the third type of funding mentioned earlier. This is why linguistic research has been less exposed to the pressures peculiar to contract-research mentioned above.

Another characteristic of current research on ethnic minorities in the Netherlands is that most projects are carried out/coordinated by Dutch researchers. Both for the development of research questions and the approach of informants, and for data collection and data analysis, knowledge available in various ethnic groups may be most valuable and even indispensable. However, not only is the number of academically schooled researchers belonging to various ethnic groups very small, also the influx of ethnic minority students at Dutch universities is extremely low. An improvement in this situation is only to be expected from special stimulation measure, comparable to the 'affirmative action programs' in the USA.

Recent summaries of current and completed ethnic minority research projects are given by Van Wijk (1984) and the ACOM (1984). Van Wijk restricts himself to (inter)ministerial contract-research, whereas the ACOM – a national advisory body for (inter)ministerial contract-research – publishes a list (adjusted each year) of a large number of research projects in approximately ten fields, funded in any of the three ways mentioned earlier. One of these fields is globally referred to as 'Education and Language'. The ACOM-list (1984) mentions 61 projects in all. In no other field is so great a research effort to be found; 'living' takes second place in the ACOM-list with 31 projects. The 61 projects mentioned concern widely divergent sectors of education and ethnic groups (both as regards origin and age). Most of the projects, however, are directed at Mediterranean groups (especially Turks and Moroccans) and at school children/ adolescents. The linguistically-oriented projects almost invariably concern the command/development of the second language, i.e. Dutch.

Finally, Penninx (1984) and Ellemers & Vermeulen (1980) contain good bibliographic surveys of socio-scientifically oriented publications on ethnic minorities in the Netherlands, whereas in 1983 the *Tijdschrift voor Taal- en Tekstwetenschap* (TTT) devoted a special issue, written in Dutch, to linguistically-oriented ethnic minority research in the Netherlands.

3. LINGUISTICALLY-ORIENTED RESEARCH AREAS

The fact that linguistically-oriented research on ethnic minorities has remained limited in size is partly due to factors which are not specific to the field of study at issue, but to the relationship between behavioural and linguistic research in general:
● in the behavioural sciences language often is not seen as a separate variable, so that language behaviour is only marginally paid attention to or is even left out of consideration completely;
● on the other hand, linguistic researchers very often keep at a respectful distance from empirical questions and methods: theories are often developed solely on the basis of intuitions about language (in particular the researcher's intuitions about his own idiolect) and most commonly no fundamental distinction is made between researcher and informant; research on language behaviour, however, makes such a distinction necessary and in many cases (such as research on language development) even unavoidable.

Table 5 presents an overview of five areas of research on language and minorities. This overview will be discussed briefly (see Extra 1982 for a more extensive discussion). To distinguish between first and second language we use the terms L1 and L2. Because L2 learning occurs outside as well as within various educational settings and extends to all age categories (children, adolescents and adults), we also use the general term L2 learners.

(a) *Dutch spoken by and spoken to non-natives*
The distinction in Table 5 made in questions three and four between the structure and tempo of second language learning is seldom found in the literature. This can be illustrated by the literature on the factor 'age' in L2 learning (see Van Els et al 1984: 104-109 for an overview). This literature is directed at the question whether young people learn *faster* than older people rather than at the certainly no less fundamental question whether young people learn *in a different way*.
  Concerning the structure/order of L2 learning: before 1970 it was generally assumed that the structure of L2 learning processes was determined by differences between L1 and L2 systems (the axiom being: differences result in learning problems, similarities do not); however, empirical studies after 1970 have produced data indicating that the influence of interference from L1 in the course of L2 learning processes has been overestimated. The structure/order of L2 learning processes seems to be strongly determined by universal laws that occur in any language learning process (L1, L2, Ln). Slobin (1973) and Clark & Clark (1977) have formulated these laws in terms of operating principles. Besides such

Table 5: Areas of research on language and minorities.

(a) DUTCH SPOKEN BY AND SPOKEN TO NON-NATIVES:

- what are the characteristics of the Dutch of non-native speakers in different contact situations with native speakers of Dutch (work, local authorities, health services, education, etc.)?
- what are the characteristics of the Dutch of non-native speakers in contact situations with other non-natives having different L1 backgrounds?
- what factors determine the structure/order of learning Dutch as L2?
- what factors determine the tempo/success of learning Dutch as L2?
- what factors determine the order and tempo of loss of Dutch when speakers are no longer in contact with native speakers (especially in the case of remigration to the country of origin)?
- How do native speakers of Dutch modify their language in addressing non-native speakers and in what situations do such modifications occur?

(b) USE OF MINORITY LANGUAGES:

- intra-ethnic varieties of minority languages spoken in the Netherlands
- L1 development in a L2 environment (possibly in comparison with the development of that same language in a L1 environment)
- maintenance, shift and loss of minority languages
- characteristics and conditions of L1/L2 switching and L1/L2 mixing

(c) LANGUAGE AND EDUCATION (for ethnic minority children/adolescents/adults)

- school career research with special attention for L1/L2 proficiency of ethnic minority groups when entering and leaving school
- structure of verbal interaction in educational settings (teacher/pupil interaction, peer group interaction)

specifically with regard to L1/L2 education:
- educational needs and educational objectives
- selection and grading of course content
- didactic procedures (including the use of audiovisual media)
- process and product evaluation (including the development of test instruments)
- educational policy and educational legislation (also in international comparative perspective)

(d) LANGUAGE ATTITUDES

attitudes of native and non-native speakers of Dutch (including local authorities, teachers, parents) with respect to:
- acquisition, use and maintenance of minority languages
- acquisition and use of Dutch as L2
- teaching Dutch as L2 as well as teaching a minority language as L1

(e) LANGUAGE AND MEDIA

- stereotypes of minority groups and minority languages in the media (press, radio/tv, educational materials, libraries)
- access of minority groups and minority languages to those media

universal operating principles, there are phenomena in L2 learning processes which cannot be retraced to the structure of the target language
(L2), but are a result of the structure of the source language (L1). Van
Els et al (1984: 59) discuss a number of factors which influence the
probability of occurrence of these interference phenomena.

The tempo/success of L2 learning processes varies considerably from individual to individual and is determined by *learner characteristics* (socio-
cultural orientation, age, L1 background, personality) and *environmental
factors* (nature and degree of L2 contact with native speakers, socio-
economic position and – as far as applicable – the quality of L2 education).
The factors mentioned are not always independent of each other and therefore cannot be investigated independently either. Moreover, the observational time span of studies on L2 acquisition is seldom longer than
one year. Therefore, not much insight has been gained as yet into possible
processes of levelling, stagnation or even regression in L2 proficiency.
However, such phenomena have been noticed frequently. For an extensive
discussion of structural and temporal characteristics of second language
learning we refer to Van Els et al (1984: 35-125).

(b) *Use of minority languages*
Because of the social and scientific emphasis on second language learning
and use (in our case Dutch), both development and use of minority
languages have received scant attention. The sparsity of research on
minority languages has other causes as well and is, moreover, not limited
to the Netherlands.

   In regard to the latter point, the asymmetry mentioned manifests itself
to a great extent in the extensive American literature about bilingualism.
Studies of the development and use of Spanish (at this moment the most
prominent minority language in the United States) are extremely limited
in number in comparison with the available literature about learning/
using English as L2. The focus on Dutch as L2 in the Netherlands is an
accurate reflection of this bias.

A cause of a completely different nature is to be found in the traditional
philological orientation of research in the Netherlands on languages such
as Turkish, Arabic, Chinese, Malaysian, Spanish and Italian. The fact that
these languages have developed into minority languages in the Netherlands
has not resulted, unfortunately, in any substantial modification of research
priorities. Nonetheless, the contribution of specialists in these areas is
indispensable to the development of research on ethnic minority languages
in the Netherlands.

(c) *Language and education*

From a social perspective, education is one of the most important users of
linguistic insights. Educationally inspired linguistic research can relate
to macro-objectives such as L1/L2 proficiency of ethnic groups when
entering and leaving school, or to micro-objectives such as the structure of
verbal interaction in educational settings (with the classical sociolinguistic
question: who says what to whom in which language and when/why?).

Research specifically directed at L1/L2 education takes up a separate
and important position. The first four domains mentioned in Table 5 are
part of what educational researchers call the 'didactic cycle' (see Van Els
et al 1984: 158ff. for an application of this concept to foreign language
teaching).

The ability to function within an educational setting places more
demands on the level of L2 proficiency of pupils than is often assumed.
Pupils have to develop not only communicative skills in order to participate in informal social interaction, but also typical 'school language skills'
including the ability to understand abstract language in textbooks and
complex verbal instructions of teachers (see Wong-Fillmore 1982 for a
global description of what such school language use requires of pupils).

As far as L1 education is concerned, responsible government agencies
have to account for what kind of instruction should be given to whom, by
whom, when/how often/how long, and why. Extra & Vermeer (1984)
evaluate national language policy with respect to each of these questions on
the basis of a ministerial report on this subject (see Van Leijenhorst 1983).

Finally, educational policy and educational legislation concerning
minority languages should also be analysed from an international perspective. For a description of the extensive jurisprudence in this field in the
United States we refer to Gray et al (1981) and Teitelbaum & Hiller
(1977).

(d) *Language attitudes*

Interest in the relationship between L2 proficiency and attitudes towards
(native speakers of) that language is not new and is central to the important and well-known study done by Gardner & Lambert (1972). It is
generally assumed that a positive attitude towards a particular language as
well as towards native speakers of that language has a positive effect on the
learning of that language. Equally well-known is the distinction Gardner
and Lambert make between integrative and instrumental orientation towards a language. Integrative orientation refers to an intrinsic interest in
or association with another language and culture, while instrumental
orientation reflects a need for proficiency in another language in order to
gain social recognition or economic advantage. The first type of orientation
is assumed to have the more positive effect on L2 proficiency. Even apart

from the question of the extent to which such a dichotomy reflects reality, research on language attitudes is complicated by various other factors.

First of all there are different ways to determine language attitudes. Until now researchers have mostly used open-end or closed questionnaires. Open-end questionnaires can be part of an interview, while closed questions are usually based on standard scaling techniques (yes/no answers or judgements on a multipoint scale). In questionnaires on attitudes towards majority/minority languages one often ends up collecting socially motivated answers, on the basis of the language of the questionaire itself or on the basis of the social prestige of the researcher who may or may not belong to the ethnic group in question.

In addition to the problem how language attitudes can best be investigated, there is the often mentioned finding that language attitudes do not constitute a stable entity, but are susceptible to change as a result of numerous personal and environmental factors. Related to this finding is the fact that success in L2 learning can be the cause as well as the result of specific language attitudes. It is assumed that acceptance of the language and culture of ethnic minority groups by important social institutions (government, media, school, etc.) has a positive influence on the former's attitudes toward the language of the majority.

(e) *Language and media*
The concept 'media' is taken as a broad one which includes not only the social institutions of press and radio/television, but also educational materials and libraries. Little research has been done in any of these areas.

Stereotypes of ethnic minority groups in educational materials were investigated by Van Dijk (1983). Wentholt (1982) used surveys and group interviews to investigate the behaviour, attitudes and wishes of first generation minorities in relation to television, radio and newspapers in general, and in particular to those television and radio programs directed at themselves. The results indicate a high interest in the existing programs for ethnic minorities, but at the same time a great deal of criticism of their marginal position within the total program of the networks.

4. CONTENTS OF THIS VOLUME

The title of our introductory contribution and the title of the volume as a whole have been phrased differently. Whereas the preceding paragraphs relate to various areas of linguistically-oriented research on ethnic minorities, the focus of the volume is on *Dutch as a second language*.

All contributions except Spoelders et al. (5) focus on ethnic minorities in the Netherlands. From a methodological point of view, the approaches to language learning are pluriform: both longitudinal and cross-sectional studies are represented, and both case studies and studies with larger numbers of subjects. L2 data relate to both oral proficiency and literacy, and are derived from both naturalistic observations and standardized tests. The same pluriformity holds for ethnic origin and age of the chosen target groups; most contributions, however, focus on Turkish/Moroccan children.

All contributions in this volume except Verhoeven & Vermeer (6) were presented in earlier versions at the seventh World Congress of Applied Linguistics in Brussels, Belgium, from 5-10 August, 1984. Marja Coenen (Department of Language & Literature, Tilburg University) has compiled the central bibliography.

2

Language Input Characteristics in Spontaneous Interaction of Native Children with Non-Native Peers

Korrie van Helvert

0. INTRODUCTION

The research project reported here is a longitudinal multiple-case study (data collection: September 1980 - July 1981) on the acquisition of Dutch as a second language by Turkish children in the Netherlands. In this project we have confined ourselves to the study of oral language development only. A second limitation is that the results only concern young children from 6 to 9 years old. Studying the process of L2 acquisition also implies that one has to make basic choices concerning the methodology in this field (see Van Els et al. 1984: 68-73). Roughly speaking there are two ways of studying the process of acquisition: the cross-sectional method and the longitudinal method. For this project longitudinal data collection procedures have proved necessary in order to answer our main research questions:

1. What developmental stages can be distinguished in the acquisition of a number of morpho-syntactic rules?
2. Do native children use foreigner talk in addressing L2 learners and is there a shift in use over time?
3. How does the L2 lexicon develop and what lexical domains are prominent in the spontaneous speech of L2 learners?
4. To what extent does performance of L2 learners on tests of specific L2 elements correlate with their use of these elements in spontaneous speech?

Only when the same subjects are studied over a longer period of time it is possible to draw conclusions about the order in which relevant linguistic aspects are acquired. One of the disadvantages of a longitudinal research design is that, because it is so laborious, only a few subjects can be studied. This means that results and conclusions can hardly be generalized. Its strength, however, is that it can suggest sensible hypotheses that in their turn can be tested in experimental studies with larger and possibly more specific groups of subjects.

The research design of this study was used before in several other comparable studies on L2 acquisition by children, such as Hakuta (1973), Wong-Fillmore (1976), Felix (1978), Wode (1981), Pienemann (1981) and Curfs et al. (1981). The data most relevant to our research questions seemed to be the spontaneous verbal interaction of the children in a naturalistic setting. The subjects in our study were five Turkish children of immigrant workers. At the start of the project all were screened for hearing or articulatory problems, mental retardation and problematic social behaviour in their own social group. Especially when working with so few subjects it is important to make sure that the sample is not too atypical. Table 1 contains some basic information about our five subjects.

Table 1: Basic information about the Turkish subjects

Name	Age	Sex	Period of residence
Nesrin	7.9	female	3 months
Belgin	7.5	female	1 month
Sefer	7.6	male	3 months
Mehmet	8.7	male	4 months
Hagan	7.9	male	1 month*

*   Hagan had been in Holland earlier, for 8 months, at the age of 4

The period of residence refers to the period of time the children had been living in Holland at the start of data collection. All children attended a special class for non-Dutch speaking children. In addition to the five Turkish subjects, seven Dutch children participated in the study. These subjects attended school in the same building and every day at playtime the children met in the playground. Table 2 gives the relevant information about the Dutch subjects. In the fourth column the names of their Turkish playmates are given.

Table 2: Basic information about the Dutch subjects

Name	Age	Sex	Playmate of	Period of participation
Sjan	6.0	female	Nesrin	Oct./July
Fanny	7.0	female	Belgin	Oct./July
Jan	6.8	male	Sefer	Oct./July
Wim	6.4	male	Mehmet	Oct./Febr.[1]
Rob	7.6	male	Mehmet	Febr./July
Bas	7.0	male	Hagan	Oct./Jan.[2]
Eddie	7.6	male	Hagan	Jan./July

[1]) Wim moved to another school at the beginning of January 1981.
[2]) During this time there was very little verbal interaction between Bas and Hagan; therefore, another Dutch playmate was selected at the end of this period.

Part of the data were collected during matched play sessions of a Turkish and a Dutch child. All sessions were recorded on audio cassette. These recordings were simultaneously transcribed and coded. The advantage of such an approach is that at the time of coding all relevant background information is available. Initially, utterance boundaries were not coded, but later on we felt the need for speech unit segmentation. Therefore, we marked single utterances in the ongoing speech of both Turkish and Dutch children. All transcripts were fed into the computer. We used SNOBOL, a higher order computer language specifically designed for string manipulation, for reorganizing and reducing the total amount of data for specific kinds of analysis.

Within this Volume, our contribution will focus on language input characteristics in spontaneous interaction of three Dutch children (Sjan, Fanny and Jan) with their Turkish playmates. First, a short characterization will be given of the general language input to the participating Turkish children (section 1). Then empirical research into foreigner talk in child/child interaction will be discussed, as well as some methodological problems connected with this type of research (section 2). The next section discusses the most important characteristics of the language input of the three aforementioned children in the experimental setting (section 3). This discussion will focus on turn distribution, turn length and utterance length (section 3.1); the absence of specific words in utterances (section 3.2); and the use of so-called clarification sequences (section 3.3). The paper concludes with some final remarks (section 4).

1. DUTCH LANGUAGE INPUT TO THE PARTICIPATING TURKISH CHILDREN

During the first stage of second language acquisition language input to the five Turkish subjects occurred in three different situations:
(a) language input in school (in particular in classroom settings);
(b) language input at home and in the street;
(c) language input within the experimental setting.
This paper focuses on the characteristics of language input by Dutch children to Turkish children within the experimental setting. The language input was transcribed in its entirety and input changes over time are described. Naturally, the input both inside and outside the classroom was of great importance to the children's L2 development. Through classroom observation and interviews with the teacher and with the children's parents an effort was made to gain insight into the nature and the extent of the language input. A characterization of both input situations will be given in this section.

(a)   Language input in school

The Turkish children came from different parts of town to a remedial class for non-native speakers run by the local authorities, after the primary school in their own neighbourhood had classified them as unable to participate in classroom interaction due to their lack of Dutch proficiency. During the year the research was carried out this remedial class was attended by Turkish children only; twenty in all. These children were taught for four days a week by a Dutch teacher who neither spoke nor understood Turkish. It was her responsibility to give the children basic instruction, in Dutch. The general teaching objective for this teacher was:
- bringing the children up to an elementary proficiency level in Dutch;
- 'adapting' the children to the teaching/learning process in the Dutch language.

The children received a further half day's in-school tuition in Turkish language and culture, taught by a native Turkish teacher. As a result of the composition of the class (Turkish children only) the verbal contacts among the children themselves were conducted mainly in Turkish. Of course, Turkish was the language of instruction during the Turkish language and culture lessons. There was no cooperation at all between the Dutch and the Turkish teacher as far as the content of the lessons was concerned. The characteristics of the language input by the Dutch teacher to the children were not explicitly investigated. Presumably, the input was in many respects the same for the five subjects. It was clear that the teacher emphasized formal aspects of the language itself rather than teaching the children to communicate in the second language. Besides these formal structural characteristics a great deal of time was spent extending the children's active and passive vocabulary. The children were seldom prompted to verbal interactive behaviour towards the teacher.

(b)   Language input at home and in the street

Encounters of Turkish children with Dutch children in the common playground were rare. In order to obtain a clearer view of the language input both at home and in the street we compiled a questionnaire for the Turkish children's parents. Together with the Turkish teacher all parents were visited at home and they were asked to respond to the questions. The primary aim of the questionnaire was to get an impression of the extent and the nature of the Dutch language input outside the classroom. The language input at home and in the street can be divided into three domains:
- contacts within the family;
- contacts outside the family;
- contacts via the media.

Contacts within the family.
All children communicate with all the members of the family in Turkish. In some of the families Dutch is spoken as well, on occasion. Nesrin sometimes speaks Dutch to her father (though not vice versa). Mehmet and Hagan, too, talk to their fathers in Dutch (and vice versa). Nesrin, Belgin and Hagan regularly speak Dutch at home when talking to their brothers and sisters. Sefer stems from a large family with many school-age children, but they never speak Dutch at home.

Contacts outside the family.
If we establish for each child how many contacts there are with Dutch-speaking children and acquaintances, it appears that Nesrin is in the most favourable situation with regard to language input. She communicates with Dutch playmates daily; at home there is regular contact with Dutch neighbours and now and then Dutch children come and play at her house, while she in turn visits them at their homes. The same holds for Sefer, although his contacts are less frequent. Mehmet's parents have Dutch friends who visit them occasionally (about once a month) and he himself regularly plays outside with Dutch children. Belgin's parents seldom (less than once a month) have Dutch friends visiting them and she never plays with Dutch children in her neighbourhood. This holds for Hagan as well. All the children's parents have Turkish friends who visit them regularly. Except for Sefer all children have Turkish playmates. Only Mehmet has Turkish neighbours and, like Nesrin, plays with Turkish children in the neighbourhood almost every day.

Contacts via the media.
The Turkish children's parents were asked whether and how often their children came into contact with Dutch and Turkish via the media. A striking result is that hardly any family ever listens to Dutch radio, although they watch TV quite often. Except in Nesrin's and Mehmet's homes, the sound is usually turned up while members of the family are watching. All children watched TV for three to four hours a day, except Mehmet, who was only allowed to watch for one hour. The families mostly watched Dutch programmes, but German programmes were watched regularly as well. Turkish newspapers were read frequently in all families; only Hagan's father also read a Dutch paper from time to time. Magazines are hardly ever read. In Sefer's and Hagan's homes there were occasionally Dutch magazines obtained from neighbours or friends. All families possessed Turkish books and two of them also had Dutch books. Children's books in both languages were available in all homes except Mehmet's. None of the children borrowed books from the (free) public library.

It is difficult to directly compare the responses by the respective parents for the purpose of drawing general conclusions about the nature and extent of the language input to the Turkish children. However, it has become clear that for some of the children the input level was very low, while for others it was fairly high. Even more important in this respect is the question whether the children, apart from input, had the opportunity to practise their Dutch fluency in natural communicative settings. Nesrin finds herself in a comparatively favourable position here. Belgin and Hagan, on the other hand, live in very protected surroundings with few Dutch contacts. Sefer and Mehmet, finally, are inbetween these two extremes.

2. EMPIRICAL RESEARCH ON FOREIGNER TALK IN CHILD/CHILD INTERACTION

In our discussion of research in the field of foreigner talk we confine ourselves to foreigner talk by and to *children*. For a general discussion of language input characteristics we refer to Van Els et al. (1984: 95-99), who give an extensive review of the research in this field. Particularly interesting is their treatment of the distinction foreigner talk vs foreigner register.

Research into characteristics of language input by native children of non-native children is sparse. To our knowledge, only two sources to date provide us with empirical data: Katz (1977) and, in Holland, Bakker et al. (1983). Both these studies show large discrepancies in relation to each other as well as to the research presented here.

Katz (1977) investigates the use of foreigner talk (henceforth FT) by an English-speaking child to a Hebrew child. He uses the following definition for FT: "the variety of language regarded as appropriate for addressing foreigners who are trying to learn the language of the host-country." Interestingly, this definition only highlights the 'learning aspect' and not also, as Hatch (1978) and others suggest, the fact that an important function of FT is to enhance the chance of communicative success, or at least to keep the communicative channels open. Katz collected longitudinal data of the English interaction between an Israeli girl, Tamar (5-6 years old), and an English-speaking girl, Lisa. Every two weeks an audio recording was made of the children's verbal interaction in a naturalistic contact situation. Katz does not specify what the actual situation was. During the period the study was carried out Tamar did not receive any formal instruction in English. According to Katz, Lisa regularly made use of FT, and it is only these FT utterances that he uses for his analyses. From a methodological point of view this is a rather curious procedure:

Katz makes a vague selection of utterances in Lisa's language use that he then labels FT, a concept of which he gives no further operationalisation. Only the final conclusion of his research will be presented here.

Lisa's FT system and Tamar's L2 use both change over time, but independently. This finding supports Ferguson's (1971) observation that FT is not a reflection of the actual language use by the L2 learner, but of the ideas the native speaker has about L2 use. As an example Katz gives a specific striking characteristic of Tamar's L2 use that was not present in Lisa's FT. The most notable feature in Tamar's language was, according to Katz, the virtually exceptionless use of *she* (third person singular) for personal reference in general. Lisa clearly indicated that she found this odd, but the same feature does not appear in her use of FT.

Although the relevant literature makes little or no mention of them, a number of fundamental methodological problems arise in the investigation of foreigner talk in children. Some of these problems are discussed below.

(a) The experimental subjects in our study were 6 to 7 years old. i.e. children who are presumably still developing their linguistic skills, not only with respect to vocabulary, but also for a number of structural and context-sensitive features of the language. Although in Holland Van Ierland (1979) investigated language use by children in the same age group, her results probably cannot be interpreted as "normative" for the rule system of children at this age. The conditions under which here data were collected differ considerably from those in our study. Therefore, since there is no clear general model of language use by Dutch children in this age group, some of the methodological decisions were necessarily taken on the basis of intuitive judgements. Is a particular deviation from the linguistic norm a reflection of the linguistic developmental level of the child at that time or is such a deviation to be attributed to the use of FT? The following examples of utterances directed at the researcher, and thus certainly not classifiable as FT, may serve to illustrate that the Dutch children's utterances do deviate from adult linguistic norms:

Sjan, week 6:   *Kunnen kinderen gestreekt worden? Gestroken... jawel Brammetje Brammetje wordt gestrijken gestrijkt*

Jan, week 11:   *Die zat ik overal naar te zoeken... hoeneer krijgen wij die mee?*

Jan, week 7:   *Oei is ie zomaar d'r uitgedoet*

Fanny, week 26:   *Waar is de station?*

(b) Although FT characteristics have been described fairly extensively in the literature, problems arise when we attempt to apply those characteristics to spoken utterances. It is generally known that spoken language is usually less explicit, less complete and less "neat" than written language. In other words, we need a clear norm that applies to spoken language and that is not the same as the one for written language (cf. Jansen 1981). Such a norm is not available for Dutch, which means that in this respect, too, intuitive decisions have to be made all the time. Is a particular deviation from the standard norm attributable to the fact that the utterance is spoken, or can we regard it as FT?

As an example, an utterance by Jan directed at the researcher in week 11: *Maar ik doe nou alles opruimen* (But I do now everything clear up). The construction "doen (*do*) + inf", which also appears frequently in utterances directed at the Turkish children, is not specifically an FT construction, but is fairly common in spoken language. Dialect influences may play a role here. A comparable construction, "gaan (*go*) + inf", appears frequently in the data of Bakker et al. (1983). In week 4 Sjan tells the researcher: *Zit niet meer watje in* (Is not more cottonwool in it), meaning: "Er zit geen watje meer in" (There is no more cotton-wool in it). From this example, and many others, it is clear that we have to be cautious in classifying a spoken utterance as FT merely because it is directed at a non-native listener.

(c) Another methodological problem is that information concerning the Dutch children in play situations with native peers is lacking. This makes it impossible to compare characteristics of verbal behaviour in both conditions. Such a comparison might reveal that certain striking features in the Dutch children's verbal behaviour should not be attributed to FT use, but for instance to behaviour that is peculiar to 'child interaction' in free play situations. In addition, such data might have shown possible idiosyncracies in verbal behaviour. In order to compensate for this problem a few variables of the Dutch children's utterances to the researcher were also looked into. Research shows (see e.g. Sachs & Devin 1976) that 5 to 6-year-olds are able to adapt their language use to the addressee. The way they talk to much younger children is different from the language they use when addressing their peers or their mothers. Furthermore, peer interaction hardly differs from mother/child interaction. Therefore, the verbal behaviour vis-à-vis the researcher has been used in our study as an approximation of verbal behaviour vis-à-vis Dutch children in general, thus including Dutch peers.

In the context of this study we have restricted ourselves to the description of characteristic features of the language input by some Dutch children to some Turkish children. Naturally, a number of these features correspond with those described in the literature as typical of FT.

3. CHARACTERISTICS OF THE LANGUAGE INPUT IN THE EXPERIMENTAL SETTING

Of the Dutch children only Sjan, Fanny and Jan participated in the experimental setting during the whole nine-months data collection and therefore only the data for these three children have been used in the analysis. Sjan was Nesrin's playmate, Fanny played with Belgin and Jan with Sefer. In the course of the school year these pairs were recorded once a week during a free play session in which the researcher, though present, participated as little as possible.

The focus of this analysis are the Dutch children's utterances because, at least in this setting, they form an important part of the linguistic input for the Turkish children. Not all the utterances of the Dutch children were explicitly aimed at their Turkish playmate. Though the Turkish child witnessed all the Dutch playmate's utterances, only those that were directly addressed to him/her are here considered input utterances. Since the aim of this paper is to describe features of verbal behaviour by the Dutch children in face-to-face communication with the Turkish children, it is reasonable to assume that any specific features only appear when the native child explicitly addresses the non-native child. All utterances by the native children were classified according to three categories, viz.:

1. T-utterances: utterances directed at the Turkish child;
2. K-utterances: utterances directed at the researcher;
3. O-utterances: other utterances (including general remarks and exclamations during play).

In doubtful cases utterances were classified in category 3, which was left out of the analysis. Categories 1 and 2 were only scored when the interaction clearly indicated that the utterances were directed at one particular addressee. The results concerning the number and features of utterances in these categories are presented in Table 3.

The most striking features of utterances classified as significant language input are the absence of specific words and the formulation of clarification sequences (repetition). Other, occasional features were non-conjugated verbs, reformulation of wh-questions as yes/no questions, use of proper names where personal pronouns would be expected (for example: "Nesrin too?" instead of "You too?"), frequent use of diminutives (though this may have been caused by the play situation, often involving playing with dolls) and finally a preference for emphatic use of subject pronouns (*jij, wij, zij*) instead of the non-emphatic, phonologically reduced forms (*je, we, ze*).

Due to their low frequency of occurrence these aspects were not quantified any further. Before we go into the results with respect to the absence of specific words (see section 3.2) and the occurrence of clarifications in the language input by the Dutch children, we will first give a general description of the proportion and length of conversational turns and utterances addressed to the Turkish playmates (3.1).

3.1. Turn distribution, turn length and utterance length

The data of the three Dutch children have been divided into conversational turns. Our operationalization of the notion 'turn' follows the one given by Huls (1982: 82): "The characterization 'what someone says in between two moments when he is silent' offers the best starting point for empirical use".

The following criteria give an indication as to how Huls subdivided her material into turns:

1. Change of speaker. A new turn starts when someone starts to speak.
2. Change of addressee. A new turn starts when a speaker addresses a different listener.
3. Change of subject. A new turn starts when the topic of conversation is changed abruptly.
4. Pause. A new turn starts after a pause longer than 1.8 seconds (...).
5. Restart. When someone tries to take the floor and makes a new attempt shortly afterwards this is classified as two turns. (Huls 1982: 82).

Criteria 1, 2, 3, and 5 have been used in the analysis below. Criterion 4 could not be used because pause length was not indicated in the transcripts. All turns by the Dutch children were classified as T-turns (directed at the Turkish child), K-turns (directed at the researcher), or O-turns (other remarks and utterances not directed at one specific listener).

Table 3 shows per child the proportion of T-turns during the first three months (period 1), the next three months (period 2) and the last three months (period 3) of the period of observation. This gives a general indication of the extent to which the Dutch children addressed their turns directly to their Turkish playmates. Table 3 also shows the total number of turns for each child. The results presented in the rest of this section apply to the total number of T-turns and, with respect to some aspects, also to the total number of K-turns.

Sjan's proportion of T-turns is highest in period 1 (36%). After that the percentage decreases (26%), recovering somewhat during period 3 (28%). In period 1 Sjan's attention is very much directed at Nesrin. As a result of Nesrin's lack of response (due to her low proficiency during that period)

Table 3: Distribution over time within each type of turn for each child, as well as percentage of turn types in relation to total number of turns

	T-turns		K-turns		O-turns		Totals	Proportion		
	N	%	N	%	N	%	N	%T	%K	%O
SJAN										
period 1	420	43.3	523	38.5	230	25.4	1137	36	44	20
period 2	311	32.0	474	34.9	427	47.1	1212	26	39	35
period 3	240	24.7	363	26.7	249	27.5	852	28	43	29
Total	971		1360		906		3237			
FANNY										
period 1	293	34.5	160	23.5	197	34.5	650	45	25	30
period 2	269	31.7	302	44.4	221	38.7	792	34	38	28
period 3	287	33.8	218	32.1	153	26.8	658	44	33	23
Total	849		680		571		2100			
JAN										
period 1	237	24.2	288	29.8	163	23.0	688	34	42	24
period 2	463	47.3	327	33.8	325	45.8	1115	42	29	29
period 3	279	28.5	352	36.4	221	31.2	852	32	41	27
Total	979		967		709		2655			

Sjan gets discouraged and in period 2 she more often addresses the re-searcher or makes general remarks. Period 3 shows an increase in the proportion of T-turns, possibly indicating a more active role on Nesrin's part, which prompts Sjan to direct herself more at Nesrin again. As regards T-turns, we see a similar development for Fanny: initially a relatively high percentage of T-turns, 45%, declining to 34% in period 2, but increasing again (strongly this time) to 44% in period 3; the same pattern emerges, possibly with the same explanation as that given for Sjan. Jan, however, shows quite a different development of turn distribution. In period 1, 34% of his turns are addressed directly to Sefer, but in period 2 this proportion increases to 42%, after which period 3 shows a decline to 32%, below the level of period 1. If we consider the absolute number (N) of T-turns for Jan, we see this number doubling from period 1 to period 2, while for Sjan and Fanny the number decreases slightly after period 1. It seems that Jan initially took a rather cautious and reserved attitude towards Sefer. Only during period 2 does the interaction really pick up, and it is then that Jan realizes that Sefer can as yet contribute little to the interaction. This would account for the decline in T-turn proportion in period 3.

It appears, then, that two of the children behave similarly in child/child interaction, whereas for the third child the same pattern only emerges later, because of a more cautious start. It is important to note here that, in this context, explanations should be interpreted as possible and plausible arguments to account for certain trends emerging in the results, rather than explanations in the sense of cause-effect relationships.

The proportion of K-turns is more or less stable for Sjan and Jan across the three periods (around 40% and 26%, respectively). The per-centage of Fanny's K-turns varies considerably, however, and seems dis-proportionate in relation to the number of T-turns. This suggests that, whenever she talks little to Belgin, she directs her attention more to the researcher.

Apart from the number of turns an interesting feature is the length of turns. Turn length is operationalized as the number of utterances per turn. All linguistic material from the Dutch children directed at the Turkish children and the researcher was divided into utterances. Dividing the number of turns by the number of utterances yields an index of turn length in terms of the mean number of utterances per turn. Not counted were one-word utterances consisting of the name of the addressee, but other single-word utterances were included. Mean turn length was cal-culated for both T-turns and K-turns. Particularly interesting in this respect are changes over time. Is it true that, as L2 proficiency develops, the mean length of turns increases? This kind of effect will be expected for T-turns, because presumably the Turkish children's comprehension will increase with their proficiency. For K-turns, however, such a systematic change over time is not expected to occur. A comparison of T-turn length and K-turn length may be interesting, though, in order to establish whether the Dutch children simplify their language input in this aspect.

In order to control for random fluctuations caused by situational factors we used the method of repeated average calculation. Every point in Figure 1 below is determined by data from three consecutive weeks (the first point represents the mean value for weeks 1, 2 and 3; the second point is the mean value for weeks 2, 3 and 4; the third point is the mean for weeks 3, 4 and 5; and so on). The resulting graph shows whether there are any clear increases or decreases in turn length over time.

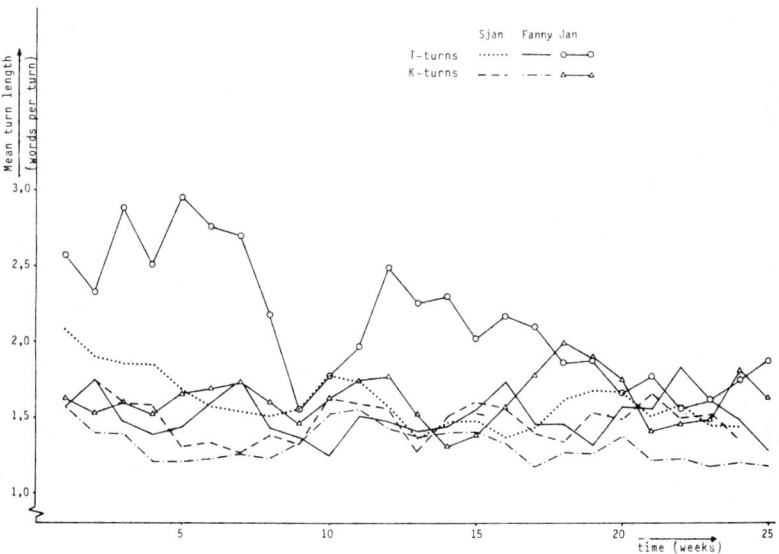

Figure 1: Development of turn length for T- and K-turns.

Turn length development is reasonably stable for Sjan, generally showing a slight decline. After a relatively high starting level turn length decreases during weeks 5 to 9, followed by a brief recovery. Subsequently turn length reaches the 1.6 level, with slight fluctuations. Fanny's turn length development yields a more variable picture without any clear trends. Jan, too, is more variable, but his turn length tends to decline over time. Striking here is the high level up to week 7 and the low level around week 9. After this week turn length goes up again, but it never reaches the initial level. From week 12 onwards there is a gradual decline in turn length. These results in no way confirm the expected trend for turn length to increase with the development of L2 proficiency. A possible explanation for this is that the Dutch children need the entire research period to become aware that they should adapt their turn length. If this were true the nine-month observation period would have been too short to draw firm conclusions.

When comparing T-turn length with K-turn length a remarkable result is that for all children T-turns are generally longer than K-turns. In the case of Jan, for instance, the highest value for K-turns is 2.0, while for T-turns it is 3.0. Otherwise there is no clear trend in turn length development for any of the children with respect to K-turns. This is in accordance with our expectations. The fact that the mean length of T-turns is higher than that of K-turns can be accounted for, however; below we will present further results with regard to the use of clarification sequences by the Dutch children. Clarification in the form of complete or partial repetition was most frequent. Although this variable was not quantified for K-turns, it is clear that repetition to the Turkish children is much more frequent than repetition to the researcher. Since these repetitions mostly fall within one turn but were counted as separate utterances, this may have resulted in T-turns containing a slightly higher average number of utterances than K-turns. In order to bring out this possible discrepancy we also calculated the mean length of utterances. The points in Figure 2 below were calculated in the same way as those in Figure 1.

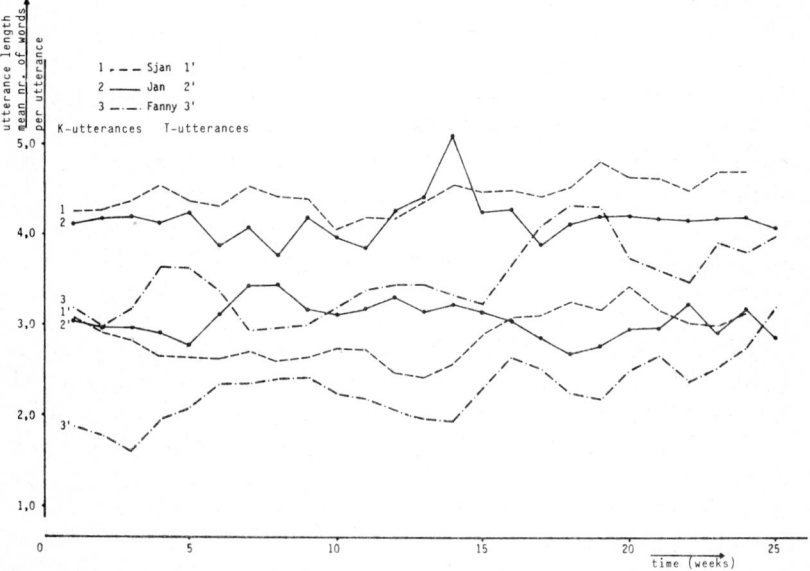

Figure 2: Development of utterance length for T- and K-utterances.

The figures for mean length of utterances are significant only if we also have an indication of the variation of values around the mean. How uniform were the Dutch children's utterances in this respect? Is there an increase in utterance length variation or is the upward trend for utterance length stable over time? Table 4 shows mean length of utterance (MLU) and standard deviation (SD) for both K-utterances and T-utterances.

These results clearly indicate that in general both MLU and SD tend to increase over time. In other words, the utterances not only get longer but there is also more variation in utterance length.

From Figure 2 it can be established that the mean length of Sjan's utterances to Nesrin increases in the course of time. Although an immediate slight decline is observable from week 1 onwards, utterance length clearly increases again from week 13 onwards, and after week 16 it stabilizes around value 3.2. For Fanny the general upward trend is much more obvious: a strong decline in utterance length immediately during the first few weeks, but from week 3 onwards a clear increase again. After some peaks and troughs her score eventually also reaches 3.2, following a strong increase during the last four weeks. Jan's utterance length curve is striking: up to week 16 his utterances are on average much longer than those of the other two children. A slight decline during the first few weeks is followed by a considerable increase and this relatively high level is maintained until week 16. After another decline in weeks 18 and 19 the final level lies around 3.0.

In short, for Sjan we observe a slight increase of utterance length, for Fanny this trend is much clearer, and for Jan the utterance length in the first weeks is the same as that in the last week, with some gradual fluctuations inbetween. That is to say, the results for two of the children point to an increase of utterance length along with an increase in the Turkish children's proficiency. Such a trend is not visible for Jan. Comparison of the development of the length of T-utterances in relation to K-utterances reveals that the K-utterances are generally longer (3.0 - 4.75 as opposed to 1.6 - 3.4 words). This means that the utterances to nonnative peers are on average shorter than those to the native adult. This result, combined with the trend found for T-utterances, suggests a modification of language use. Finally, the length of K-utterances is constant for Sjan and Jan, while Fanny shows a slight upward curve with many peaks and troughs. It is not clear how this last result should be interpreted. Figure 3 shows the development of T-utterance length together with the development of the utterances produced by the Turkish children in the same observational setting.

Table 4: Mean length of utterance (MLU) and standard deviation (SD) per child per period for T-utterances and K-utterances

| | T-utterances | | | | | | K-utterances | | | | | |
| | Sjan | | Fanny | | Jan | | Sjan | | Fanny | | Jan | |
	MLU	SD	MLU	SD	MLU	SD	MLU	SD	MLU	SD	MLU	SD
period 1	2.1	1.6	2.0	1.3	3.1	1.8	4.5	2.4	3.4	2.0	4.2	2.2
period 2	2.8	1.1	2.3	1.3	3.1	1.9	4.4	2.5	3.4	2.1	4.3	2.4
period 3	3.3	1.8	2.6	1.1	2.9	1.9	4.7	2.6	3.9	2.2	4.2	2.2

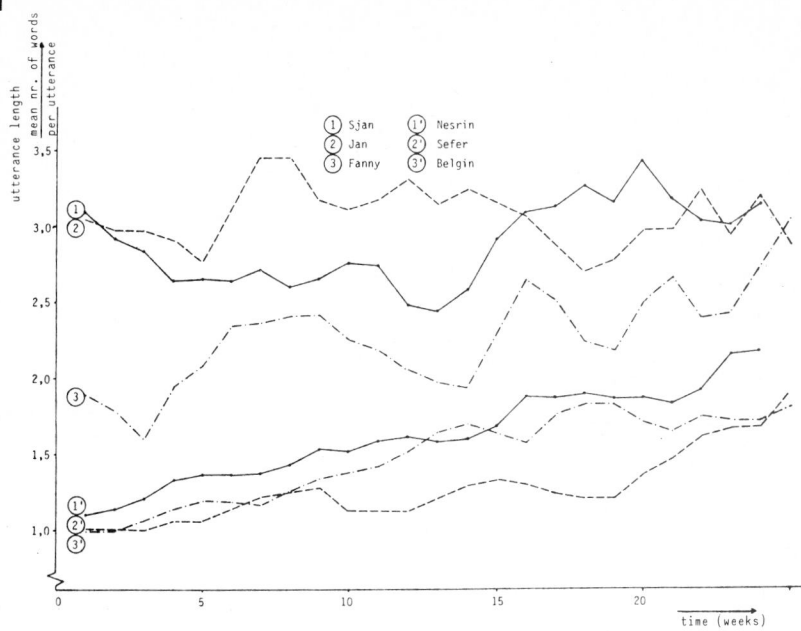

Figure 3: Development of utterance length for T-utterances and utterances by Turkish children.

Notably, the peaks and troughs in Jan's curve correspond with those in Sefer's language use. This may indicate monitoring of Sefer's language by Jan. On the other hand, it has also been suggested repeatedly (Katz 1977, Ferguson 1971) that language output like Sefer's may be strongly determined by features of language input, in this case the length of utterances. The developmental patterns of Fanny and Belgin show rather a reverse effect. Clear troughs for Fanny coincide with slight peaks for Belgin. Even if a direct relationship can be established between language input features and spontaneous L2 behaviour, a different process from the one seen for Jan and Sefer confounds the results here. Except during the first four weeks the curves for Sjan and Nesrin are similar in their gradual upward trend. In short, we observe that there is a general gradual increase in the length of utterances of both the Turkish and the Dutch children.

3.2. *Absence of specific words in utterances*

All T-utterances by the Dutch children have been evaluated for the conspicuous absence of words that could be expected to occur on the basis of intuitions about language in the given context. As has been indicated above, there was no norm available that could be used in this analysis. The notion 'obligatory context' frequently employed in the literature was here used in a restricted sense, in that obligatoriness was determined on the basis of intuitive linguistic judgements on the part of the researcher. Absent words were classified according to word class. The general results with respect to the absence of words in both T-utterances and K-utterances will be discussed first, with particular attention to the development over time. The aim of the analysis was to determine, not only what word classes the absent words belonged to, but also what function they had in the sentence configuration. If an absent word functioned as subject, verb or object in the sentence this was indicated separately.

It frequently occurred that words were absent in obligatory contexts. To give an impression of the decisions involved in establishing the absence of a word in an utterance, some examples are listed here for each child. By # we indicate where in the utterance a word has been left out. After each utterance the word class the absent word belongs to is given in parentheses.

Sjan: week 5:   *nou zijn we# oma*
                    [now are we # grandma's] (preposition)
         week 14:   *ikke ook mama#*
                    [me too mother #] (copula)

Fanny:week 16:   *nee, die# voor mij*
                    [no, that-one # for me] (copula)
         week 18:   *ga je mee naar # trein?*
                    [come you along to # train?] (article)

Jan: week 23:   *Sefer,# wij dit samen doen?*
                    [Sefer, # we this together do?] (auxiliary)
         week 13:   *waar is# telefoon?*
                    [where is # telephone?] (article)

Table 5 shows for each child the percentage of utterances with one or more absent words in the three testing periods. These percentages are related to the total number of utterances in the same period (see Table 3).

With respect to this analysis we formulate three expectations.
1. The proportion of T-utterances with absent words will decrease over time.
2. The proportion of K-utterances with absent words will remain constant over time.

Table 5: Mean percentages of utterances with absent words, per child per period, for T- and K-utterances

	Sjan		Fanny		Jan	
	T-utterances	K-utterances	T-utterances	K-utterances	T-utterances	K-utterances
period 1	20.4	3.9	6.3	4.4	5.7	2.9
period 2	9.1	3.4	9.5	3.1	4.7	4.2
period 3	4.9	4.7	15.4	4.8	10.4	2.8

3. The proportion of T-utterances with absent words will be larger than that of K-utterances with absent words.

The percentage of utterances where an obligatory word is absent declines for Sjan during the period of testing. A steep decline for the T-utterances is particularly clear from period 1 to period 2. This is the expected pattern, considering that Dutch children leave out words as a strategy to adapt their use of language to the proficiency level of their Turkish playmates. For the K-utterances, as expected, there is no declining trend. For Sjan the percentage of utterances with absent words is near a stable 4% in all periods. The absence percentage for T-utterances in period 3 is approximately the same as the 'basic absence percentage' of the K-utterances. This may indicate that Sjan saw no more need for this kind of adapted verbal behaviour in period 3.

In Fanny's case the trend for the percentage of T-utterances with absent words is the reverse of Sjan's. From period 1 to 3 a steady increase of absence percentage occurs, although the proportion is again close to 4% in all periods for the K-utterances. An increase of the percentage of utterances with absent words over time is not in concord with the expectations formulated. Apparently Fanny feels increasingly obliged to adapt her linguistic performance in this way.

The same picture can be drawn for Jan. Once again there is an increasing percentage of absent words in the T-utterances, particularly in period 3. After a slight decline from period 1 to 2 the absence percentage goes up to 10.4% in this period. For Jan also, there is a fairly stable pattern for the K-utterances, hovering between 3% and 4%. The sudden increase in the percentage of utterances with absent words in the last months of observation is again contrary to expectations.

In short, only in Sjan's case can we establish the expected pattern, i.e. a steady decline in the proportion of utterances with absent words. Jan and particularly Fanny display a reverse trend which is very surprising and hard to account for.

A comparison of the children with respect to the absence percentages in the K-utterances indicates substantial agreement. For all the children the absence percentage in utterances addressed to the researcher is stable and lies around 3% to 4% during the whole period of observation. In this respect, then, there is no indication of atypical or idiosyncratic use of language for any of the children. This observation reinforces the remarkable nature of the fluctuating results and unexpected trends in Fanny's and Jan's T-utterances.

It is clearly important to know not only how often words are left out, but also which words they are and exactly what *function* they have in the utterance. The absence of an article is thus much less crucial to the communicative value of the utterance than the absence of a subject or verb. A count was done of the absence of the three most important functions in the utterance, i.e. subject, verb (including copula and auxiliary) and object. We expect the number of cases where words with important functions are absent to be small. Where this percentage does turn out to be high, utterances will suffer significantly as far as comprehensibility is concerned. The central question in this analysis is: do the data suggest that absence of subject, verb or object is typical of language input to those in the early stages of L2 acquisition? Should this be the case, we expect:

- the absence percentage of subject, verb or object to decline during the 9 months of testing;
- the absence percentage of these words to be higher, on the whole, for the T-utterances than for the K-utterances.

Table 6 shows percentages of the total number of absent words with one of the three functions mentioned before.

Table 6: Percentage of cases, per child per period, for the T- and K-utterances, where the absent words functioned as subject, verb or object

	T-utterances			K-utterances		
	Sjan	Fanny	Jan	Sjan	Fanny	Jan
period 1	12.3	4.6	4.3	1.3	2.4	2.0
period 2	5.6	3.5	5.3	1.0	1.6	3.6
period 3	2.5	3.8	5.4	1.3	2.0	0.7

In Sjan's case we see, for the T-utterances, a gradual decline in the number of absent words with important functions in the sentence. Fanny's score shows a slight decline, though on the whole the percentages for the three periods hover around 4%. The same goes for Jan. Here again, then, a clear and expected trend for Sjan, and for Fanny and Jan a pattern which neither confirms nor contradicts expectations. Sjan and Fanny's K-utterances display comparable trends. The percentage of absent words with important functions in the sentence remains fairly constant across periods for both children: roughly 1% for Sjan, around 2% for Fanny. The percentages for the K-utterances are significantly lower than those for the T-utterances in all cases. We do see indications of a specific feature of linguistic input to a non-native hearer. Consequently we feel that the aformentioned research question should be answered affirmatively.

There are some final remarks to make concerning the distribution of absent words over the subject, verb and object functions. In the T-utterances the function most absent for all children is the verb. Taken over the whole period the percentages are as follows: Sjan 85.3%, Fanny 73.6%, and Jan 68.6%. The overall percentage for absence of verbs is at least 65%. The second most absent function is subject, with 13.2% for Sjan, 19.4% for Fanny, and 22.4% for Jan. Absence of object is the least frequent category. The percentages are: Sjan 1.5%, Fanny 6.9% and Jan 8.9%. For the K-utterances the distribution is different. Absence of verbs takes up 45.9% for Sjan, 23.5% for Fanny, and 35.0% for Jan. The percentages for Fanny and especially Jan should be interpreted with caution, as the absolute numbers of absent words with important functions are very small in the K-utterances. In the case of the K-utterances it can be said for all the children that the subject is left out most often. The percentages for absence of subject are: Sjan 48.6%, Fanny 58.8%, and Jan 65.0%. The object in the utterance is rarely left out. This category represents 17.6% of the total number of important words left out. The percentage for Sjan is 5.4%, and in Jan's K-utterances the category does not feature at all.

Summarising, we can state that verbs and to a lesser extent subjects and objects, get left out in language input for L2 learners, whereas in interaction with the researcher the subject is most likely to be absent, followed by verb and object. This applies to all the children.

As far as the absence of different word classes is concerned, we would first of all expect content words to be left out less often than function words. This expectation is based on the fact that content words are the typical carriers of meaning and therefore central to the communicative process. Also, function words will more often be left out owing to their often unmarked and unaccentuated nature.

Apart from the word classes presented below only one noun and one proper noun were left out. These absences have been left out of the following analysis because of their incidental nature. The absent words can be categorised according to whether they are function words or content words. The content word category contains only verbs, and then only those which functioned as full verbs in the respective utterances. The absent function words were: auxiliaries, copulas, articles, pronouns, prepositions and adverbs. These word classes are shown in Table 7. For each period can be seen which percentage of the total number of absent

Table 7: Distribution of absent words over respective word classes, per child per period, for T- and K-utterances

	T-utterances			K-utterances		
SJAN	Period 1	Period 2	Period 3	Period 1	Period 2	Period 3
Content words						
Full verbs	7.9	9.5	26.8	–	8.7	12.0
Function words						
Auxiliary	24.0	14.3	27.8	6.7	17.4	–
Copula	20.6	19.0	5.5	6.7	17.4	–
Article	34.7	33.3	5.5	50.0	21.7	37.0
Pronoun	5.3	19.1	27.8	30.0	31.0	36.0
Preposition	8.0	2.4	5.5	–	–	4.0
Adverb	–	2.4	–	6.7	4.3	12.0
FANNY	Period 1	Period 2	Period 3	Period 1	Period 2	Period 3
Content words						
Full verbs	25.9	5.3	10.0	11.1	–	–
Function words						
Auxiliary	29.9	–	11.4	–	–	16.7
Copula	1.1	18.4	17.1	–	–	8.3
Article	14.8	36.8	25.7	11.1	16.7	16.7
Pronoun	1.5	26.3	30.1	77.7	75.0	58.4
Preposition	–	7.9	2.9	–	–	–
Adverb	0.4	10.5	4.3	–	8.3	–
JAN	Period 1	Period 2	Period 3	Period 1	Period 2	Period 3
Content words						
Full verbs	14.3	17.4	19.2	–	4.8	18.8
Function words						
Auxiliary	14.3	10.9	13.5	–	4.8	6.3
Copula	5.7	–	9.6	–	4.8	–
Article	40.0	28.3	32.7	15.4	14.3	50.0
Pronoun	17.3	34.7	23.0	69.3	47.6	12.5
Preposition	–	–	–	–	9.5	–
Adverb	–	4.3	–	15.4	9.5	12.5

words belonged to a particular word class. The results are given per child and they represent both the T-utterances and the K-utterances.

Our expectation that content words are less likely to be left out than function words is confirmed. We shall confine our discussion to the main trends. On the whole, articles, auxiliaries, copulas and pronouns are left out relatively often in T-utterances. In the K-utterances articles and pronouns are absent most often. Verbs are much less likely to be left out.

The following results can be given concerning changes over time in the distribution of absent words across periods. In Sjan's case the number of articles and copulas clearly decreases in the T-utterances, whereas the number of full verbs, pronouns and to a lesser extent prepositions, increases. The auxiliaries show a steep percentual increase in period 3 after a slight decline in period 2. In short, there is no clear overall picture. For Fanny percentages for word categories vary strongly over time. There are large differences per class between periods, the shifts varying in both direction and size. No clear inter-class shifts can be seen for any of the children.

Summarising: apart from a general insight into the classes of words which are particularly likely to be left out, and the ways in which T-utterances and K-utterances differ in this respect, this analysis does not warrant further conclusions. Clear shifts over time cannot be distinguished for any of the children.

The distribution of the first 75 words by the Turkish children over the respective word classes is discussed in another part of the research project from which this article is drawn. Some results are: the ratio of content words to function words is 50/50; nouns constitute the largest subgroup of the content words; the largest subgroup with the function words are count nouns, adverbs and pronouns, whereas auxiliaries, copulas, articles and prepositions are very infrequent. Comparing these aspects of the language behaviour of Turkish children in the first period with the absent words in the language input of the Dutch children in the same period,

In general it can be said that word classes used frequently by the Turkish children (nouns, count nouns, adverbs) are hardly, if ever, absent from the language input of the Dutch children. Conversely, those categories not used very often by the Turkish children (full verbs, articles, prepositions, adjectives and copulas) are left out relatively frequently in the language input of period 1. These findings tie in with the correspondence, suggested by Katz (1977), between features of language input on the one hand and features of L2 use on the other. We found one exception to this trend in our material, i.e. the pronoun class. Pronouns feature frequently in L2 use by Turkish children, but they are rather frequently absent from the language input. We will not venture here an opinion as to the strength or weakness of the correspondence (in Katz's terms), nor do we address the question of whether the native speaker adapts the language input on the basis of the L2 use of the hearer, or rather that the L2 learner specifically adopts those elements which feature relatively prominently in the language input.

3.3. *The use of clarification sequences*

The verbal interaction between the Dutch and the Turkish children was at times an extremely painstaking process. Particularly in the beginning, but also later, there were frequent misunderstandings between the children, and the Turkish children very often did not understand at all what they were told or what was expected of them. The Dutch child had two options in these cases. Sometimes the attempt was abandoned immediately. Occasionally the Dutch children went to a great deal of trouble to get their meaning across in the second instance. These repeated attempts we will call *clarification sequences*. They will be extensively discussed in this paragraph. The extent to which Dutch children engage in these clarification sequences will be gone into, as well as the means by which children attempt to get their meaning across after having failed to do so in the first instance.

The trouble a Dutch child takes to make himself understood despite problems depends mainly on the child's own interest in being understood. When Jan wants Sefer to hand him some object, he engages in long and varied attempts to get this across:

Jan, week 7   *Give me one... give me... one of those... give me one of those give me one of those... with one of those on... no no give me another one*

These clarification sequences warrant closer examination in several ways. First of all the extent to which children make use of this strategy can be looked into. Willingness to repeat and clarify utterances which are not understood is an indication of the Dutch children's attitude towards their Turkish peers in play situations. Furthermore, the clarification sequences themselves are worth closer scrutiny. How will the Dutch child attempt to make himself understood? How will the child clarify his previous utterance? Insight can be gained into the child's hypotheses as to what will be easier to understand from the way he explains his utterances. Basically, there are five strategies a child can use in a clarification sequence:

1. literal repetition
2. partial repetition

3. expansion of the utterance
4. reformulation of the utterance
5. change in word order of the utterance.

The five strategies mentioned above only apply to segmental aspects of language behaviour. Suprasegmental changes in word accent and sentence intonation can of course also be looked into. These are often used to establish meaning when a first attempt at communication has failed. The system of transcription however did not allow for these aspects to be considered in the analysis: the transcripts do not contain information about intonation contours. Wherever literal repetition is mentioned below, this concerns segmental aspects only, and no suprasegmental ones. Even in a case of literal repetition, therefore, we may very well be dealing with an attempt at clarification.

All the utterances in the transcripts which were addressed to a Turkish child we checked for clarification sequences. Where a sequence occurred, each step was scored for one of the five criteria mentioned above. Criterion 5 is the only one that can occur in combination with any of the other four. Criteria 1 through 4 are mutually exclusive. Thus, a single sequence can be scored for more than one criterion. The following examples illustrate this.

Jan, week 6:

moet jij met de trein mee Sefer?	must you go along on the train, Sefer?
trein mee? (cat. 2)	along on the train?
trein mee? (cat. 1)	along on the train?
jij ook mee? (cat. 4)	you also along?

Fanny, week 25:

zwart haar heeft ie	black hair he has
hij heeft zwarte haren (cat. 5)	he has black hairs

Sjan, week 4:

jij dalijk ook	you also later
jij dalijk ook mooi maken (cat. 3)	you also make up later

The following research questions will be discussed consecutively:
1) Is there, over the period of observation, a shift in the percentage of clarification sequences in relation to the total number of utterances?
2) Are there individual differences concerning the use of clarification sequences?
3) Which strategy is generally used most frequently, and can any shifts be distinguished over time concerning the five strategies?

4) Are there individual differences in the use of the five clarification
sequences?

Question 1

In order to indicate changes over time and to keep the influence of situational variables down to a minimum we used the mean values of three
sessions each to determine one point in the graph. Each point in the graph
is the result of three different consecutive sessions, calculated by the
method of repeated averages. The results for the clarification sequences
for the three Dutch children are represented in figure 4.

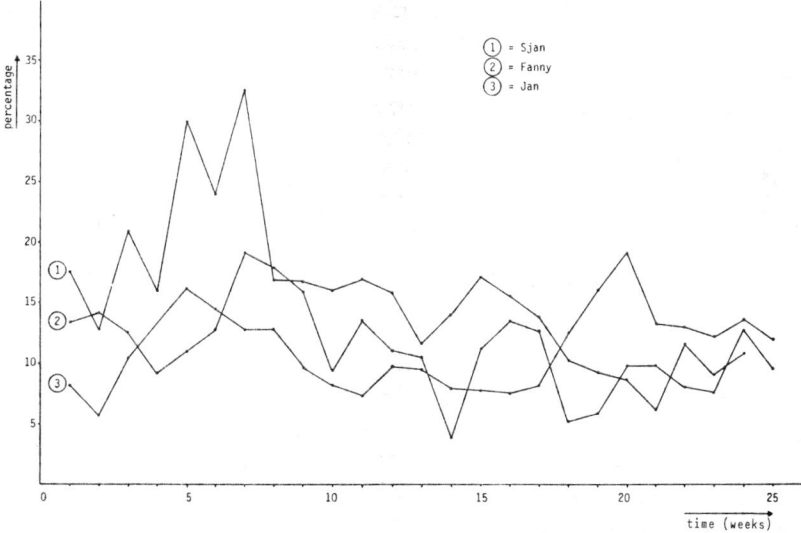

Figure 4: Development of proportions of clarification sequences over time.

The course of the percentages of clarification sequences in relation to
the total of utterances indicates a gradual decline for Sjan. Initially this
percentage stays close to 20%. From week 8 onwards the percentage
goes down to about 15% and declines very gradually after that. This is an
expected development. As the listener's L2 proficiency increases the
native speaker is less and less obliged to clarify utterances. The proportion
of clarifications at the end of the test period is roughly 10%. In Fanny's
case the graph shows a different developmental pattern. The percentage
generally hovers around 10% to 12% during the whole period. Up to
week 10 the percentage is slightly higher than later on, but there is no
sign in the data of a clearly shifting trend. Despite her playmate's ongoing
L2 acquisition process Fanny's clarification percentage remains stable. Jan
starts his very first encounters with a rather low percentage of clarifications,

less than 10%. The percentage soon goes up to about 15% in week 5, after which it goes down to 8-9% until week 17. After week 17 there is a clear rise again and from that week onwards the average percentage is higher than for the first 8 weeks. This is a striking development. The increase after a low start can be explained by the fact that Jan realises he is not understood and hence clarifies more often. After week 8 the need for this apparently diminishes, since the percentage goes down. After 8 weeks Jan may have adopted a more or less preventive manner of speech, obviating clarifications. There is no need for clarifications because he has adapted his language use. If this is so, the rise from week 17 onwards is surprising. Has Jan discarded the adaptions in his language input, so that clarification is once more called for? This does not follow from the other analyses. The length of utterances is declining in this period and it does not increase until the last four weeks: the utterances, then, are not longer. Could the intermediate drop in the proportion of clarifications be due to the fact that Sefer did not understand Jan's utterances, even when they were repeated, so that Jan suspended his efforts for the time being? The increase in week 17 would then point to a second attempt, prompted by Sefer's increased L2 proficiency. Another possibility is that Sefer, in the last period, is more capable of indicating his lack of understanding to Jan. No conversation analysis was carried out to check on this possibility, but it must be borne in mind as a possible explanation. Although clarifications were in the majority of cases prompted by the speaker's failure to communicate his intentions, signals such as 'Hmm?' or shrugging of shoulders can also invite clarifications. On the whole, Sefer manifested himself more and more explicitly in verbal interaction as time went on.

Question 2

Table 8 shows the number and percentage of clarification sequences in relation to the total per period and per child.

Table 8: Number and percentage of clarification sequences in relation to the total, per period and per child

	Sjan		Fanny		Jan	
	N	%	N	%	N	%
period 1	165	22.5	52	12.1	77	12.6
period 2	64	13.9	41	10.2	87	8.9
period 3	36	9.7	47	10.4	66	13.3
Total	265		140		230	

The children's percentages of clarification sequences per period vary considerably. In period 1, Sjan's percentage is nearly double those of Fanny and Jan. In period 2 the proportions are closer together. Even so Sjan's percentage is clearly highest. In period 3 there is a striking reversal. Sjan's percentage is lowest (9.7%) and comes close to Fanny's. Jan's relative score is highest in this period. No single child, then, scores the highest percentages in all periods. This suggests that the amount of clarification is no characteristic of individual speakers, but rather that it is conditioned by the situation in which the conversation takes place.

Question 3

As indicated earlier, there are five strategies available, in principle, to a speaker whose utterance is not understood or at least does not activate the desired response. This desired response may involve concrete participation in play, but it may also consist of the answer to a question. The frequency of each of the five clarification strategies was analysed. As the numbers per strategy per session are very low, the results are once again shown per three-month period. In table 9, percentages indicate the relative frequencies of strategies per period for each child. The overall distribution of the respective strategies across the whole period of observation is also given. The column headings are as follows:

Table 9: Percentages of each of the five clarification strategies, per child and per period

SJAN	LR	PR	E	R	C
period 1	33.3	33.3	17.6	13.3	2.4
period 2	37.5	28.1	10.9	21.9	1.6
period 3	33.3	38.9	16.7	8.3	2.8
whole period	34.7	33.4	15.1	14.5	2.3
FANNY	LR	PR	E	R	C
period 1	59.6	23.1	5.8	9.6	1.9
period 2	61.0	17.1	4.9	14.6	2.4
period 3	48.9	12.8	19.1	14.9	4.3
whole period	56.6	17.7	9.9	13.0	2.9
JAN	LR	PR	E	R	C
period 1	29.9	29.9	11.7	20.8	7.8
period 2	37.9	25.3	20.7	12.6	3.4
period 3	36.4	30.3	18.2	13.6	1.5
whole period	34.7	28.5	16.9	15.7	4.2

LR   literal repetition
PR   partial repetition
E   expansion of the utterance
R   reformulation of the utterance
C   change in word order of the utterance

The results indicate that literal repetition is most frequent for all children. Next is partial repetition, followed by expansion and reformulation, which are about even. Change of word order is clearly the least frequently used strategy. These results are the same for the three children. Looking at the distribution of strategies across periods, we can observe some striking shifts. For Sjan, the proportion of literal repetitions remains constant over time. Partial repetition and expansion are relatively less frequent in period 2 than in periods 1 and 3, whereas reformulation is actually more frequent in period 2 than in periods 1 and 3. The reason for these shifts is not clear. For Fanny, period 3 shows a clear decline in the proportion of literal repetitions and a clear increase in the proportion of expansions. In the course of the three periods the percentage of partial repetitions goes down. After period 1 the proportion of reformulations goes up strongly. In Fanny's case we can conclude that, over time, literal and partial repetitions give way to expansions and reformulations. This pattern is to be expected, owing to the growing L2 proficiency of the Turkish interactant. Literal and partial repetitions may be characterised as the most primitive clarification strategies. Literal repetition leads to higher redundancy, and partial repetition can be seen as a form of simplification.

Expansion or reformulation of an utterance is of no use unless the non-native hearer is capable of understanding the alternative formulations. Only when the hearer has more linguistic means at his disposal is there any point expanding an expression with familiar words, or replacing unfamiliar words with familiar ones. These alternatives do not become available as ways of clarifying an expression until later on in the L2 acquisition process.

For Jan the proportion of literal repetitions and expansions increases after period 1. Partial repetitions and reformulations show a relative decline after period 1, and the same goes for changes in word order. From period 2 onwards the proportions remain almost constant for the respective categories, with an increase of partial repetitions and a further decline of changed word order. There is no indication of any systematic shifts over time. Literal and partial repetitions are the most frequently used strategies in all periods, followed by expansion and reformulation. With the exception of period 1, changes in word order for clarification of utterances are as rare for Jan as they are for the other children.

Question 4

This question has already been answered in a general way. The results of question 3 already indicated a high degree of similarity among the Dutch children. It can be stated as a general trend for all three children that clarification sequences mainly consist of literal and partial repetitions of the previous utterance. Actual percentages do vary from one child to the other, however. The two strategies roughly represent 1/3 each of Sjan's total of clarifications. In Fanny's case the two together account for 3/4 of the total number of clarifications, literal repetitions outnumbering partial ones 3 to 1. The two strategies make up something like 60% to 70% of Jan's clarifications, devided about evenly between the two of them. Expansion and reformulation take up 10% to 16% each for all three children. Change in word order is a dustbin category, taking up 2% to 4% of clarifications.

In conclusion, the three children apparently agree on how best to clarify an utterance that is not understood. Shifts over time may be related to the changing L2 proficiency of the Turkish child addressed. It cannot be determined to which extent the selected strategies are linked to the phenomenon of FT. For such a link to be made, the clarification sequences used by the Dutch children to either other Dutch children or to the researcher would have to be analysed in the same way. This is problematic for several reasons. First of all, the utterances directed at the researcher contain so few clarification sequences as to inhibit a straight comparison on these grounds alone. Futhermore, the nature of communicative breakdowns between native speakers is a different one from the nature of those problems occurring because the listener's mastering of the language is inadequate or altogether absent. In the first instance, lack of communication will be caused by such factors as sloppy articulation or too much background noise. Clarification strategies often observed in such situations are a raised voice or emphatic articulation. Apart from the odd case where the Dutch speaker became almost impatient, these strategies do not feature at all in our data. The Dutch speakers were quite conscious of the fact that it was their interlocutor's inadequate language proficiency which was at the core of communicative breakdowns. From this point of view the frequent use of literal repetitions by all children is surprising. In a number of cases the aim was clearly to boost the interlocutor's attention. Literal repetitions of utterances were very often preceded or followed by the name of the child addressed. Since no structurally or content bound expansions are involved, these cases are classified as literal repetitions. Mentioning the name may however indicate a request for extra attention. To the Dutch children the idea may be that the same utterance, taken in carefully, will be understood the second time around.

4. FINAL REMARKS

Language input in general.
As far as L2 input in general is concerned some small differences emerge
for the individual children. The linguistic input in the classroom can
safely be assumed to be nearly identical for all the children. The input at home and in the street however is a matter of considerable variation.
On the whole we can say that Nesrin and Sefer had most access to input,
Hagan had a little less contact, whereas Belgin and Mehmet had least
opportunity to hear Dutch at home or in the street.

Turn distribution, turn length, utterance length.
The length of the input turns and input utterances generally increases
during the 9 months of verbal interaction. Occasionally the first few
weeks show relatively long utterances and turns. This can be explained as
follows: the Dutch children initially talk to their Turkish playmates the
way they would to other Dutch children. Not until later on in the process
of interaction does it become clear to them that the situation poses
different demands and that they are often not understood. As soon as the
children have established this the length of turns and utterances decreases,
either to remain constant from then on or to increase again during the 9
months of verbal interaction.

Absence of specific words in utterances.
A striking characteristic of linguistic input in the absence of specific words
in utterances. Our prediction that the absence of words would diminish over
time was only confirmed by Sjan's results. In the case of Jan and Fanny
we saw an opposite trend. Hence, no unequivocal conclusion can be drawn
at this point. The analysis of the classes of words which are most likely to
be left out leads to the following conclusion: articles, auxiliaries, copulas
and pronouns are left out relatively often. Absence nearly always involves
function words rather than content words.

Use of clarification sequences.
As a last point of interest we looked at the ways in which Dutch children
may attempt to clarify utterances not understood in the first instance.
The rationale of this analysis is that it indicates in what ways Dutch
children imagine they can simplify their language use. From an analysis
of the clarification sequences used the following conclusions can be drawn.
● The extent to which Dutch children clarify their utterances seems to
be a situationally triggered communicative strategy rather than a characteristic of individual speech style.
● In the course of the 9-month period of observation Sjan's utterances

show the predicted decline in proportion of clarifications (from 22% to 10%). The percentage of clarified utterances remains constant during the whole period of observation for Fanny and Jan (between 9% and 13%). No systematic changes over time were observed for those two children.

• Turning to the types of clarifications the children use we conclude that literal and partial repetitions are particularly frequent. In most cases the literal repetition is preceded by the name of the Turkish child concerned in order to draw his attention. In the case of partial repetition, the words most likely to be left out are function words. Reformulations and expansions are less frequent throughout the period of observation, whereas none of the children made use of changes in word order more than incidentally.

3

Moroccan and Turkish Children in The Netherlands: The Influence of Social Factors on Tempo and Structure of L2 Acquisition

Anne Vermeer

0. INTRODUCTION

Foreign workers' children tend to show a decrease in the speed of acquiring Dutch as a second language after some time. Teachers report that during the first year in primary school children learn Dutch very fast, but after that year their tempo seems to come to a halt and their progress becomes more difficult to observe (see the continuous line in Figure 1).

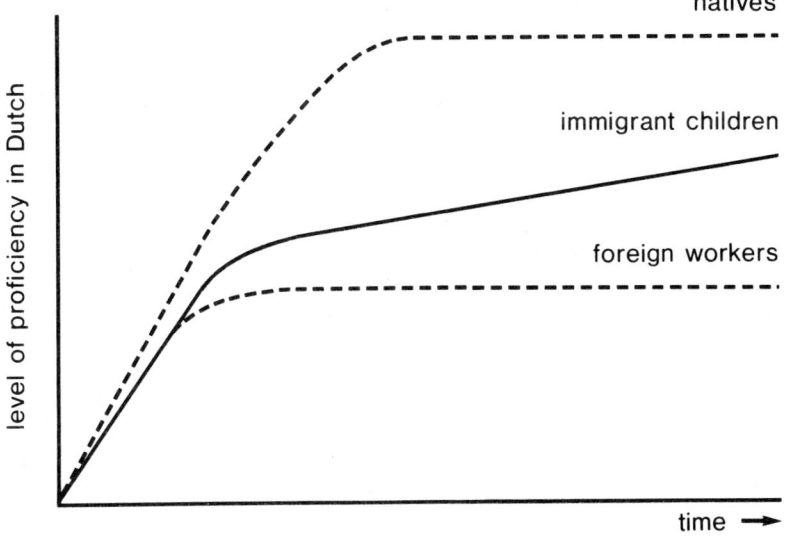

Figure 1. Schematic representation of three hypothetical courses of language development in Dutch.

A similar phenomenon is reported as a pattern of stabilisation in dialect speaking children after some years at school (Stijnen & Vallen 1981). Research on foreign workers shows that the second language acquisition

1 With thanks to Pieter Niewint and Marianne Sanders for correcting my English.

process of adults comes to a halt at a level which is often far below that of near-native proficiency (see Figure 1). Socio-economic and socio-psychological factors seem to account for the level of proficiency in a second language (see McLaughlin 1978).

In this paper the following two points will be discussed: firstly, does the tempo of L2 acquisition indeed slow down after one year at primary school? And secondly, which of the socio-cultural factors, such as motivation and contacts of the children and attitudes of their parents, contribute most to the childrens' success in acquiring a second language?

1. STRUCTURE AND TEMPO OF L2-ACQUISITION

In studying *temporal* aspects of L2 acquisition, that is, in studying the speed at which the various steps towards a higher level of proficiency are taken, one has to distinguish different *structural* aspects of L2, such as conjugations and inflections, word order, etc. There is yet another reason to distinguish these two aspects (structure, or order, and tempo, or success) of the process of acquiring a second language.

The structure of L2 acquisition is mainly defined by cognitive strategies and has a strongly universal character. The order in which people with different L1 backgrounds learn a second language is remarkably similar. Even when learners are forced to produce structures, but haven't got that far yet, as far as their L2 development goes, they will follow the principles of natural acquisition (see Felix 1981). In the 'creative-construction-process' model (Dulay & Burt 1974) the successive intersystems of the language acquisition process are highly systematic and predictable: a particular structure or rule B is acquired only when a particular structure or rule A is mastered, and not the other way around.

In contrast with these universal regularities in the structure of language acquisition, tempo of language acquisition differs from individual to individual. Beside factors like age and aptitude, the tempo in which and the success with which a second language is learned is determined for the greater part by the socio-economic background and socio-cultural orientation of the learner and by the kind and intensity of contact with the second language. In first language acquisition it is the family that forms the main language environment of the child. A child learning a second language however, is dependent on playmates at school and in his neighborhood. His own will and ability to build up relations with L2 speakers are also crucial predictors of second language success.

2. THE RESEARCH PROJECT

The two aspects distinguished here are objects of a four-year longitudinal research project called 'Tempo and structure of second language acquisition of Turkish and Moroccan children', which started in June 1981. In this project, 32 foreign workers' children are being followed in their acquisition of Dutch during their first three years in primary school. Two recordings of the level of L2 oral proficiency are made every year. The main variables within the project are given in Figure 2.

informants	controlled variables	recordings	
8 Turkish boys	age 6;5 – 7;5	1 Jan 82	every 6 recordings:
8 Turkish girls	1st year in prim.school	2 Jun 82	– elicitation tasks &
8 Moroccan boys	1 year kindergarten	3 Nov 82	spontaneous
8 Moroccan girls	SES 1 or 2	4 Apr 83	speech
	'immersion' model of	5 Oct 83	– questionnaire
	L2 learning	6 Mar 84	

research variables & operationalisations

L2 data:	elicitation tests	spontaneous speech
• vocabulary	+	+
• syntax	+	+
• morphology	+	+
• MLU		+

sociocultural orientation & contact (filled in by teacher)
• language choice, motivation and Dutch contacts informant
• Dutch proficiency, attitudes towards school and Dutch contacts parents

Figure 2. Main variables within the project.

The informants are 16 Turkish and 16 Moroccan children in various schools in Tilburg, an industrial town of 150,000 inhabitants in the southern part of the Netherlands. Each group contains an equal number of girls and boys. They are all working class children who at the first recording were 6½ to 7½ years old, and had one or two years of kindergarten. It was their first year at primary school. All children were at monolingual Dutch schools, with one or two hours of extra L2 tuition every week. With an interval of five months two kinds of data were collected at six moments in time: data on second language proficiency and various socio-cultural data. Two kinds of L2 data were gathered: spontaneous speech samples based on dialogues between teacher and child, and elicitation tests, all productive ones. Both types of data have been chosen to get as accurate a description as possible of the L2 proficiency of the children. Tests produce standardized data of phenomena that might have been avoided in spontaneous speech, and they can function as a check on the spontaneous data. On the other hand, the results on standardized tests tend to be misleading and can be verified by spontaneous data (for a discussion see Adams 1978). There were several tests: a vocabulary test of 100 items, in which the informant had to name a picture; two sentence imitation tests, in which syntactic phenomena were analyzed; and morphology tests on inflection and conjugation.

Beside vocabulary, the same morphological and syntactic phenomena were examined in spontaneous speech. Every five months a conversation between child and teacher was recorded. That conversation, which lasted 20 minutes or so, was half about a picture book, half about playmates, school, holidays and so on. This procedure (teachers themselves carry on the conversation) has the advantage that children are at their best in natural situations like these and show less variation than in an interview with an unknown researcher.

Finally, at six moments in time data are gathered on childrens' and parents' socio-cultural orientation towards and contact with the Dutch language and Dutch speaking people. Various researchers report that particularly these variables contribute to success in L2 acquisition of children, as well as adults. They point to the importance of the ratio of native and non-native speakers in classes and at schools, and of other social contacts with L2 speakers that can give the input and context that is necessary to acquire a second language (Wong-Fillmore 1976, Pfaff 1981). With regard to the second factor, socio-cultural orientation, the importance of motivation and attitude is frequently pointed out (see for instance the work of Gardner & Lambert 1972). There are only a few reports on attitudes of children. Wong-Fillmore notes that one of her informants, Nora, learned English rapidly because she identified herself with the people who spoke English, she wanted to be *like* them. Finally, the attitude of the parents, at least in the first phase of primary socialization, influences that of their children. It is very likely that parents who show interest in school, visit school very often, transmit a more positive attitude with respect to school than parents who not do so.

Socio-cultural orientation has been operationalized by a set of 40 written questions. These questions are answered by the teachers, who are appointed at a school to give extra lessons in Dutch for the benefit of non-Dutch speaking children. They are pre-eminently capable of answering questions on social contacts and aspects of attitudes, because they generally have very close contact with the parents. The questionnaire asked whether the parents visit school if they are invited, or whether they come of their own accord, how many times they come in a month, and whether they show interest in the activities of the school. There were questions about parental contacts with Dutch speaking people and their level of proficiency in Dutch, on a five-point-scale. Then there were questions about the child himself: what language he chooses to speak with brothers and sisters or other fellow-countryman at home, in the street, and at school; if he takes great pains to learn Dutch at school. Finally, to define the contacts of the child with native speakers of Dutch we asked what the nationality of his playmates was, and that of his closest friend, and what his activities outside school were (in sportclubs and so on). The percentage of non-Dutch speaking children in the class and at school also defined the factor contact. In this way we distinguished 6 socio-cultural and contact variables: language choice, motivation and Dutch contacts of the children; and Dutch proficiency, attitude towards school and Dutch contacts of the parents.

Our sixth and last recording was made in April 1984. At this moment we have analyzed most of data from the first four recordings, that is, data of Turkish and Moroccan children during their first two years in primary school, in an age range from 6; 9 to 8 years. In some cases data are presented up to the childrens' 9th year.

3. STRUCTURE OF SECOND LANGUAGE ACQUISITION

Firstly, some structural aspects. In contradistinction to the individual differences in tempo, the structure of L2 acquisition shows universal regularities. We did not find in our data differences between Turks and Moroccans, or between boys and girls, in the order in which particular linguistic subsystems were acquired.

Two examples are given: the plural of nouns and the past participle.

a	/-ə(n)/	tent	– ten*ten*	(tent)
b	fin. cons. modification +/-ə(n)/	/hant/	– han*den*	(hand)
c	/-s/	sleutel	– sleutel*s*	(key)
d	mid vowel (+ fin. cons.) modification +/ə(n)/	sch*i*p	– sch*epen*	(ship)

Fig.3. Plural of nouns in Dutch.

The plural of nouns in Dutch is mainly formed by adding /-ə(n)/ to a word, as in *tent – tenten* (see a in Figure 3), in addition to which in some cases the final consonant has to be modified as in *hand – handen* (see b).

After liquidae an /-s/ forms a plural, as in *sleutel - sleutels* (see c). Finally there are some nouns in which the vowel (and sometimes the final consonant) has to be modified, as in *schip - schepen* (see d).

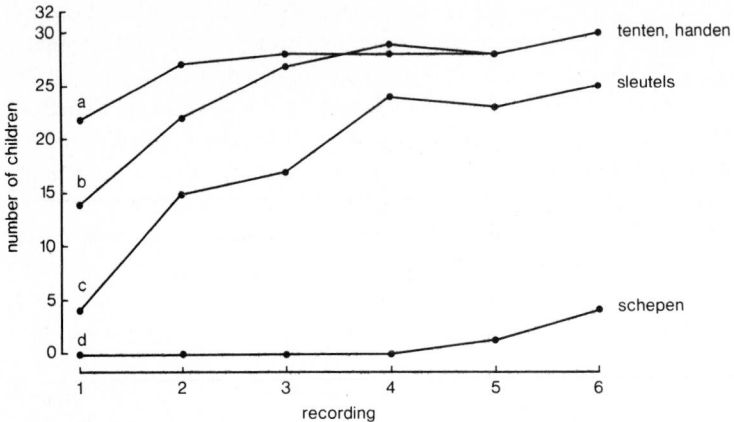

Figure 4. Order of acquisition of 4 noun plural formation rules (5-month interval).

Figure 4 makes clear that the basic rule (a) *tent - tenten* is acquired first: 22 out of 32 children obeyed that rule in 80% of the obligatory cases at the first recording (for that criterion, see Andersen 1978), whereas at that time rule c (*sleutel - sleutels*) was acquired by only 4 children. No one had acquired rule d. After two years 30 children had acquired rule a and b, 25 rule c, and 5 rule d. Two of them did not even master rule a yet. All children acquired the rules of the plural in the same order, only the tempo was different.

Figure 6 offers the same pattern of acquisition for five rules to form the past participle. The past participle is formed mainly by a discontinuous suffix, /ge/ before and /t/ or /d/ after the stem as in *stop - gestopt* (a) or by /ge/ before and /-en/ after the stem, with modification of the vowel (b, c, d).

		present	past	past part.		
a	/ge-/ + /-t//-d/	a	b	a	stoppen *gestopt*	(stop)
b	/ge-/ + vowel change + /-en/	a	b	b	*vallen viel gevallen*	(fall)
c	/ge-/ + vowel change + /-en/	a	b	c	*drinken dronk gedronken*	(drink)
d	/ge-/ + vowel change + /-en/				*breken brak gebroken*	(break)
e	irregular					

Fig. 5. Past participle in Dutch.

Apart from regular forms (a) and irregular forms such as *brengen gebracht* (e), in past particle three other forms should be distinguished as can be seen in Figure 5. (b) for example in *vallen viel gevallen,* so present tense and past participle have the same form, except for the prefix *ge.* (c) for instance in *drinken dronk gedronken,* and (d) in *breken brak gebroken.*

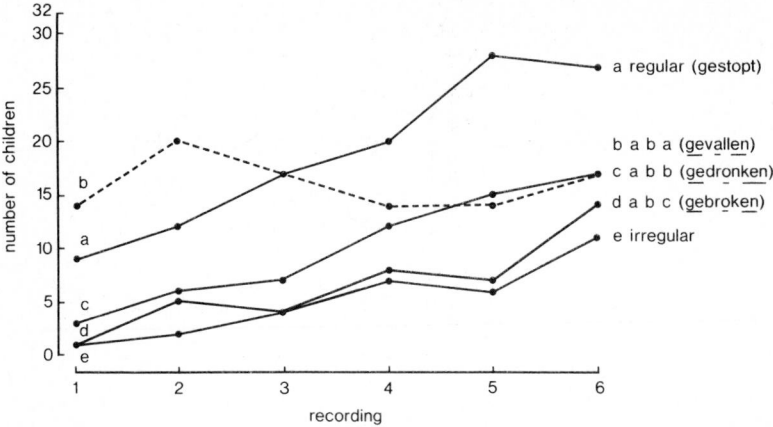

Figure 6. Order of acquisition of 5 past participle formation rules (5-month interval).

Figure 6 makes clear again that the rules are acquired in the same order. There is one remarkable phenomenon: rule b is acquired first, but after some time the rule is forgotten and acquired again after two years. This phenomenon can be explained in the following way. Present tense and past participle of b-type verbs have the same mid-vowel. Later on, rule (a) is discovered as the rule to form the past participle, and overgeneralized in forms like *gevalt.* This phenomenon is also known from first language acquisition. Felix (1977) called this phenomenon 'repetitive order of acquisition': a second language learner masters a particular rule, does away with that rule because he is learning another one, and having acquired that other rule, he learns the first rule again.

4. SPONTANEOUS SPEECH DATA VS. TEST DATA

From the examples given it can be seen that the order of acquisition of these rules proceeds along the same lines. These examples were taken from the elicited production tests, but the spontaneous speech data show the same results. Overall, there is a strong correlation between the different tests and the spontaneous speech data. As can be read from the cross-tables in Figure 7, all correlations are significant at the 1% level, except for two of them at the 5% level.

Spearman .01++ .05+ (n=32)	recording 1 VOCAB	MLUT	SYNT	2 VOCAB	MLUT	SYNT	3 VOCAB	MLUT	SYNT	4 VOCAB	MLUT	SYNT
MORPH	.70++	.71++	.62++	.62++	.36+	.79++	.71++	.59++	.51++	71++	.62++	.58++
VOCAB		.61++	.49++		.45++	.59++		.53++	.41+		.42++	.43++
MLUT			.56++			.44++			.57++			.45++

Fig. 7. Correlations between elicited production data (morph, vocab, synt) and spontaneous speech data (mlut) in 4 recordings.

Morph, vocab and synt indicate the three tests of in each case 100 items
or more. MLUT is the cumulative index of the mean length of non-elliptic
utterances, the mean length of elliptic utterances, and the mean length of
the ten longest utterances of a corpus, 200 utterances, each informant,
and for each recording. A distinction is made between elliptic and non-
elliptic utterances to make up for the fact that some children are less
talkative than others. In that case they produce relatively more – elliptic
– answers to questions of teachers. By definition those answers are shorter
than non-elliptic utterances. The third measure, the mean length of the ten
longest utterances, can be conceived as the maximal verbal capacity of a
speaker. Between MLU of non-elliptic utterances and MLU-10 there is a
very high correlation.

Taking into account the correlations in Figure 7 we may conclude that
both elicited production data and spontaneous speech data give similar
impressions of the verbal capacity of the children. Gathering these two
kinds of data has proven to be very fruitful: the standardized data can be
verified by non-standardized data and the other way around: some phenomena, very scarcely used, and perhaps avoided in spontaneous speech,
appear in the tests not to have been acquired.

5. TEMPO OF SECOND LANGUAGE ACQUISITION

Figures 8 and 9 give an impression of temporal aspects of second language
acquisition.

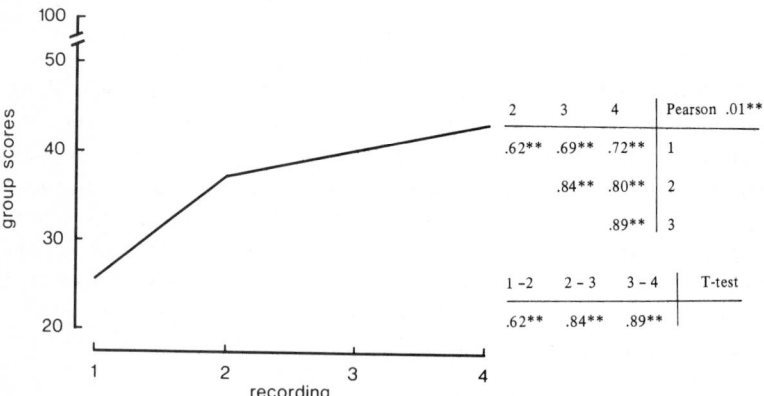

Figure 8. Group scores on vocabulary.

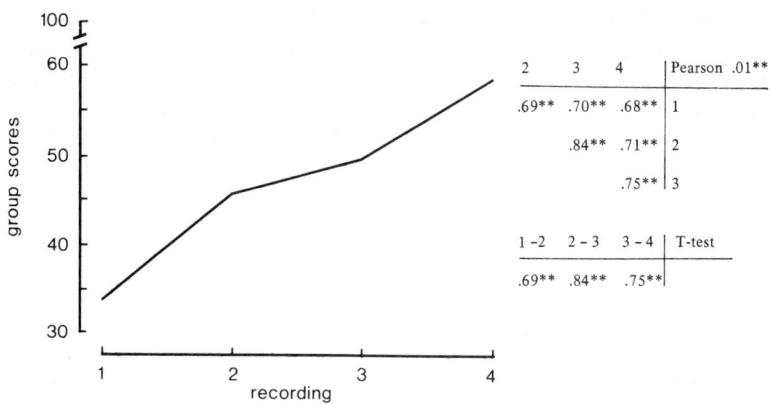

Figure 9. Group scores on morphology.

At all recordings the children make progress on vocabulary and morphology. Differences between scores are significant, as is shown by the T-Test. The childrens' achievements are very constant, as can be seen from the cross tables. The best performers on the first are the best ones on the second, third and fourth recording, and those who achieve low scores, always have low scores. This also applies to MLU, but there is no progress in MLU: the top seems to be reached at 6 words for mean length of non-elliptic utterances, and at 13 words for mean length of the ten longest utterances. Because of this ceiling effect the MLU for all children stays around 5 and 9 for non-elliptic utterances and MLU-10 respectively.

Conclusion: in spite of the reports of the teachers that the L2 acquisition of Turkish and Moroccan children seems to come to a halt, the children still make progress in vocabulary and on the morphological and syntactic level. But all that glitters is not gold. There are large differences between children in tempo, there is an enormous variation among them. As can be seen in Figures 4 and 6, at the sixth recording, after at least one year in kindergarten and three years in primary school, there are still two children who eight out of ten times cannot correctly form a plural of a noun in Dutch, not even the most simple variant, and these two and a third child did not acquire the past participle rule.

Is it possible to find an explanation for these differences in the socio-cultural data?

6. SOCIO-CULTURAL ASPECTS

As mentioned before, we distinguished six socio-cultural and contact variables: language choice, motivation, and Dutch contacts of the children on the one hand, and Dutch proficiency, attitude towards school and Dutch contacts of the parents on the other hand. Each of these variables is based on a homogeneous cluster of questions. In Figure 10 correlations between all variables are given.

Dutch proficiency of the parents	motivation at school of the children	parental attitudes towards school	Dutch contacts of the children	Dutch contacts of the parents.	Spearman $.01^{++}$ $.05^{+}$
$.66^{++}$	.00	.08	$.50^{++}$	.20	language choice of the children
	.05	.28	$.38^{+}$	$.44^{++}$	Dutch proficiency of the parents
		$.34^{+}$	.12	−.05	motivation at school of the children
			−.08	$.44^{++}$	parental attitudes towards school
				−.19	Dutch contacts of the children

Figure 10. Correlations between socio-cultural and contact variables of the children and their parents.

The proficiency of the parents in Dutch correlates significantly with the language choice of the children: a high level of Dutch proficiency of the parents is related to the children's choice of Dutch as their medium of communication. Secondly, there is a significant correlation between attitudes of the parents and motivation of the children: great parental interest in school is related to high motivation of the children to learn Dutch. Furthermore, there is a significant correlation between the language choice of the children and their L2 contacts: frequent contact with Dutch children is related to a choice to speak L2 with brothers and sisters. For the rest there are strong correlations between the three parent-variables: high parental proficiency in Dutch is related to frequent parental contact with the Dutch, as it is related to a great interest in school. Taking the three child-variables together as clustered socio-cultural orientation, proficiency in Dutch is strongly related to socio-cultural orientation, and this holds for various linguistic levels: morphology, vocabulary and syntax (the tests) and the MLU-measures (based on spontaneous speech data). Especially vocabulary has high scores; the four recordings .46, .40, .49, .45 respectively, all significant at the 1% level.

The socio-cultural orientation of the parents does *not* correlate significantly with the proficiency of the children in Dutch. Only vocabulary correlates sometimes (at first and third recordings) at the 5% level. From this, it is concluded that the children's level of proficiency in Dutch is related to their socio-cultural orientation, and not to that of their parents. But which one of the different variables of socio-cultural orientation is related to proficiency, and which one is not?

recording	1			2			3			4			Spearman .01++ .05+ (n=32)
	LANG	MOTIV	CONT	LANG	MOTIV	CONT	LANG	MOTIV	CONT	LANG	MOTIV	CONT	
	.79++	.06	.36+	.53++	.20	.07	.63++	.05	.36+	.34+	-.06	.15	Morph
	.72++	.02	.25	.63++	-.01	.24	.70++	-.19	.31+	.39+	-.23	.37+	Vocab
	.52++	.00	.29	.17	.24	.14	.41+	.01	.04	.47++	-.03	.22	Mlut
	.51++	.45++	.19	.54++	.35+	.06	.34+	-.02	.21	.23	-.11	.11	Synt
		.00	.50++		.03	.41++		-.36+	.44++		-.39+	.32+	Language choice of the children
			.12			-.01			-.21			-.16	Motivation at school of the children
													Contacts of the children with Dutch

Figure 11. Correlations between socio-cultural and L2 variables of 32 Moroccan and Turkish children in 4 recordings.

Figure 11 shows that at all four recordings the L2 proficiency of the children correlates significantly with the language choice the children make in interaction with brothers and sisters, and with their contacts: a frequent choice for Dutch is related to a high level of L2 proficiency. That language choice is all the time closely bound up with their contacts with Dutch people.

In spite of our expectations, there is no significant correlation between proficiency and motivation, as can be seen from the tables. After one year at primary school there is even a significant negative correlation between motivation and language choice. (-.36⁺ and -.39⁺ at the third and fourth recordings). That is, in the second class, there is a relation between a high motivation to learn Dutch in school, and a choice for the mother-tongue as medium of communication with brothers and sisters. So in the first class, 6 and 7 year olds really prefer to speak Dutch in all situations, whilst later on language is chosen according to situational circumstances. This phenomenon has been noticed earlier by teachers, who observed that first class children don't want to speak their mother-tongue anymore, even with their Turkish or Moroccan playmates. But after one year or so they will choose their mother-tongue again. Gradually they seem to realize that there are different situations in which sometimes the one, and sometimes the other language is appropriate. However, it should be mentioned that the operationalization of "motivation" in our study is probably weak. It is the only factor of which the teacher had to give a highly subjective opinion, on a five-point scale. All the other factors are defined by more objective measures: what nationality has the childs friend, how many times do the parents come to school, etc. Motivation is also the only variable that changes in the course of the recordings, in contrast to the other socio-cultural and contact variables. What we need is a more refined instrument to measure children's ambitions to learn a second language.

The main results of this study are that the level of proficiency in Dutch is strongly related to the language choice and the contacts of the children and not to their motivation or the attitude of their parents. In an indirect way, parents of course do have their influence: the language choice and the contacts of the children continually correlate significantly with the proficiency of the parents in Dutch. Furthermore, at the third and fourth recordings, the contacts of the parents correlate at the 1% level with the language choice and the contacts of the children.

We found that the structure of L2 acquisition, i.e. the order of acquisition of various morpho-syntactic elements showed a very regular pattern, independent of L1 background, sex or such socio-cultural factors as contact or orientation towards language or school. On the other hand, the tempo of L2 acquisition differed from child to child, dependent on language choice and the contacts the children had.

7. CONCLUSION

We can now return to the question we posed in the beginning: why do teachers think that second language learners show a decrease in the speed of their acquisition after one year or so? We believe there are two reasons for this.

The first reason is that initially second language learners make fast progress on a few linguistic devices: one rule for plural formation, one rule for past tense formation, etc., mainly basic communicative needs. Later on they learn to make use of many forms and phenomena at the same time: different rules for plural formation, irregularities, etc. So in the beginning they seem to run fast on a narrow path, picking up the basic rules they need for that moment, whereas later on they walk along a broad language-avenue, picking up all the rules they encounter.

The second reason may be that tempo is a relative notion: interpretation of it is related to other tempi. In the first class at primary school children read stories that are no match for their cognitive abilities because of the difficulty of the process of reading: simple words, short sentences, short stories, many repetitions. So Dutch and non-Dutch speaking children learn reading in the same tempo. But once the technical aspects of the reading process have been mastered, the Dutch children speed up as compared to their non-native peers, and texts become relatively more difficult to understand. Scores on vocabulary tests show that the relative distance between Dutch and non-Dutch speaking children becomes greater as time goes by (Verhoeven & Vermeer, in this volume). This phenomenon is known as the process of divergence. Children do not slow down in their tempo of L2 acquisition, but their Dutch classmates increase their head start over them.

4

Structural and Temporal Aspects of Turkish Children's Reading Dutch as a Second Language

Ludo Verhoeven

1. INTRODUCTION

From the very beginning, language instruction at primary school is mainly devoted to reading and writing. In the first few months of reading instruction, the relationship between the alphabetical code and speech is emphasized. Children discover that words can be represented as strings of phonemes, and that graphemes are representations of these phonemes. Once they have grasped this principle, they can assign a pronunciation to words they have never seen before and arrive at the meaning of these words by spelling them out loud. After frequent practice they will reach the stage where they can read words more directly. At that stage attention can be focussed on the understanding of larger units such as phrases, clauses and relations between sentences (Perfetti & Lesgold 1977 and 1979; La Berge & Samuels 1974).

In deciding what is the best approach to teach bilingual children to read, an important question is whether the alphabetical principle is better taught using L1 or L2. Bilingual children who have mastered this principle in one language do not have to start from scratch in the second language: what they have to learn is a new written code (see Thonis 1970).

In the Netherlands, ethnic minority children are rarely given initial reading instruction in L1. In the vast majority of cases instruction is L2-based from the first year of primary school. In some cases first language teachers will start reading instruction in L1 at the same time, but this usually takes place without the two programmes being adequately geared to each other. Research conducted in the United States and Europe into L2-reading results of bilingual children indicates that they frequently lag behind their monolingual peers in reading ability (Hatch 1974; Cummins 1980); they have a relatively low reading rate and a poor comprehension of the text. According to teachers bilingual children who receive reading instruction mainly in L2 seem to show poor reading results as well. This

---

1 This research project is supported by the Netherlands Foundation for the Advancement of Pure Research (Z.W.O.).

paper gives a description of the design and the first outcomes of a longitudinal study on Turkish children's process of learning to read Dutch as
a second language. Their acquisitional process was followed for a period
of two years. The two central questions (see also Verhoeven & Extra
1983) in this study are:

1) what features of learning behaviour are evinced by Turkish children in
   L2 reading processes as compared with Dutch children involved in
   learning to read in L1?
2) what learner variables can account for individual differences in L2
   learning results of Turkish children?

The first question deals with structural aspects, the second with temporal
aspects of learning to read Dutch as a second language. The study has both
theoretical and practical implications. Problems that occur in, or are
related to, concrete teaching situations form the basis of the study.

With respect to the first question posed in the present study, the
behaviour of Turkish children learning to read in L2 is compared with
that of Dutch children learning to read in L1. After five, ten and twenty
months of instruction the process of reading of both groups in different
kinds of reading tasks will be compared. The learner characteristics of the
two groups of children are subsequently subjected to linguistic analysis in
order to discover the similarities and differences in learning behaviour
between Dutch and Turkish children. With respect to the second question
individual variation in L2 reading performance of Turkish children in
Dutch after a one-and two-year period of reading instruction will be
accounted for. In choosing relevant learner characteristics we have em-
phasised those aspects which are closely related to the linguistic and
socio-cultural background of the children. Three hypotheses are tested.
In the first place, a causal relation is posited between oral proficiency in
L2 and metalinguistic intuitions about L2 on the one hand, and reading
results on the other. In testing this relation an attempt will be made to
determine as accurately as possible what linguistic components are important in learning to read. The assumption here is that the act of reading
can be analysed as a collection of constituent components that interact
(see Carr 1981: 100-107). Secondly, it will be determined whether poorly
developed oral L1 proficiency inhibits the development of oral proficiency
in L2. In testing this hypothesis, the nonverbal cognitive skill variable is
taken as a covariate. In fact, this part of our investigation seeks to gain
empirical evidence for the interdependency hypothesis (cf. Cummins
1979, 1982). Finally, it is hypothesised that socio-cultural orientation
will affect L1 as well as L2 development. Thus, identification with the
home language and culture will have a positive effect on L1 develop-

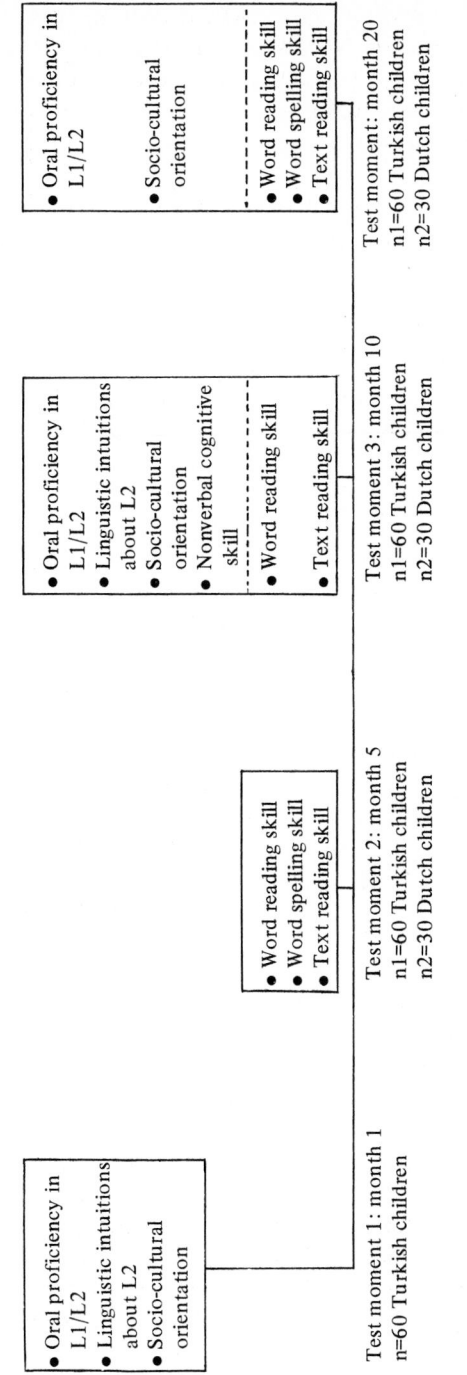

Figure 1. Schematic representation of research design.

ment, while identification with Dutch culture and language will favourably affect L2 development. Non-identification is expected to have the opposite effect.

In Figure 1 a schematic representation of the design of the project is presented.

2. PREVIOUS RESEARCH ON SECOND LANGUAGE READING

Earlier studies on *structural* aspects of the second language reading process have concentrated primarily on an analysis of the miscues observed in first and second language learners reading a text out loud. The observed miscues were then accounted for in terms of graphonological, morphosyntactic or semantic strategies related to the target language, or in terms of strategies that are based on interference from the source language. In this way the importance of both *intralingual* and *interlingual* developmental features of the second language reading process will be explored (see Van Els et al. 1984: 47-67). Goodman & Goodman (1978) tried to find support for the universal character of L1/L2 reading strategies. They analysed the reading behaviour of children with widely varying L1 backgrounds (Spanish, Navajo, Samoan and Arabic) reading English texts. The miscues made by these four groups showed a remarkable degree of similarity. Moreover, the pattern of miscues greatly resembled that of English speaking children who had learned to read in their first language. A study conducted by Rigg (1977) arrived at comparable results. In studying the pattern of miscues among children with the same L1 backgrounds as mentioned above, she concluded that learning to read in a first or a second language will basically yield universal strategies. On the basis of a miscue analysis with Arabic children reading in English, Haddad (1981) concluded that first and second language reading processes involve greatly similar processes. The same conclusion was arrived at by Romatowsky (1973) concerning the pattern of miscues of Polish children reading in English as a L2. However, besides strategies comparable to those of L1 learners, these children also made use of strategies that can only be accounted for in terms of the syntactic system of Polish.

Studies investigating the L2 reading behaviour of adults also come to the conclusion that developmental features in the second language reading process are universal or intralingual to a high degree. Connor (1981) found that adult Vietnamese students while reading English texts produced miscues similar to those produced by English students, although the former group appears to delete especially those word-final features that do not occur in L1. Furthermore, Cziko (1980) concluded that if second language learners have a reasonable L2 proficiency, they are able to process contextual cues in a manner similar to first language learners.

Apart from the reading of the text proper, some studies have investigated the occurrance of graphonological interference in reading and spelling of words in L2. Hatch (1974) reports evidence of such interference with Spanish children reading English words. Slembek (1980) examined the role of phonological interference in Turkish children's spelling of words in German. She concluded that the error pattern of children who had learned to read in Turkish (L1) first, can largely be explained in terms of Turkish orthography, while the errors of children who had learned to read in German (L2) first was better explained in terms of German orthography.

With regards to *temporal* aspects of second language reading the relationship between oral and written language proficiency has been highlighted. French (1981) stressed that in oral and written discourse both first and second language learners make use of comparable strategies. A positive correlation between oral L2 proficiency and success in second language reading was demonstrated in a number of studies. Talbott (1976) showed a significant relationship between these variables with children from grades one to six. The same result was found by Matluck & Mace-Matluck (1977). Furthermore, Goodman & Goodman (1978) found that as the level of oral L2 proficiency increases, the L2 reading process in children gets more efficient. Cziko (1977 and 1980) came to the same conclusion concerning the L2 reading process of adults. Whereas readers with a relatively low level of oral L2 proficiency seem to take decisions predominantly on the basis of graphical information, L2 learners with high L2 proficiency level are able to use both graphical and contextual information during the reading process. Similar conclusions were arrived at in studies on reading cloze-texts in L2. Lapkin & Swain (1977) and Oller et al. (1972) found that in such tasks the reading strategies of L2 learners become more efficient as their oral proficiency in L2 increases.

Some authors claim that in learning to read in L2 a basic mastery of both oral-receptive and oral-productive aspects of that language is required (see Hatch 1974). In studying the reading performance of both monolingual and bilingual children Matluck & Tunner (1979) indeed conclude that the likelihood of success in reading English as a second language depends on a certain threshold level of oral proficiency in that language. They assume that this threshold level corresponds to the mean level achieved by monolingual English speaking first-graders on a measure of oral proficiency.

In addition to oral proficiency in L2, other factors that may predict success in learning to read in a second language have been paid attention to. The intuitions that children have developed about language have been mentioned as universal prerequisites in learning to read.

The metalinguistic ability to segment speech into phonemic units (phonemic segmentation) and to combine such isolated units to form words (phonemic synthesis) have proved to be especially relevant (see Golinkoff 1975). Furthermore, Connor (1983) found a relationship between success in L2 reading on the one hand and instructional and sociocultural variables on the other hand. Her conclusion was that the number of students in a class, their first language background, the degree of English spoken at home and paternal occupation all contributed to a positive prediction of L2 reading success.

In brief, earlier research in second language reading can be summed up as follows. From a structural point of view two types of evidence have been found: on the one hand the presence of intralingual developmental features can be observed in particular in studies of morphosyntactic and semantic strategies used in reading a text; on the other hand, the importance of interlingual developmental features is mainly based on studies of phonological strategies in reading and spelling isolated words. From a temporal point of view success in L2 reading seems to be related primarily to the level of oral proficiency in L2, whereas metalinguistic intuitions and socio-cultural variables also seem to play a role.

In the following sections some preliminary findings of our own study are presented. Two research questions were investigated. With reference to the structure of their reading process, the L2 reading comprehension results of Turkish children are compared to the L1 reading comprehension results of Dutch children after one year of reading instruction. With reference to the L2 reading success of Turkish children, the individual variation in L2 reading comprehension after one year is related to the variation in oral proficiency in L2 and metalinguistic intuitions about L2 measured at the beginning of reading instruction.

3. DESIGN OF THE PRESENT STUDY

3.1. Informants

A group of 70 Turkish children was selected from the first forms of ten primary schools in several cities, with 20-50 per cent of the pupils per class belonging to ethnic minority groups. All the children have Turkish as their mother tongue and have been living in the Netherlands for at least two years, during which period they attended nursery school. The reading method used, *Veilig leren lezen,* was the same for all schools. This method is used by 85 per cent of the Dutch schools and is generally applied fairly strictly. The group of Turkish children was supplemented with a group of 110 Dutch children. The Dutch children were recruited from the same forms and their socio-economic background is as similar as possible to that of the Turkish children.

3.2. Tasks

In order to investigate children's reading comprehension ability in Dutch three different tasks were developed bearing on three different aspects of text cohesion: anaphoric reference, implicit relations and sequential principles.

The *Anaphora Task* is based on referential relations between sentences in a text. Children's understanding of anaphora is thought to be an important intersentential device in reading comprehension in that the choice between possible antecedents presupposes sophisticated syntactic, semantic, pragmatic, inferential and evaluative abilities (see Webber 1980). From earlier research it can be concluded that with regard to different types of anaphoric expressions, a hierarchy of comprehension difficulty or an order of acquisition can be identified (Bormuth, Manning, Carr & Pearson 1970; Lesgold 1974; Richek 1976-77). A task was constructed in which four types of anaphora are distinguished: personal reference, reference to space or time, verbal reference and clausal reference. Each of these anaphoric types was assumed to be syntactically characterized by specific anaphor-antecedent pairs.

In the Anaphora Task six texts are presented. Each text is followed by four multiple-choice questions, referring to the earlier types of anaphora. In Figure 2 one of the texts with questions is presented. The questions successively refer to spatial, personal, clausal and verbal antecedents. The children are asked to read the texts silently and then to tick the right answers on testforms.

The *Inference Task* measures implicit relations between sentences in a text. Previous studies have shown that children as young as six years or even younger can make inferences of various kinds (Paris & Lindauer 1976; Trabasso, Riley & Wilson 1975). Furthermore, MacNamara, Baker & Olson (1976) have shown that there is a developmental trend in making inferences of various sorts. As to the understanding of semantically complex propositions in some predicates, they conclude that assertion, presupposition and implication can be seen as distinct propositional com-

Ali zit op het dak van de schuur.
Daar kan hij veel zien.
Hij ziet Kees en Roos in de tuin.
Ali roept naar hen.
Dat heeft moeder gehoord.
Ze komt naar buiten.
Ali moet van het dak af.
Moeder is erg boos.
Vader ook.

Ali is sitting on the roof of the shed.
From there he can see a lot.
He sees Kees and Roos in the garden.
Ali calls out to them.
His mother has heard that.
She goes outside.
Ali is ordered to get off the roof.
Mother is very angry.
So is father.

1. Waar kan Ali veel zien?

    A.   Op het dak van het huis
    B.   Op het dak van de schuur
    C.   In de schuur
    D.   In de tuin

1. Where can Ali see a lot?

    A.   On the roof of the house
    B.   On the roof of the shed
    C.   In the shed
    D.   In the garden

2. Naar wie roept Ali?

    A.   Naar Kees
    B.   Naar vader en moeder
    C.   Naar Kees en Roos
    D.   Naar moeder

2. Who does Ali call out for?

    A.   Kees
    B.   His father and mother
    C.   Kees and Roos
    D.   His mother

3. Wat heeft moeder gehoord?

    A.   Dat Kees en Roos in de tuin zijn
    B.   Dat Kees en Roos naar Ali roepen
    C.   Dat Ali naar Kees en Roos roept
    D.   Dat Ali op het dak klimt

3. What has mother heard?

    A.   Kees and Roos playing in the garden
    B.   Kees and Roos calling for Ali
    C.   Ali calling for Kees and Roos
    D.   Ali climbing on the roof

4. Wie is erg boos?

    A.   Ali
    B.   Moeder
    C.   Vader
    D.   Vader en moeder

4. Who is very angry?

    A.   Ali
    B.   Mother
    C.   Father
    D.   Father and mother

Figure 2. A text of the Anaphora Task with multiple choice questions (on the right an adapted version in English is given).

ponents. According to Carrell (1977) the understanding of implicit meaning as displayed in presupposition or implication is much harder than that of simple propositions for both L1 and L2 learners.

The inference task which we developed consists of four texts. Each text is followed by three questions related to assertion, presupposition and implication respectively. Figure 3 presents one of the texts with its questions in the order just mentioned. In this task the children are asked to read the text aloud. After each reading of a text the child is asked three questions.

The *Sentential Sequence Task* is the third reading comprehension task that has been constructed. Twenty groups of four sentences are displayed that together build a mini-story; however, the sentences are presented in an illogical sequence. In half of the 20 mini-stories children are asked to point at the initial sentence of the story; in the other half the last sentence is asked for. Because the former instruction seems to demand a less intensive use of context it is expected to be easier than the latter (see Spiro 1980). In Figure 4 two examples of items of the Sentential Sequence Task are given.

Figure 5 shows the learner characteristics under investigation and the way in which these characteristics have been operationalised. The number of items in each task is indicated in the last column.

The receptive phonology task requires children to distinguish words that differ in one phoneme, or in the position or the number of phonemes (Dutch examples: *kas/kaas, dorp/drop, strik/stik*). For each pair of words, children are asked to indicate whether the words are the same or different.

In order to measure lexical skills, productive and receptive vocabulary tasks have been developed. The productive vocabulary task uses pictures for recognition; the receptive vocabulary task is a multiple-choice test which involves listening to a particular word and selecting the correct referent out of four pictures. The procedure adopted in constructing the vocabulary tests has been to rank the items in order of supposed difficulty.

Morphosyntactic skills are measured by means of a sentence imitation test. The aspects under investigation are specified beforehand and fall into three subcategories: function words, word-final markers and specific word order characteristics.

Metalinguistic intuitions the children have formed about L2 are investigated using four separate tasks. Knowledge of grapheme/phoneme correspondences is determined by means of a grapheme and phoneme dictation task. Furthermore, phonemic segmentation and phonemic synthesis tasks have been constructed in which words of increasing ortho-

Ali wacht op zijn vader.
Daar komt hij al aan.
Ali vraagt hem of hij morgen mee gaat fietsen.
Morgen is het zondag.
De vader van Ali hoeft dan niet te werken.
Ali wil graag met de fiets naar het bos.
Als het mooi weer is, wil vader wel mee.
De volgende morgen is Ali al vroeg wakker.
Hij kijkt vlug naar buiten en zegt:
"wat jammer dat het regent."

1. Regent het, als Ali 's morgens naar buiten kijkt?
2. Vindt Ali het fijn dat het regent?
3. Gaat Ali met zijn vader fietsen?

Ali is waiting for his father.
There he comes.
Ali asks him to go and cycle with him tomorrow.
Tomorrow it will be Sunday.
Then Ali's father does not have to work.
Ali would like to go by bike to the woods.
If the weather is good father is willing to join him.
The next morning Ali wakes up early.
He looks outside saying:
"what a pity that it rains!"

1. Is it raining when Ali looks outside in the morning?
2. Does Ali enjoy the rain?
3. Will Ali go cycling with his father?

Figure 3. A text of the Inference Task with questions (on the right an adapted version in English is given).

1. Cross the initial sentence of this story.

   A I am getting a large piece of it.
   B Mother is making dough.
   C She is baking a pie.
   D She is lighting the oven.

2. Cross the *last* sentence of this story.

   A The alarm clock is ringing.
   B He is leaving for his work.
   C Father is waking up.
   D He is putting on his clothes.

1. Met welke zin moet het verhaaltje beginnen?

   A Ik krijg er een groot stuk van.
   B Moeder maakt deeg.
   C Ze bakt een koek.
   D Ze doet de oven aan.

2. Wat moet de *laatste* zin van het verhaaltje zijn?

   A. De wekker loopt af.
   B Hij gaat naar zijn werk.
   C Vader wordt wakker.
   D Hij trekt zijn kleren aan.

Figure 4. Two items of the Sentential Sequence Task (on the right an adapted version of English is given).

Learner characteristics	Operational definition	Number of items
Oral proficiency in L2	– receptive phonology task	50
	– receptive vocabulary task	108
	– productive vocabulary task	80
	– sentence immitation task	250
Metalinguistic intuitions about L2	– knowledge of grapheme/phoneme correspondences	33
	– phonemic segmentation task	20
	– phonemic synthesis task	20
	– reading concepts	20
L2 Reading comprehension	– anaphora task	24
	– inference task	16
	– sentential sequence task	20

Figure 5. Operational definition of learner characteristics.

graphic complexity must be split up into segments and must be recognised by joining segments, respectively. Finally, a task has been developed in which reading concepts such as 'word', 'sentence', etc. are asked for.

In all cases, before the tests are administered, the subjects are given detailed instructions in L1, followed by additional instructions in L2.

3.3. Procedure

With regard to the first research question the subscores on the three reading comprehension tasks were determined after one year of reading instruction. For each task a two-way analysis of variance (ANOVA) was computed on the mean number of correct subscores of each subject. The between-subjects factor was ethnic group (Turkish vs. Dutch) and the within-subjects factor was type of subscore. On the Anaphora Task this factor referred to the subscores personal reference, space/time reference, verbal reference and clausal reference. On the Inference Task the sub-scores assertion, presupposition and implication were involved, while on the Sentential Sequence Task the subscores initial sentence and last sentence were referred to.

It was hypothesized that on each reading comprehension task the main effect of type of subscore would be significant. Furthermore, on the basis of instructional practice it was expected that the main effect of ethnic group would also be significant. However, because of the supposed similarities in L1 and L2 reading processes the interaction between this factor and ethnic group was not expected to be significant.

As to the second research question, the following procedure was adopted. At the beginning of reading instruction, the oral proficiency in L2 and the metalinguistic intuitions about L2 of the Turkish children were recorded on the basis of the tasks mentioned in Figure 2. After one year of reading instruction, the above-mentioned reading comprehension tasks were administered. Step-wise multiple regressions were then computed in order to estimate the percentage of variance in the reading comprehension measures which could be accounted for by oral proficiency in L2 and metalinguistic intuitions about L2 respectively. The added standard scores on the three reading comprehension tasks were used as dependent variables.

4. RESULTS

4.1. L1 and L2 reading comprehension compared

Table 1 shows the statistics of a 2 × 4 ANOVA on the Reference Task. It can be concluded that the main effects of ethnic group and of type of reference are both significant. The interaction between these factors, however, proves not to be significant.

Table 1: 2 × 4 ANOVA statistics on the Reference Task (**$p<.01$)

Source	Sum of squares	DF	Mean squares	F
Ethnic group	136.4	1	136.4	19.0**
Error	1210.4	169	7.2	
Type of reference	67.3	3	22.5	22.4**
E × T interaction	3.9	3	.5	1.3
Error	507.7	507	1.0	

As can be seen in Figure 6, Dutch children obtain higher scores on the Reference Task than do Turkish children. Furthermore there is a gradual and comparable increase in difficulty with respect to the four referential subtasks: reference to person and time/space is easier than clausal or verbal reference.

78   *Ludo Verhoeven*

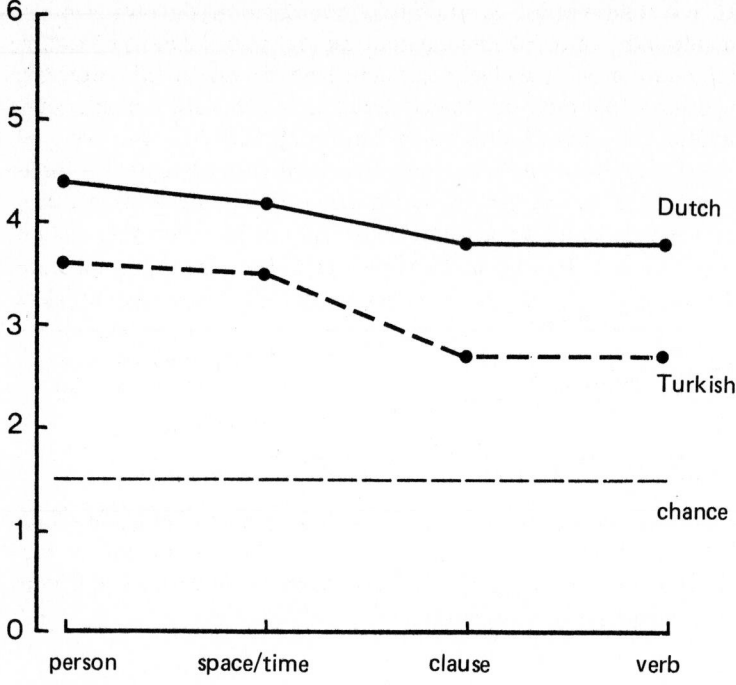

Figure 6. Graphic representation of the mean correct scores on the referential sub-tasks (6=maximum score, 1.5=chance score)

The ANOVA results computed for the Inference Task are presented in Table 2. Again it is shown that the between-factors ethnic group and type of inference result in significant main effects, while the interaction between those factors appears not to be significant.

Table 2: 2 × 3 ANOVA statistics on the Inference task (**p<.01)

Source	Sum of squares	DF	Mean squares	F
Ethnic group	22.1	1	22.1	7.3**
Error	311.3	103	3.0	
Type of inference	9.6	2	4.8	9.9**
E × T interaction	.1	2	.0	.1
Error	99.8	206	.5	

In Figure 7 these results are graphically displayed. Again similar effects are found: the Dutch children obtain higher scores than the Turkish children, and there is a gradual and comparable increase in task difficulty: presupposition items appear to be easier than implication items, while assertion items seem easier than presupposition items.

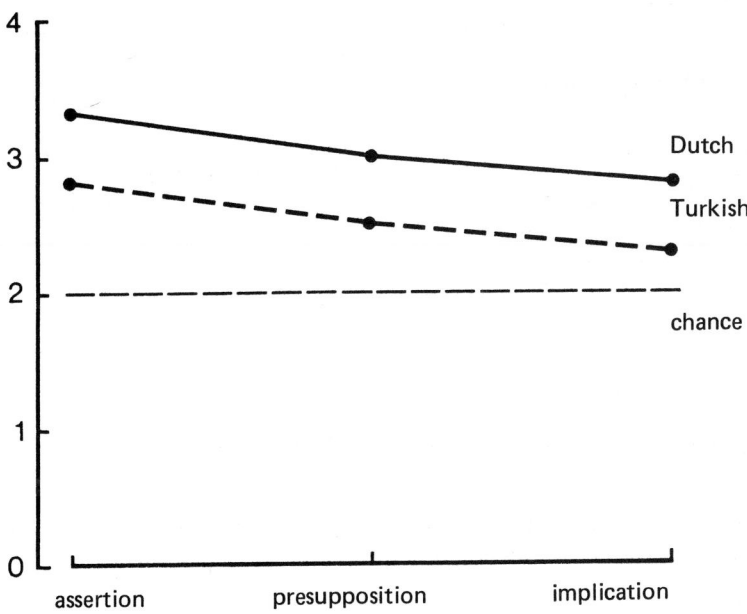

Figure 7. Graphic representation of the mean correct scores on three inferential tasks (4=maximum score, 2=chance score)

Table 3 displays the ANOVA statistics for the Sentential Sequence Task.

Table 3: 2 × 2 ANOVA statistics on the Sequence task (**p<.01)

Source	Sum of squares	DF	Mean squares	F
Ethnic group	308.3	1	308.3	34.7**
Error	1564.7	176	8.9	
Type of sequence	76.7	1	76.8	28.1**
E × T interaction	4.4	1	4.4	1.6
Error	480.3	176	2.7	

The main effects ethnic group and type of sequence prove to be significant, while the interaction between those factors is not. The graphic display in Figure 8 shows that Dutch children perform better on the tasks than the Turkish children and that for both groups it is easier to find the initial sentence of a text than the last one.

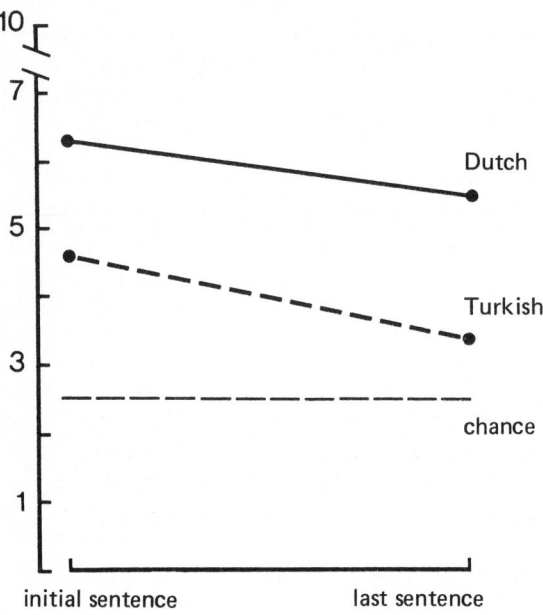

Figure 8. Graphic representation of the mean correct scores on two sequential tasks (10 is maximum score, 2.5=chance score)

From the results in this part of the study it can be concluded that Turkish and Dutch children show comparable features on each of the three reading comprehension tasks. Though the scores achieved by the Dutch children are higher than those of the Turkish children, the order of difficulty of semantic aspects within each of the tasks is the same.

4.2. Individual variation in L2 reading comprehension

In Table 4 the means and the standard deviations of the predictor variables at the onset of the reading instruction are presented.

Table 4: Means and standard deviations (sd) on predictor variables at the onset of reading instruction

Task	Mean	Sd
Phonological discr. (PD)	34.0	6.0
Receptive vocabulary (RV)	23.8	12.0
Productive vocabulary (PV)	8.4	4.7
Sentence imitation (SI)	117.7	49.1
Graph/phon. knowledge (GPK)	4.3	4.4
Phon. segmentation (PS)	3.0	2.2
Phon. synthesis (PSy)	3.9	3.1
Reading concepts (RC)	11.9	3.7

From the numerical values of the standard deviations of these variables it can be concluded that the individual differences of Turkish children on both the L2 oral proficiency tasks and the metalinguistic intuition tasks are considerable. As compared to native Dutch children (see Mommers & Van Dongen 1983) the mean scores on both types of tasks appear to be low.

Table 5 displays the correlations between the predictor variables.

Table 5: Correlations between Turkish children's scores on the predictor variables

	RV	PV	SI	GPK	PS	PSy	RC
PD	.35	.36	.51	.11	.42	.17	.36
RV		.76	.64	.00	.21	−.02	.43
PV			.70	−.06	.28	.12	.45
SI				.00	.40	.05	.41
GPK					.23	.37	.35
PS						.38	.33
PSy							.30

The correlations between the L2 oral proficiency tasks (phonological discrimination, receptive and productive vocabulary, sentence imitation) on the one hand, and between the metalinguistic intuition tasks (grapheme/ phoneme knowledge, phonemic segmentation, phonemic synthesis and reading concepts) on the other hand appear to be relatively high.

Table 6 shows the statistics of the multiple regression analysis with L2 reading comprehension as dependent variables and L2 oral proficiency tasks as predictor variables.

Table 6: Multiple regression statistics with L2 reading comprehension as dependent variable and L2 oral proficiency tasks as predictor variables (*p<.05; **p<.01)

Dependent variable	Predictor variable	Beta	Multiple R
L2 reading comprehension	Receptive vocabulary	.39*	
	Phonological discr.	.19*	
	Sentence imitation	.10	
	Productive vocabulary	−.10	.51**

L2 oral proficiency as measured by the four tasks mentioned explains 26 percent of the total amount of variance in L2 reading comprehension scores. The variable receptive vocabulary contributes significantly to this explained variance. To a lesser degree the variable phonemic discrimination shows a reasonable contribution on its own.

Table 7 presents the statistics of the multiple regression analysis again with L2 reading comprehension as the dependent variable, but with linguistic intuition tasks as predictor variables.

Table 7: Multiple regression statistics with L2 reading comprehension as dependent variable and linguistic intuition tasks as predictor variables (*p<.05; **p<.01)

Dependent variable	Predictor variable	Beta	Multiple R
L2 reading comprehension	Reading concepts	.37*	
	Graph/phon knowledge	.04	
	Phonemic synthesis	.02	
	Phonemic segmentation	.00	.39**

The Turkish children's metalinguistic intuitions, as measured with the four tasks that were used, explain only 15 percent of the total amount of variance in L2 reading comprehension scores. This explained variance appears to be accounted for in its totality by the variable reading concepts. The other variables hardly contribute to the explanation of total variance in reading comprehension scores.

Furthermore, in determining the relative importance of the above mentioned groups of predictor variables two more multiple regression analysed were carried out, treating one group of variables as predictors and the other group of variables as covariates. If the L2 proficiency tasks are taken as predictors with the linguistic intuition tasks as covariates, the prediction proves to be significant ($p < .05$). However, taking the linguistic intuition tasks as predictors while treating the L2 oral proficiency tasks as covariates does not result in a significant prediction of L2 reading comprehension scores.

Finally, in Table 8 a combined multiple regression model is given with the five best predicting variables out of the eight L2 oral proficiency and linguistic intuition variables. These variables explain about 30 percent of the total amount of variance in L2 reading comprehension scores. Again, receptive vocabulary proves to make the largest contribution to this explained variance.

Table 8: Multiple regression statistics with L2 reading comprehension as dependent variable and the five best predicting L2 oral proficiency tasks and linguistic intuition tasks as independent variables (*$p < .05$; **$p < .01$)

Dependent variable	Predictor variable	Beta	Multiple R
L2 reading comprehension	Receptive vocabulary	.31*	
	Reading concepts	.13	
	Phonemic discrimination	.15	
	Grapheme/phoneme knowledge	.11	
	Sentence imitation	.07	.54**

5. DISCUSSION AND PERSPECTIVE

The results of the first part of this study show that semantic complexity as measured in three different reading comprehension tasks does show comparable features in Turkish and Dutch children. Although Dutch children achieve higher scores on each of the tasks than Turkish children, the order of difficulty of semantic aspects within each of the three tasks is the same.

Understanding reference to persons and time/space proves to be easier than clausal and verbal reference for both Turkish and Dutch children. Linguistic devices that imply a relationship between anaphor and antecedent seem to have different impacts on the L1/L2 reading process. The fact that in the first stage of reading development clausal and verbal reference are relatively hard for children can tentatively be explained. In clausal reference it must be understood which of the preceding events in the text forms the antecedent of an anaphoric term. This presupposes a high level of understanding of previous context. Verbal reference, on the other hand, can be seen as a specific syntactic device in the target language Dutch that is primarily used in written discourse. Due to the high processing loads of the initial reading process the association between this anaphoric type and its antecedent will only be learned with difficulty.

As to making inference, both groups of children find presuppositions easier to understand than implications, and assertions easier than presuppositions. It seems that the more implicit items are harder to answer correctly than the more explicit ones. This finding corresponds to the more general finding that both first and second language learners (Cummins 1979) have more difficulty with reading as the text gets more decontextualized (see Scribner & Cole 1981).

Finally with respect to sequential principles of sentences in a text, the search for initial sentences proves to be easier than the search for final sentences for both groups of children. From a linguistic point of view this can be explained by the fact that initial sentences in a text are generally marked by nominal reference, whereas in the other sentences pronominal referents are usually used. From a cognitive point of view it can be added that in the search for the last sentence of a text the whole text must be understood. Initial sentences, on the other hand, can also be found on the basis of a partial understanding of the text.

On the basis of these findings it is claimed that L1/L2 reading comprehension processes have highly universal characteristics. In learning to read in a second language it is primarily the structure of the target language that accounts for various comprehension difficulties and *not* the structure of the source language. This finding is in line with the outcome of most of the studies cited in section 2 of this chapter.

The second part of this study shows that in the initial stages, Turkish children learning to read Dutch as a second language manifest remarkable individual differences in their oral L2 proficiency and their metalinguistic intuitions. However, as a predictor of L2 reading success after one year of reading instruction, L2 oral proficiency proves to be much more important than metalinguistic intuitions (explaining 26 and 15 percent of the variance in reading comprehension scores respectively). The finding that oral L2 proficiency is a good predictor of L2 reading success corresponds with similar conclusions from earlier mentioned research in this field.

Furthermore this study provides insights in the common and relative contribution of the best predicting linguistic variables of L2 reading comprehension ability. Five variables together turn out to explain 30 percent of the total variance in reading comprehension scores. Receptive vocabulary proves responsible for the highest contribution. The efficiency of L2 reading strategies seems to be primarily related to the size of L2 vocabulary.

In a later stage we will analyse more data in order to develop a more extensive theoretical framework with respect to structural and temporal aspects of Turkish children's process of learning to read Dutch as a second language. From a structural point of view the miscues that Turkish and Dutch children demonstrate while reading Dutch texts aloud will be analyzed so that the syntactic and semantic strategies within both groups of subjects can be compared. Furthermore, we will compare the graphonological strategies both groups use while reading lists of isolated words. Finally, the reading results of Turkish children in three different bilingual instructional conditions will be evaluated so that the efficiency of the various methods of instruction can be revealed.

From a temporal point of view we will investigate the role of underlying variables that might be relevant in explaining individual L2 reading results of Turkish children. As such the predicting power of the oral language proficiency of Turkish children in their mother tongue as well as their socio-cultural orientation will be determined.

5

The Brussels Foyer Bicultural Education Project: Socio-Cultural Background and Psycho-educational Language Assessment

Marc Spoelders, Johan Leman & Ludo Smeekens

0. INTRODUCTION

Foyer is a relatively small socio-educational non-profit organisation for migrants in Brussels. Amongst other activities a Bicultural Education Project (BEP) has been set up. Indeed, for some years now, Foyer has been – at least in Flanders – best known for its specific model of bilingual education for migrants in the Brussels context. It is, so to speak, a kind of field laboratory in which educational research in this domain is initiated. The Foyer model aims at a positive reorientation of the specific languages-in-contact/conflict situation for migrant children in Brussels by providing an adequate educational setting in which integration of the home culture and the host culture is promoted.

Though BEP is currently extending to other target groups of migrant children (of Spanish, Moroccan and Turkish origin) as well as to the kindergarten level (totalling 155 children September 1, 1984), the data on language assessment reported here refer to the first group of Italian children. In 1981, at the beginning of the school year, the parents of seven Italian (mostly Sicilian) children were invited to take part in the project (henceforth BEP-It). With the cooperation of a school in the neighbourhood whose language of instruction is Dutch, educational facilities were created for splitting up the first year of the primary school into two parallel classes: one for BEP-It, the other one for their autochtonous peers (BEP-F1). The motto was "the proof of the pudding is in the eating". Before going into the educational and didactic realisation of BEP at the classroom level (the Foyer model), we will briefly sketch the socio-cultural background against which BEP is projected. In a last section we will elaborate on the psycho-educational language assessment. By way of conclusion these data are again related to some more general aspects of migration.

* We gratefully acknowledge the cooperation of Mrs. Coppens, H. De Smedt, R. Lamberti, L. Marchi, I. Morreel and Gr. Vercamme who spent many hours assessing the speech of the Italian and Flemish children for this study.

1. SOCIOCULTURAL BACKGROUND

About one quarter of the total population of Brussels (which has about one million inhabitants) is of foreign origin: in decreasing order, Moroccan, Italian, Spanish, French, Turkish, Greek, British, Zairese, and Dutch. In some quarters of the city, migrants from the Mediterranean area - who are considered by autochtonous people to be the really 'foreign' group and with whom this paper is concerned - make up more than fifty percent of the population. In kindergarten and primary school, figures even amount to eighty and ninety percent. Indeed, this is probably becoming the real challenge for the year 2000.

At present Brussels is a multicultural and multilingual city, with a predemonantly French street image. As an economic and geographical centre, however, it is situated in a multilingual country, with a Dutch speaking majority. For each citizen of Brussels, and thus for every migrant who lives there, proficiency in Dutch gains in importance every day. The ethno-cultural and linguistic complexity is colouring the Brussels situation in a unique and fascinating way. From an educational point of view the following aspects should especially be taken into account:

- the actual family situation
- the predominant street image
- the real employment possibilities
- the educational opportunities for the child in case the parents decide to return later to their source country
- the child's cultural rights
- other, for instance, sociolinguistic arguments for an efficient development of the language of origin.

In the Brussels migrant families the respective home-languages could hardly be identified with the respective standard languages. The home languages vary from regional or local dialect (which on the morphological level sometimes differs strongly from the standard language) to mixed language or - in some cases - French which is often the first language of socialisation. However, we share the opinion of many interested in this field that French-Dutch bilingualism is becoming more important than it was some years ago, when French dominated completely.

As far as employment is concerned - and this is especially true for the more qualified jobs - a thorough proficiency in Dutch becomes more and more a necessity. Proficiency in Dutch seems to have made a jump not only in the job-requirements parade but also, for example, in the advertising business in the last years.

For some time the idea of returning has grown among some migrants, especially the more successful ones. It should be remembered that immigration to Brussels by ethnic groups from the Mediterranean is of fairly recent date (from the sixties onwards). When parents decide to return, they expect their children to have a good command of the standard language of their home country. This too forms part of the socio-linguistic and educational situation of the migrant family. Having the opportunity to develop one's mother tongue is, of course, one of the cultural rights of the child. Native language has, indeed, a solidarity-creating effect and is "the very lifeblood of human self-awareness, it is the carrier of identity, the safe repository of a vast array of affective and cognitive templates making up the total web of personality" (Guiora 1984:10).

Though second generation children are sometimes socialized in a language other than the so-called mother tongue, we are not tempted to isolate or overaccentuate this fact thereby placing them outside the broader diachronic and synchronic context of migration. Indeed, an important aspect of language and speech lies in the implicit continuous reference to the history of the specific language speakers as a group, at least when this language is experienced as mother tongue, i.e. a language that refers to the culture of origin. To speak a certain language as a mother tongue does not so much mean that there is a special relation with the language of the parents or guardians, or that the use of this language is narrowed to the preschool first socialization but refers rather to the establishment of restoration of a link with the history of people who recognize themselves in this mother tongue as a group or community.

But why talk about a bicultural education project in a trilingual situation and not in a multilingual one? Even though Brussels has a multicultural character, the migrant is basically faced with three languages: his own mother tongue, French and Dutch. Because of this specificity, the Foyer model, described in the next section, does not pretend to offer solutions for conditions other than those found in Brussels.

2. THE FOYER MODEL

The Foyer model functions on the level of kindergarten and primary school of the Dutch educational system in Brussels. It essentially tries to achieve that the apparently divergent and sometimes contradictory language stimuli are filtered out in school to the benefit of the child. The model consists of a gradual and guided integration of, in principle, one migrant subgroup in each school. In this process as much emphasis as possible is put on the maintenance and strengthening of the migrant's own identity, on the condition, however, that this does not have a negative effect on the rest of the educational process. In the 1984–85 school year the first group of Italian children were in the 4th year, and the oldest group of Spanish children in the 3rd year of elementary education. A 'replay' Italo-Flemish group started September 1, 1984, in the first year and groups of Moroccan and Turkish children were introduced on kindergarten level. For a better understanding of this mono-ethnic approach it should be remembered that most quarters in Brussels, even if they are of a pluri-ethnic type and thus are typical migrant twilight zones (Rex 1973), have their own dominant ethnic subgroup. And it is this dominant subgroup which is integrated in each quarter. Furthermore, the schools involved are rather small.

The children spend three years in kindergarten: from three to six years of age. Half the week they play separately; communication proceeds in their first language. The general aim of a (bicultural) kindergarten is to provide sound guidance of the developmental process of the individual toddler through the creation of educational settings in which experiences in several domains can be gained. Toddlers are helped to sort out or deepen their understanding of these experiences so that they become ready for primary schooling. A major part of the activities is devoted to (home) language development. But Dutch is also 'taught': the children are familiarized with this language as a functional medium in the discourse with, for example, their Dutch speaking peers.

The six years of primary school are divided into the two first school years and the period that follows. The objective is a gradual integration of both allochtonous and autochtonous groups of pupils. In the first year 60% of the curriculum is devoted to 'eduation in their language and culture' (EOLC), 30% to 'Dutch as a foreign language' (DFL), and 10% to 'integrated activities' (IA). Reading and writing skills are taught in the language of origin. In the second year these figures are: 50% EOLC, 20% DFL, and 30% IA (as soon as possible a shift within mathematics is made from EOLC to Dutch). In this second year attention to the child's own language continues. But at the same time the children are taught a new code, i.e. the Dutch writing system. Figure 1 illustrates the gliding of languages for the Italo-Dutch group. From the third year onwards IA makes up 90%, and EOLC 10%. At that moment the two groups (of about ten children each) are merged in an 'integration class'.

Meanwhile most of the children have been gradually absorbing French, usually street and T.V. language, and possibly also, albeit fragmentarily, the language spoken at home. During the third year and the years to follow, while the mother tongue is developed further (4 hours a week)

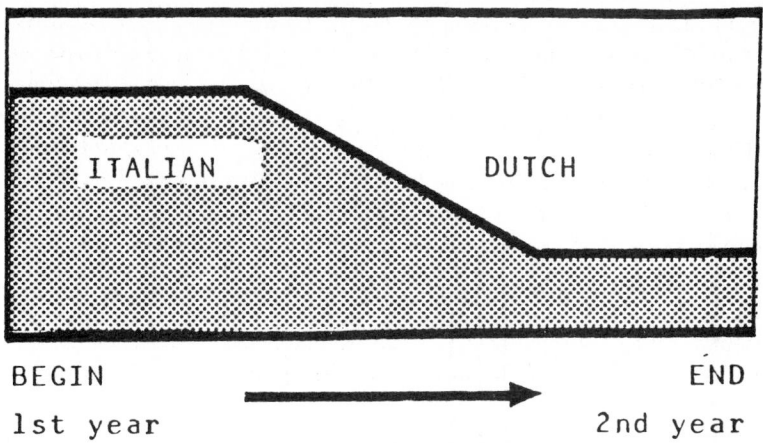

ITALIAN   DUTCH

BEGIN   END
1st year   2nd year

Figure 1. Gliding of languages for BEP-It.

and Dutch is activated as the medium of instruction, the children are taught French writing, to which the same amount of time is devoted as it is to Flemish-speaking children in the Brussels area. Within the model it should be possible that towards the end of the primary school those allochtonous children are becoming trilingual.

3. PSYCHO-EDUCATIONAL LANGUAGE ASSESSMENT OF THE FIRST ITALO-FLEMISH GROUP

It lies beyond the scope of this contribution to elaborate extensively on the present state of the project (see Foyer-stuurgroep: Bicultureel 1983 for a first evaluation). Furthermore, the project has not been finished yet and firm conclusions cannot be drawn from the data based on the low number of children reported on here. Some first data resulting from Italian, French and (more specifically) Dutch language assessment will be presented. Though the real value of this work probably lies in the clinical in-depth analyses of different individual cases, the report only presents some overall quantitative results. From the beginning of the second school year we have been screening BEP-It, BEP-F1 and 'control' NONBEP-It and NONBEP-F1 with several language testing devices. We obtained a wealth of data and were able to make a lot of observations.

3.1. 'Experiment' and 'control' classes

Our investigation took place in three different school settings: A, B & C.

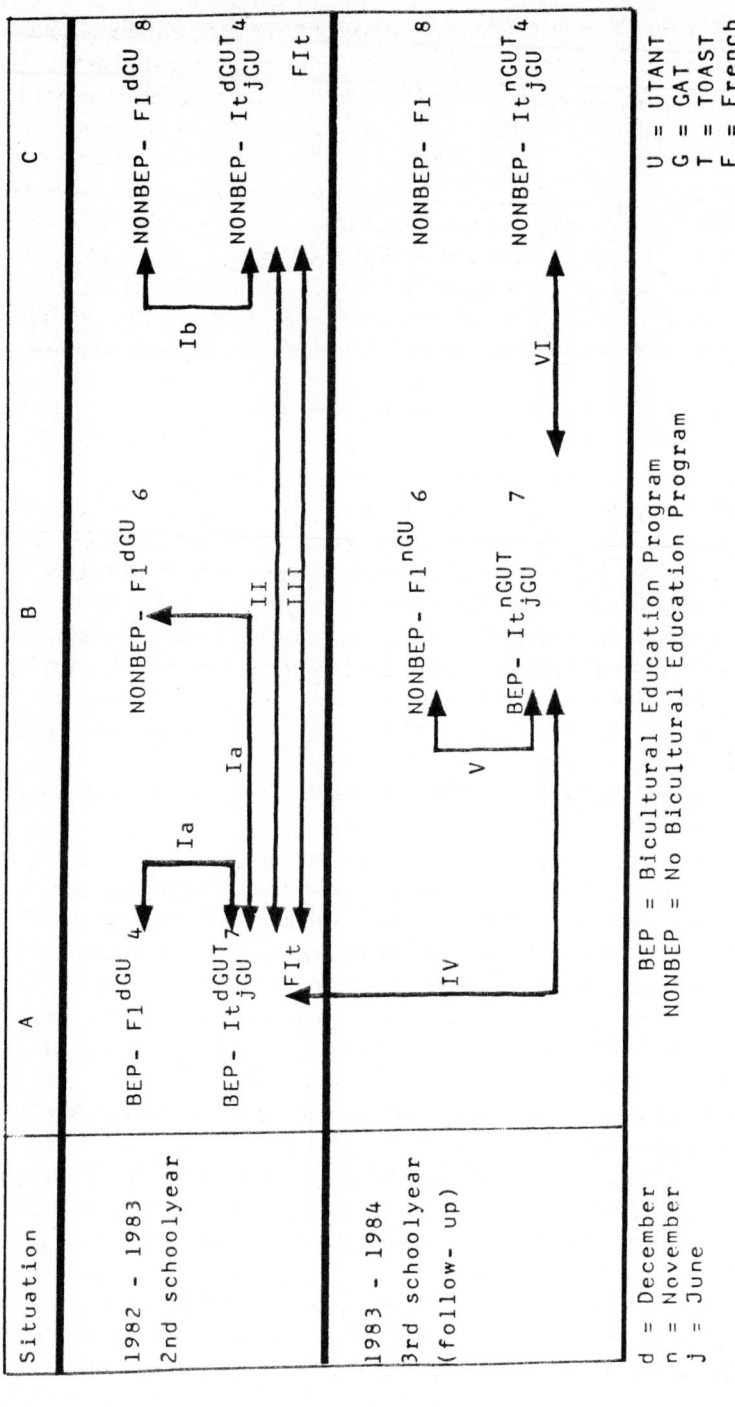

Table 1. Classes involved and research questions.

Situation A refers to the intake classes (BEP-It and BEP-F1; 7 and 4 pupils respectively). Situation B is a school in which we studied a 'normal' 2nd year (3rd year in 1983–1984). From the beginning this class was in the running to become the integration class for BEP-It. This group consisted of 6 Flemish pupils (NONBEP-F1). In situation C there were four Italian children in the second year. However, no special arrangements for them had been made: from kindergarten onwards allochtonous children follow a monocultural regime (either Dutch or French). Table 1 also shows the testing periods: in principle (and as to Dutch), pupils were tested on four occasions, i.e. December 1982, June 1983, November 1983 and June 1984.

3.2. Research questions

The following questions guided our research (see Table 1):
Ia Do 2nd year BEP-It children function on a proficiency level in Dutch that will allow them to get instruction in Dutch only, from the third year onwards? To answer this question we compared BEP-It, NONBEP-F1 and NONBEP-It.
Ib Do 2nd year NONBEP-It pupils have a proficiency level in Dutch that corresponds to that of their autochtonous, NONBEP-F1 peers? Comparisons Ia and Ib were to allow us to find a kind of class norm.
II How do BEP-It and NONBEP-It pupils compare on some Dutch language proficiency tests?
III How do BEP-It and NONBEP-It compare on proficiency in Italian and French?
The following questions regard the follow-up study, performed in 1983–1984, when the pupils were in their third year of study in primary school.
IV What is the progression of Dutch proficiency of BEP-It?
V How do BEP-It relate to NONBEP-F1 compared to 1982–1983?
VI How do BEP-It relate to NONBEP-It compared to 1982–1983?

3.3. Instruments

Throughout the study we made use of the following more or less currently used language tests:
(a) UTANT (Utrechtse Taalniveau Test, Kohnstamm et al. 1971): an ITPA-(Illinois Test for Psycholinguistic Abilities) like test containing subtests on receptive word proficiency, analogies and contrasts, morphological rules, and giving descriptions;
(b) GAT (Grammaticale Analyse Test, Van Geert 1975) which measures the syntactic capacity of children aged 5 – 9. It is an experimental paper and pencil test which consists of two parallel forms. We used form 1 as a

complement to the morphology-subtest of UTANT because of its in-depth analysis of syntactic competence thus rendering a wealth of information for remediation.

(c) TOAST (Taal Onderzoek via Analyse van Spontane Taal, Moerman-Coetsier & Van Besien 1982), an experimental instrument which uses a corpus of spontaneous speech to determine the language proficiency of the child. TOAST defines the general proficiency level of the child (by means of MLU, mean length of utterance), the extendedness of vocabulary (by means of type-token ratio in a corpus of 100 words), an index of intelligibility (number of completely intelligible words in 100 utterances), and an index of communicative competence (the proportion between responses of the child and the number of direct stimuli by the adult researcher). Another index of pragmatic competence (i.e. the proportion between the total number of spontaneous utterances of the child and the total number of responses to questions and other stimuli) was also used in the follow-up. In addition to those quantitative pragmatic measures, a more qualitative analysis of speech acts based on Dore's functional taxonomy (1975) was performed. It should be noted that none of the tests used here is specifically designed for use with migrant children. This is especially true for UTANT. Because we had some doubts about the validity of our instruments, we asked the teacher of the third class in C for a rank-ordering of his BEP-It and NONBEP-F1 pupils on Dutch proficiency (leaving out of account pronounciation). Spearman rank correlations with our UTANT interpretations were, however, high (.93 for Bep-It and .82 for NONBEP-F1).

To answer the third question (skill in and knowledge of French and Italian), the evaluators, a French-speaking speech therapist and a qualified native Italian staff member of Foyer, made use of the following tests:

(a) (for French) the TERMAN-MERRILL subtest of word knowledge, an ad hoc device based on DESCOEUDRES (1948) and UTANT measuring analogies and contrasts, two subtests of a clinical test developed by BO-REL-MAISONNY (1960) ('Construction de phrases', 'Complètement de phrases'), and an ad hoc test corpus, based on TOAST for the analysis of spontaneous speech;

(b) (for Italian) CESPEE (Bruni), i.e. four subtests 'Abilità di recezione per canale uditivo', 'Uso di parole adatte ad un contesto analogico', 'Trovare delle relazioni significative tra imagini', 'Conoscenza della morfologia del nome e dell' uso del verbo' were administered. In addition to those four subtests of the 'Complesso per l'esame dello sviluppo psicolinguistico in età evolutiva', the spontaneous speech of the Italian children was evaluated by the Italian teacher.

3.4. Results and discussion

In this section we bring together the results of the language assessments and discuss them briefly. The reader is invited to check Table 1 for the respective research questions to which the data refer.

Ia

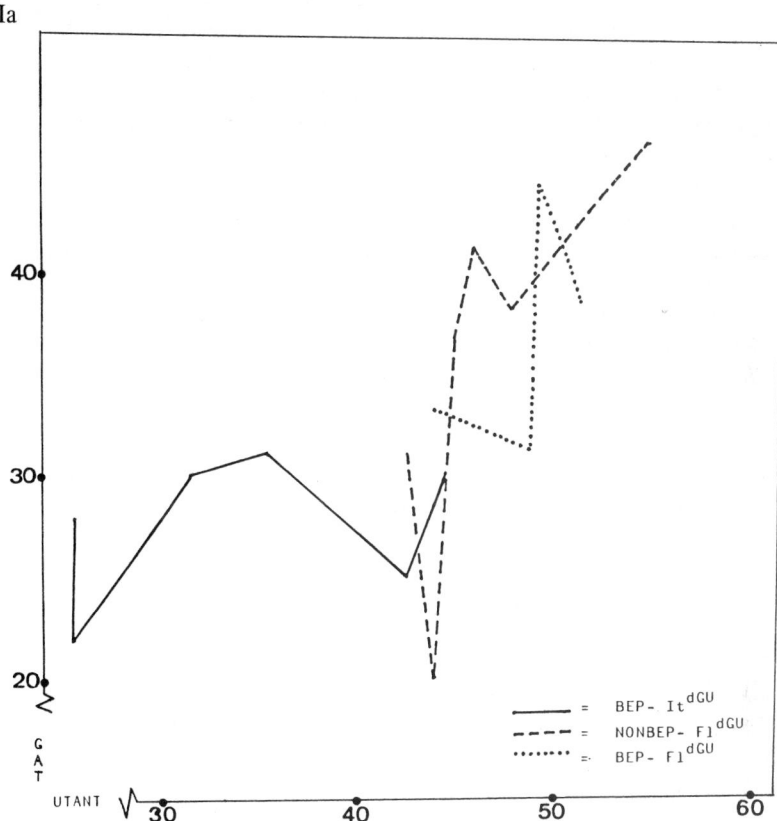

Figure 2. Comparison of BEP-It, BEP-F1 and NONBEP-F1 1982–83 on UTANT and GAT.

In this and analogous figures a subject receives a place in function of two coordinates, i.e. his results on two tests. The different places are then connected.

Scores obtained by BEP-It on the different subtests of UTANT differ considerably from child to child. Some Italian children, however, approximate their native peers. Most problems arise within the subtest of morphological rules. It should be remembered that BEP-It only received 7 hours of instruction per week during the first school year, with an emphasis on comprehension rather than on explicit knowledge of grammar. The BEP-It class mean is 34.8 (on 80 max); mean scores for BEP-F1 and NONBEP-F1 (B) are 48.5 and 46.75 respectively. All in all scores are rather low for all classes tested. Probably the norms of UTANT – originally defined on a population in the Netherlands – are not tailored to the Flemish population. The same general trend can be observed as to GAT: BEP-It mean score is 27.7 (on 50 max); the mean scores for BEP-F1 and NONBEP-F1 (B) are 36.5 and 35.3 respectively. In all groups the interindividual differences scores obtained by the 'best' BEP-It children approximate those of the low scoring NONBEP-F1 and BEP-F1 peers.

Ib

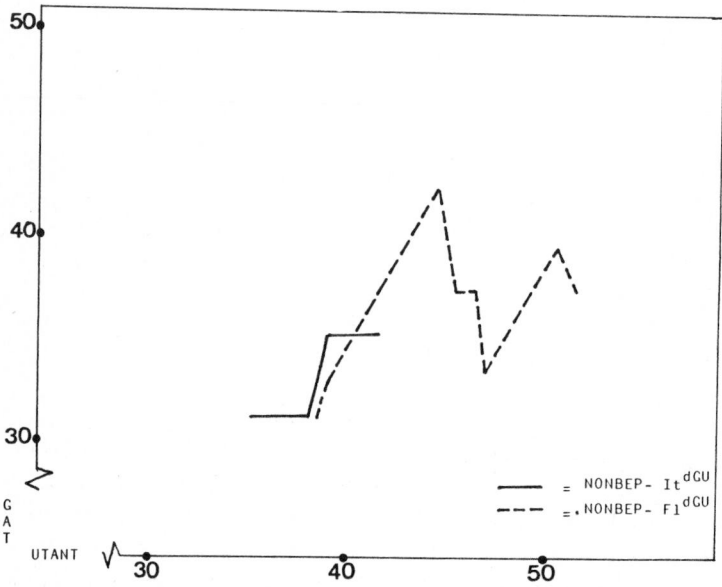

Figure 3. Comparison of NONBEP-It and NONBEP-F1 1982–83 on UTANT and GAT.

On all subtests of UTANT the interindividual differences are high. Compared to the other Flemish children examined NONBEP-F1 (C) results are low. The scores of NONBEP-It 'fit' into the range of scores of NONBEP-F1 (C). However, on the subtest 'Analogies and contrasts', scores are clearly lower. Some NONBEP-It children show better results in the subtest 'defining' than do some NONBEP-F1 (C) peers. The mean scores are 38.4 and 45.4 for NONBEP-It and NONBEP-F1 (C) respectively. As could be expected from the results on the subtest 'morphology' of

UTANT, scores on GAT are rather low. But here too, NONBEP-F1 (C) achieve less well than the other Flemish children tested. The scores of NONBEP-It can already be situated within the range of scores obtained by NONBEP-F1 (C). The mean scores on GAT are 33 and 36.1 respectively.

II

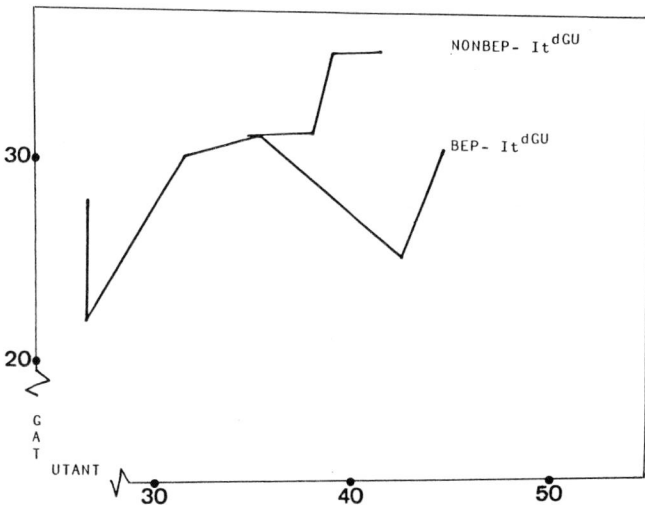

Figure 4. Comparison of BEP-It and NONBEP-It 1982–83 on UTANT and GAT.

Judged from the test results of December 1982 on UTANT & GAT (for means, see above), the general picture is that BEP-It score lower than NONBEP-It. The area which presents most difficulties is grammar. Almost all children make the same kind of errors: the difference between the groups is rather a matter of quantity. The spontaneous speech corpus reveals interference as well as developmental errors (for example in the endings of declined or conjugated words). Examples of the former are, on the level of syntax, French word order in Dutch sentences "nu gij ga lachen" or, on the lexical level, the insertion of French words "Italia of Amérique, ik heb met de bateau geweest". In June 1983 both groups had made progress in Dutch (as measured by UTANT & GAT). Most striking are the results of BEP-It on the subtest dealing with morphology, analogy and contrasts. Clinical examination of the children confirms this observation. Figure 5 clearly shows the shifting of the curves.

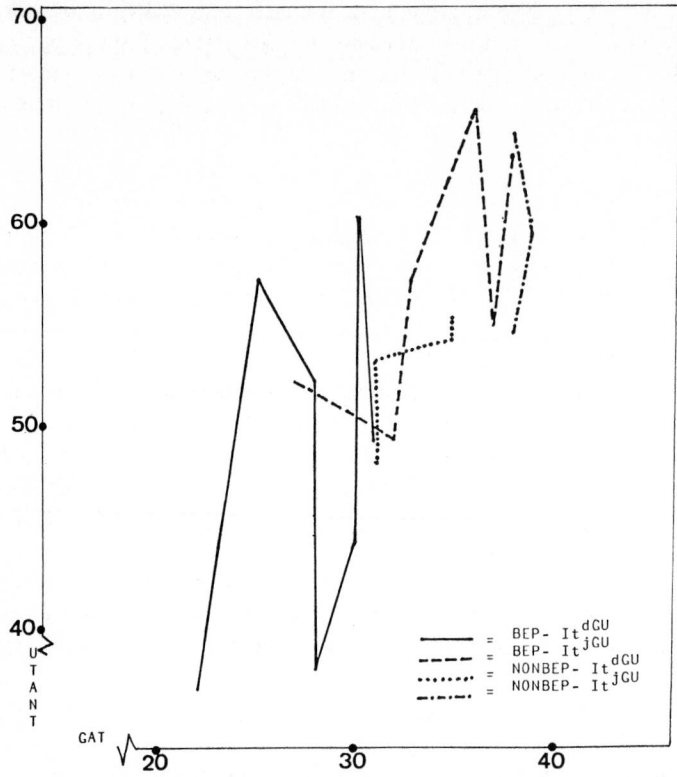

Figure 5. Comparison of BEP-It and NONBEP-It 1982–83 (December & June) on UTANT and GAT.

III

As could be expected BEP-It are more skilled in Italian than NONBEP-It. Most striking is the fact that the latter seem to pass through a phase of stagnation as far as their mastery of Italian is concerned. which at the age of 8 and 9 puts them on a level comparable with that of 4 to 5 year old Italian children in Italy. Also, spontaneous use of Italian with NONBEP-It is very limited. On the other hand, BEP-It show normal to very good progress in Italian, though it is obvious that the starting point cannot be compared with that of Italian children in Italy. The influence of the factors home and environment certainly has something to do with this. It appeared to the Italian research-assistant that a kind of stagnation can be observed outside the project versus progress within the project. This means probably at the same time that in the former case stagnation will gradually turn into regression, because the school system does not promote Italian language and culture. At the end of the project we hope to examine whether this regression, besides being a lost opportunity for learning the Italian language and culture, also influences further achievement in school which is not directly linked to the Italian language and vice versa.

As far as French proficiency is concerned. the clinical interpretations offered by the French speech therapist point in the direction of a more favourable evolution for BEP-It than for NONBEP-It. This finding may relate to the fact that BEP-It have been in a kindergarten where French is spoken.

Given these results, there were no strong counter-indications to assume that BEP-It could join the Flemish children of the integration class, at least as far as Dutch language proficiency is concerned. We even feel encouraged to believe that the slight dropping behind in Dutch will disappear towards the end of the primary school (based also on Skutnabb-Kangas and Toukomaa 1976) and that, in general, their achievement in school will proportionally be better and remain that way, in addition to maintaining the advantage of a high proficiency in the Italian language. We hope that the four hours of Italian/week from the third year onwards will be sufficient.

IV

Figure 6 gives a general view on the evolution of BEP-It as to Dutch language proficiency (as measured by UTANT & GAT). The same evolutionary picture appears with almost all children: a sharp positive rise in June 83, a fall in November 83, and a clear jump forwards in June 84. This 'kink' is illustrated in Figures 7 & 8 (for UTANT & GAT, respectively). Mean scores on UTANT: November 40.36, June 44.5. Mean scores on GAT: November 33.71, June 36. The distribution of the scores, especially on UTANT, remains wide, reflecting the heterogeneity of BEP-It children. This heterogeneity can also clearly be demonstrated by means of a close examination of the scores obtained by the different children on the TOAST-indexes: from December 82 to November 83 a slight progression could be observed on the means of MLU (from 3.69 to 4.9), TTR (from .55 to .65), II (from .92 to .93), and CI (from .84 to .93/from 79.43 to 87.14). However, on some indexes certain children score lower in November 83 than in December 82. But although the distribution of the results is more dispersed for TTR and MLU (reflecting great differences in the use of words and the length of utterances) the intelligibility becomes better (i.e. the range of scores is becoming smaller for this index).

A possible explanation for the 'kink' in the overall evolution could be

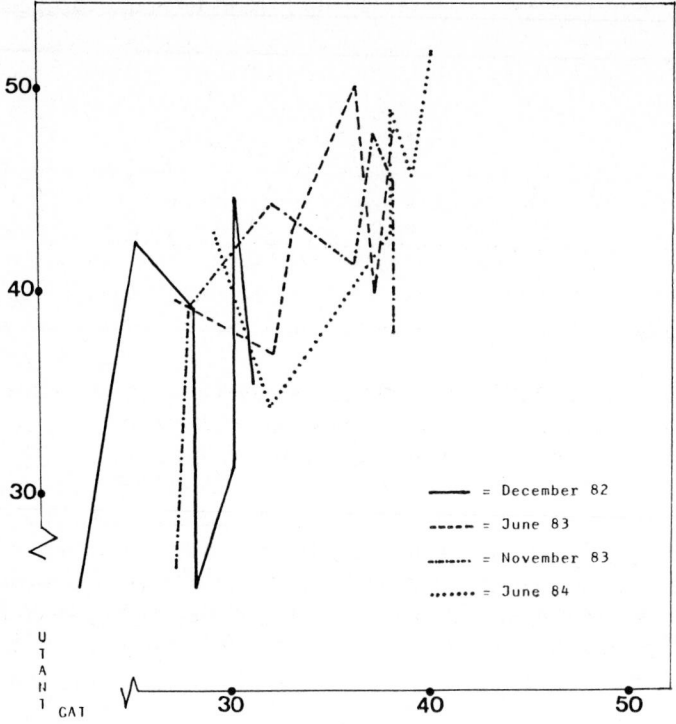

Figure 6. Evolution BEP-It on UTANT and GAT.

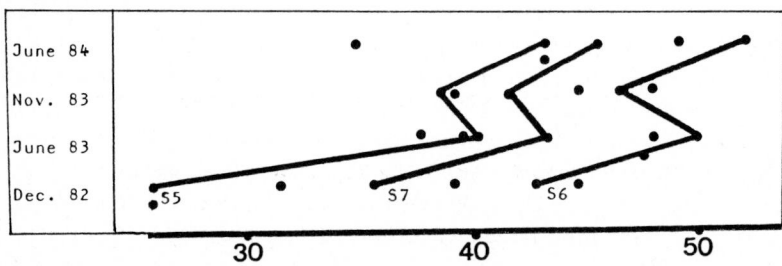

Figure 7. Evolution BEP-It on UTANT (Profile illustrations of Ss 5, 6 & 7).

the relatively long vacation period (two months) preceding the November testing in a dominant Italo-French setting. It should also be taken into account that in the third year no special, 'tailored' Dutch lessons for Italian migrants are being taught (still 9 hours/week in the second year). However, there are more hours in which Dutch is used as the language

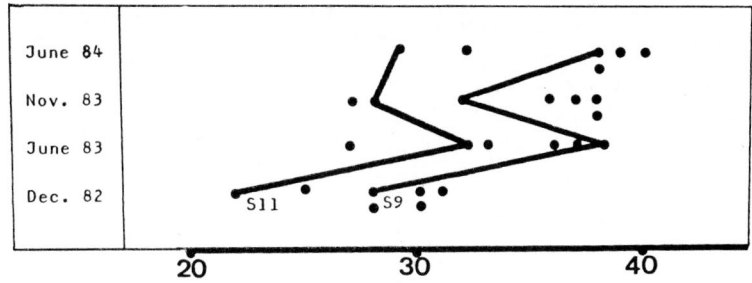

Figure 8. Evolution BEP-It on GAT (Profile illustrations of Ss 9 & 11).

of instruction. Since NONBEP-It children also show a similar evolution and since they do not receive any special tutoring either, the (negative) influence of the holidays seems to have the most explanatory value.

V

The differences in mean scores on UTANT and GAT become smaller (from approximately 7 points in December 1982 to less than 4 points in November 1983 for GAT; from about 12 to about 9 for UTANT). Figures 9 & 10 show that in November 83 BEP-It 'fit' better in the scores of NONBEP-F1 (B). The errors made in November 83 remain of the same kind as in December 82.

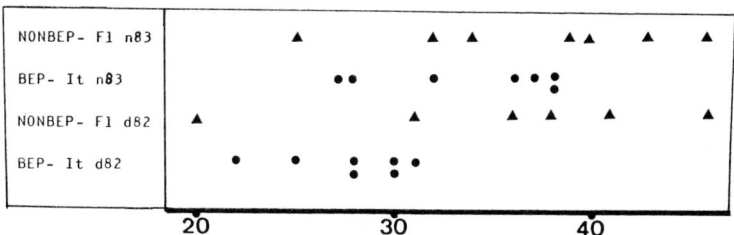

Figure 9. GAT results of BEP-It and NONBEP-F1 (B) on two occasions.

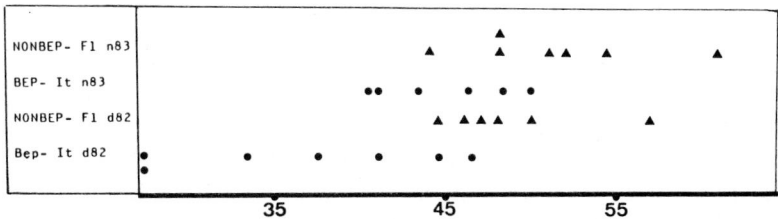

Figure 10. UTANT results of BEP-It and NONBEP-F1 (B) on two occasions.

VI

The difference in mean scores of BEP-It and NONBEP-It on UTANT becomes larger (to the advantage of the latter): 3.5 in December 82, almost 6.5 in June 84. On GAT, on the other hand, the difference in mean scores becomes smaller (from 5.3 to 2.2).

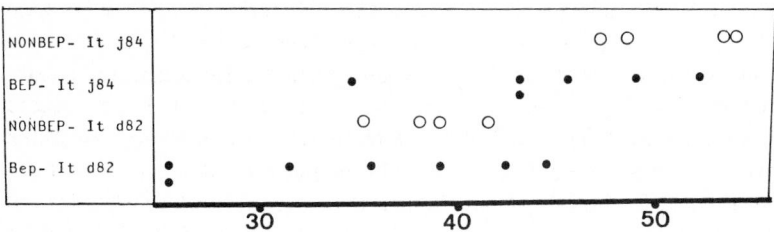

Figure 11. UTANT results of BEP-It and NONBEP-It on two occasions.

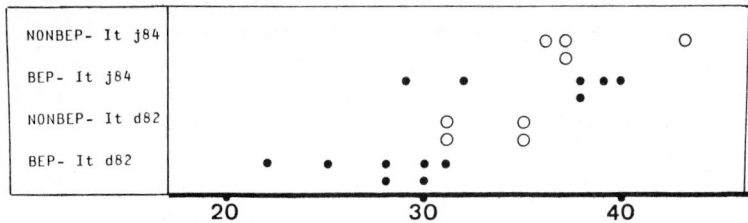

Figure 12. GAT results of BEP-It and NONBEP-It on two occasions.

4. CONCLUSION

It would be unwise to 'eyeball' the data presented here and not relate it to the real lifeblood of the language learning processes that take place in BEP. We are aware of the fact that in this report much attention has been paid to formal aspects of language knowledge (knowing that), rather than to more functional aspects (knowing how) of language skill. Indeed, the communicative ability of BEP-It did not come into focus so far. Yet, TOAST data at our disposal point in the direction of growing communicative competence. This is confirmed by two other observations. (a) A qualitative analysis of the spontaneous speech utterances revealed that all language functions (as suggested in TOAST, based on Dore's system of classification), such as giving information, asserting, regulating, giving answers, asking for information or action, etc., were realised by

BEP-It (with a pronounced preponderance of asserting). (b) Observation in the classroom during a Besellian-like class conversation (see Van Damme 1982) revealed that BEP-It actively engage in conversation: they turn up as astonishingly active and spontaneous communicators. Observations such as these also point to the relevance of a more ethnographically oriented methodology for studying communication-in-action.

In BEP we try to incorporate language-like questions into a broader framework of process-like characteristics of the migration of specific ethnic minorities into the Brussels area (see Leman 1982). Speaking about language education and language proficiency has more implications than just language related ones. In fact, the status attributed to a language in the educational process implies a cultural option which relates to the cultural identity of the future adult. Supporting this cultural identity need not be a disadvantage for the social adjustment of the migrant children involved or for their loyalty towards the host country and its autochtonous people. On the contrary, not supporting cultural identity will enhance the probability of irrational revendicative actions which could lead to disintegration of society (see Cohen 1974, Despres 1975, De Vos & Romanucci-Ross 1975, Epstein et al 1978; Glazer & Moynihan 1963, 1975; McKay & Lewins 1976, and Roosens 1979).

We would finally like to point to the particular situation experienced by the so-called second generation (see Leman 1979 & 1980). This generation, at least during the school period, seems to be most of all inclined to assimilate the characteristics of its autochtonous environment. Often this process involves some kind of aggressiveness towards the host country. This almost certainly relates to the fact that this generation consists of children who at a very early age, i.e. at the start of their period of schooling, have seen their authority poles – who represented their language and culture – discredited de facto (though usually unconsciously), in favour of new authority poles, namely the teacher of the autochtonous educational system, representing the culture of the host country. It seems a wise pedagogical principle, to attribute precisely at the beginning of the school period an important role to allochtonous adults, teachers who are as closely as possible connected to the culture of the migrant families. Part of the success of BEP should be ascribed, not only to the clear bilingualism-with-diglossia character of the endeavours, but above all to the genuine 'engagement' of these teachers. They deeply believe that their efforts, based on the solicited cooperation of the parents, will lead to intercultural education from which all will benefit, both ethnic minority and majority children.

6

Ethnic Group Differences in Children's Oral Proficiency of Dutch

Ludo Verhoeven & Anne Vermeer

1. INTRODUCTION

In almost all schools in the Netherlands Dutch is the medium of instruction from the very beginning for both Dutch and minority children. Such a 'submersion' model makes high demands upon minority children's communicative competence in Dutch: in the beginning they are not used to speaking Dutch, whereas later on the instruction patterns in school become more complex and formal. Among minority children there are great differences in Dutch language proficiency: some of them show a very low proficiency level, whereas others seem to have the same competence in Dutch as their native speaking classmates. So within school classes there is a very wide range of competences in Dutch.

Most minority children start learning Dutch when they enter kindergarten, at their fourth year. With respect to Dutch language development the relative distance between minority and Dutch children appears to be one year or more, which is hard to make up for within a few years. It is reported that this gap is not bridged but becomes even wider in the course of time. Stijnen & Vallen (1981) mention that dialect-speaking children in the Netherlands show a pattern of stabilisation in their acquisition of the standard language after some years in school. Molony (1982) reports that the relative distance between Moluccan children learning Dutch and their Dutch classmates becomes greater, a process referred to as 'divergence': at entering school Moluccan and Dutch children show fewer differences in Dutch competence than in the final classes of primary schools.

In an educational setting with great individual differences in language proficiency between children, teachers need procedures and instruments to evaluate the childrens' competence in Dutch: what aspects do they master, what are their lacunae, do they make progress in learning Dutch?, i.e. they need a diagnostic evaluation procedure. In this section an outline is given for such procedures and instruments.[1] Furthermore, these procedures will be applied in studying the variation in oral proficiency of Dutch in children of different age levels of two minority groups: Surinam and Turkish children. Both groups appear to be good representatives of the linguistic minorities that have recently immigrated to the Netherlands. The Surinam group can be seen as a representative of the groups from former Dutch colonies. The Turkish group represents the foreign workers from Mediterranean countries who have migrated to the Netherlands since the early sixties and whose stay became more permanent, when during the seventies they were allowed to let their families come over.

The language backgrounds of both groups are quite different. In Surinam, Dutch is the colonial language used at school. However, to a lot of Surinam people who have come to the Netherlands, Dutch norms and values and hence also Dutch language are experienced as unfamiliar. What the impact is of these supposed experiences on the actual proficiency of Dutch in Surinam children who attend Dutch schools by now, remains an open question. On the other hand, the first generation of Turkish immigrants can be seen as predominantly Turkish speaking persons. Their children, most of whom were born in the Netherlands, seem to form a generation that undergoes a truly bilingual development. However, it is unclear to what extent these children succeed in a native-like development of both languages.

This paper is structured as follows. In the next paragraph (2) theoretical aspects of the study of language acquisition and of language abilities assessment in minority children are discussed. Paragraph 3 gives the design of a study in which the individual variation in oral proficiency of Dutch in Surinam and Turkish children is determined and compared with that of Dutch children. In paragraph 4 the results of the above mentioned study are given. In a final paragraph (5) these results will be discussed.

2. LANGUAGE ACQUISITION AND DEFINING LANGUAGE ABILITIES

Language acquisition can be conceived as a creative process in which a learner, in interaction with speakers of the target language, picks up characteristics of the target system. On the basis of language input he forms hypotheses about the rules of the system, which are right or wrong, at least according to the target norms. During the process of acquiring the target language, those hypotheses are constantly adjusted and newly formed. In the course of time the learner's language is made up of successive interlanguages, the last of which finally (nearly) equals the target language.

In this process of 'creative construction' (Dulay & Burt 1974) the successive interlanguages are highly systematic and predictable. Various studies show that the order in which people, from different L1-backgrounds learn the elements and rules of a second language, has a remarkable resemblance as regards the deviations from the L2 norm (Cancino, Rosansky & Schumann 1975). A particular structure or rule B is acquired only when a particular structure or rule A is mastered, and not the other way around. Basically, this holds for both second and first language learners (for Dutch, see Extra 1978). This fact offers interesting educational perspectives. Firstly, it makes it possible to determine the position of a learner in the language acquisition process. From this position it may be deduced what has already been acquired and what has not. Given that a learner has acquired rules K, L and M, and not N and O, a teacher can deduce that A - J has been acquired too, and not yet P-Z. Secondly, because of considerable order similarities between first and second language learning processes, it is possible to compare the level of proficiency of second language learners with that of first language learners. Especially in the latter case it is necessary to avoid culture-bound procedures and materials (see Brière 1973, Leemann 1981).

In our study of variation in Dutch proficiency of Surinam and Turkish children furthermore the notion of proficiency will not be conceived as a monolithic ability. The assumption is that speaking a language involves distinct sub-skills that can be acquired in differential individual patternings (see Snow & Hoefnagel-Höhle 1978: 335). Following Levelt & Kempen (1976) the language user will be defined as a hierarchically built grammatical system consisting of four ability levels:
- phonological abilities directed to the discrimination and production of sounds;
- lexical abilities directed to the comprehension and production of words;
- syntactic abilities directed to the comprehension and production of sentences;
- textual abilities directed to the comprehension and production of discourse.

Figure 1 displays the hierarchical relationship between these four ability levels. As can be seen, lexical abilities imply phonological abilities, syntactic abilities imply lexical abilities and so on.

Figure 1. Hierarchical relationship between different language abilities

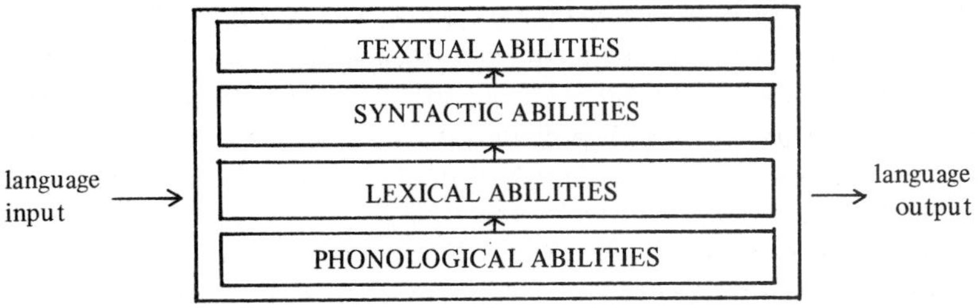

In the present study the variation of oral Dutch language proficiency in Surinam and Turkish children is investigated and compared with that of native Dutch children by tracing the results of each group on linguistic tasks that differentially refer to the above mentioned linguistic ability levels. In order to get insight into developmental stages in a cross-sectional design, we assigned the tasks to children of three age levels: four, six and eight years old. In studying the variation of oral proficiency in Dutch both temporal and structural characteristics will be treated.

As to the results of the study several expectations can be held beforehand. Firstly it is expected that Dutch children will exhibit higher levels of Dutch oral proficiency at each age level than their Surinam and Turkish peers. Furthermore we expect that, owing to a smaller degree of Dutch language input, Turkish children will achieve lower scores than Surinam children. The relative distance in proficiency moreover, is expected to be greater as measured linguistic abilities are placed higher in the hierarchical system of the language user (see Figure 1), due to the fact that these abilities are less automatized. From a structural point of view group specific patterns are expected only at the phonological level. Garnica & Herbert (1979) have shown that at this level source-language specific factors play a significant role. However, at the other linguistic levels no first language influence will be expected. Behavioral patterns within each group are rather expected to be interpretable in terms of specific attributes of the target language Dutch. This final expectation is in line with earlier studies that stress universal characteristics in first and second language development (see McLaughlin 1978).

3. DESIGN OF THE STUDY

3.1. Informants

Out of the heterogeneous population of non-Dutch speaking minorities Turkish and Surinam children were selected, the former representing the largest group of Mediterranean immigrants, the latter representing the largest group of former colonial immigrants. Dutch children formed a reference group, for reasons of comparison (see 2). Within each ethnic group three age levels were selected (i.e. 4, 6, and 8), being the lowest, the in between and the highest age group the test constructed is aiming at respectively.

In October and November 1983   208 children from various schools, most of them in the southern part of the Netherlands, were tested by students of the Department of Language & Literature of Tilburg University[2]. Table 1 shows the number of informants in each group.

Ask Carol Pfaff
for review

Date   18-9-1985.

To the editor of Language in Society,
attn.: Prof. Dell Hymes, Review Editor,
Dept. of Linguistics, Univ. of Linguistics
PHILADELPHIA – PA 19104, / USA.
Herewith you receive a copy of

"Studies on Language Acquisition"

Author	Guus Extra & Ton Vallen
ISBN	90 6765 114 1
Price	Dfl. 55,20 / US $ 22.

Dear Editor,

Since we assume that the readers of your journal are interested in the subject(s) dealt with in the enclosed publication, we herewith send you a copy for review.

If you are willing to give special attention to this book, please state the price and ISBN number, as mentioned on this form, and send us a copy of the journal in question.

Thank you very much for your co-operation.

FORIS PUBLICATIONS HOLLAND/USA
P.O. Box 509 - 3300 AM DORDRECHT, THE NETHERLANDS
and
P.O. Box C-50 - CINNAMINSON, NJ 08077, USA

Table 1. Number of informants in each group

	age 4	age 6	age 8
Dutch	26	28	29
Surinam	7	14	12
Turkish	30	29	33

The informants, equally devided over boys and girls, are all working-class children (SES 1 and 2), who had at least one year of kindergarten (except for the four-year-olds). The informants all attend monolingual Dutch schools, some of them with one or two hours of extra tuition in L2 weekly. Unfortunately, we could not reach as many Surinam children as we wanted. Especially the number of 4-year-olds is low.

3.2. Linguistic tasks

For each of the four linguistic ability levels that were mentioned in Figure 1 both receptive and (re)productive tasks were developed. At the phonological level an Auditory Discrimination Task and a Word Imitation Task were developed, measuring discrimination and reproduction of speech sounds respectively. At the lexical level a Receptive and a Productive Vocabulary Task were developed. Furthermore, a Productive Morphology Task was constructed.

At the level of syntax a Sentence Comprehension Task and a Sentence Imitation Task were developed, appealing to receptive and reproductive syntactic abilities respectively. Finally, at the level of discourse a Receptive Text Comprehension Task was developed. A short description of each of the tasks is given below.

Auditory discrimination

The Auditory Discrimination Task assesses the ability to distinguish between minimal pairs of Dutch phonemes. The task requires children to distinguish words that differ in one phoneme, or in the position or number of phonemes (examples: *kas–kaas, dorp–drop, strik--stik*). After an aural presentation of a word pair by a native speaker children are asked to indicate whether the words are different or not. All together 50 word pairs are administered: 36 different and 14 identical word pairs. In the different word pairs vowels are contrasted in 16 cases, and consonants in 10; in the remaining 10 cases different phoneme distribution patterns are contrasted. The score on the Auditory Discrimination Task is determined by calculating the number of correctly discriminated items.

Word imitation

The Word Imitation Task requires children to identify and to articulate Dutch speech sounds. The children are asked to imitate a sample of isolated Dutch words when spoken by a native speaker. This sample is made up of 44 monosyllabic words that contain a maximal variation of Dutch phonemes in initial, medial and final position. 15 items obey a consonant-vowel-consonant structure; the remaining items contain consonant clusters in initial and/or final position. The subject's score is given as the total number of correctly imitated words.

Productive vocabulary

The items of the vocabulary tasks were selected from a corpus of 6785 words, evaluated by teachers on the question whether they thought that a particular word on the list, given in a context, had to be understood by six-year-old native Dutch children (Kohnstamm et al. 1981). For the vocabulary tasks, words are placed in the order of teachers' ratings, from 100 to 30% agreement. So for the first words nearly every teacher agreed that a six-year-old had to know that word, whereas for the last words only 30% of the teachers thought so. Because the words are ordered according to a decreasing percentage of teachers' ratings, it is assumed that the words increase in difficulty.

The Productive Vocabulary Task consists of 100 pictures of objects and actions, that have to be named by the informant. The test assistant gives the verbal stimulus *"this is a"* or *"he/she is"*, to be completed by the informant. This procedure is similar to the Vocabulary Usage Test (Nation 1972), in which besides this kind of verbal stimuli one is also allowed to point at details, and to ask the informant to be more specific.

Because of the supposedly increasing difficulty of the items, a break-off point is used, as is accepted in similar kinds of tests (Peabody Picture Vocabulary Test). The score on the productive vocabulary task is given as the total number of correct items.

Receptive vocabulary

In the same way as for the Productive Vocabulary Task, for the Receptive Vocabulary Task 108 items were selected, based on the corpus of Kohnstamm et al. (1981) and rankordered in (assumed) degree of difficulty. For each word, four pictures are made, one being the right referent of that word. The test assistant presents the word and the informant has to point to the intended picture. In this subtask too, a break-off point is used. The subject's score is determined by the total number of correct items.

Morphology

The Morphology Task consists of six subtasks, with regard to inflection of nouns (plural and diminutive) adjectives (comparative and superlative) and conjugation of verbs (past tense and past particle). For each subtask the most frequent alternants are selected (each alternant four items), to get as accurate an insight into the ability of the informant as possible. To give an example, Figure 2 shows the inflection of the noun plural in Dutch.

Figure 2. Plural of nouns in Dutch (four alternants)

a.	/-ə(n)/	tent	– tent*en*	(tent)
b.	final cons-modification + / –ə(n)/	/han*t*/	– han*den*	(hand)
c.	/-s/	sleutel	– sleutel*s*	(key)
d.	midvowel (+ fin. cons.) modif. + / –ə(n)	sch*i*p	–sch*epen*	(ship)

Noun plurals in Dutch are mainly formed by adding /-ə(n)/ to a word, as in *tent-tenten* (see a. in Figure 2), in addition to which in some cases the final consonant has to be modified as in *hand – handen* (see b. in Figure 2). For both alternants, further on indicated by -( )en, parentheses stand for (optional) final consonant modification. After liquidae an /-s/ forms a plural, as in *sleutel – sleutels* (see c.). Finally, there are some irregular nouns in which the vowel (and sometimes the final consonant) has to be modified, as in *schip – schepen* (see d.). For each of these alternants, four items are constructed. The other subtasks are operationalized in the same way. The test assistant shows the informant two pictures, with a verbal stimulus like *"this is one key", "these are two ..."*, where the informant has to complete the last sentence. The score is determined by the total number of correct items.

Sentence imitation
Three subtasks, varying in sentence length and difficulty of items, consist of sentences with syntactic elements like negations, *wh*-words, auxiliaries and conjunctions, and syntactic patterns such as inversion, NP-constructions, VP-constructions, and subject/object clauses. In subtask 1 the sentences are 4, 5, 6 and 7 words long respectively, each length occurring 5 times, as is the case in subtask 2, where the length is 7, 8, 9 and 10 words, respectively. Subtask 3 finally consists of 4 × 3 sentences of 10, 11, 12 and 13 words long. In those 52 sentences 88 syntactic elements and patterns are distinguished. The elements have to be reproduced fully accurately, and for the patterns deviations are scored as correct if the order of elements in the pattern remains the same (e.g. *een groot tekening - een grote tekening*). Only the intended syntactic elements and patterns are taken into account. The informant has to reproduce the whole sentence. If a sentence is broken off half-way, the whole sentence is repeated once by the test assistant. The total of correctly reproduced items determines the subjects' score on the Sentence Imitation Task.

Sentence comprehension

In the items of the Sentence Comprehension Task three pictures are given, together with an aural production of a Dutch sentence by a native speaker. The meaning of the sentence corresponds with one of the pictures. The child is asked to point to the correct picture. The task breaks up into two subtasks. In the first subtask explicit relations within and between word groups in a sentence are tested. Relations within word groups are tested by presenting a sentence from which an element can be related to different word groups. For example, in the sentence *The hat of the man on the bike is black* the predicate *black* should refer to *the hat* and not to *the bike*. Relations between word groups are tested by contrasting the semantic roles of constituents within sentences. For example, in the sentence *The boy puts the box in the car* the roles of object and locative are contrasted. Utilizing Fillmore's Case Grammar (1968), a large variety of role contrasts has been strived for.

In the second subtask implicit meaning in sentences is tested. Two types of linguistic phenomena are asked for: presuppositions and modal terms. Four types of presuppositions are tested. The first one is implicative verbs (i.e. *to succeed, to remember*) of which an implied proposition can be asserted or denied. The second one is factive predicates (i.e. *to know, to pretend*) which imply the (un)truth of their complement. The third one is subordinated sentences that express temporal, causal or conditional relations. The last one is comparative relations between constituents in a sentence that imply the existence of the case being compared. The modal words that are tested all represent a certain modality of the predicate in a sentence, among other things repetition (*again, another one*) and time (*not yet, not any more*).

For the Sentence Comprehension Task the score is determined by the total number of correct items.

Text comprehension

In the Text Comprehension Task six successive short texts are read by a native speaker. Both mean word length and mean sentence length in the texts gradually increase so that the later texts can be assumed to demand a higher level of comprehension ability. After a text is read, four questions are asked. Two questions refer to information that is explicitly given in the text; two other questions refer to implicit information in the text.

3.3. Procedure

The children of the three ethnic groups were individually tested in a separate room in the school. The linguistic tasks that have been described earlier were administered in a fixed order and in two separate sessions of

45 minutes each. For each of the linguistic tasks a 2 X 2 analysis of variance (ANOVA) would be done. It was expected that the two main effects, being age and ethnic group, would be significant on each task. With progression of age higher scores were expected with each ethnic group. In addition Dutch children were expected to score higher than Surinam and Turkish children, while the scores of the Surinam groups were expected to be higher than those of the Turkish groups. It would be determined exploratively whether the Ethnic group X Age interaction turned out to be significant as well. Such an interaction could point to a relative change in Dutch language proficiency over time.

Furthermore, it was investigated to what extent children from different ethnic groups show comparable developmental features at each of the linguistic levels assessed. At the phonological level we wanted to find out whether the auditory discrimination of consonants, vowels and phoneme distributions yield different score patterns. In addition the score patterns on the CVC and CC subtasks of the Word Imitation Task would be compared. At the lexical level the question would be to what extent the order of difficulty on the two vocabulary tasks within each ethnic group corresponds to the order of difficulty as predicted by primary school teachers. At the level of syntax first the acquisition order of subsets of morphological rules for each ethnic group would be compared. Secondly it would be determined whether in the Sentence Comprehension Task implicit items prove to be more difficult than explicit ones for each ethnic group. Thirdly in the Sentence Imitation Task the question would be whether the imitation of syntactic elements and syntactic patterns yield differential results over ethnic groups. At the level of discourse the aim would be to see whether the different ethnic groups show comparable patterns as to text-explicit and text-implicit items. Finally, the extent to which the linguistic components that were presupposed in this study can be derived from the data structure of both Dutch and minority children would be determined. Therefore, with respect to both groups a factor analysis would be carried out, clustering the scores on the linguistic tasks that had been assessed. The degree of correspondence of the two factor structures would then be compared with the original devision of oral proficiency into four linguistic levels.

4. RESULTS

4.1. Phonology

4.1.1. Auditory discrimination
In Table 2 means and standard deviations on the Auditory Discrimination

Task are presented. It can be seen that Dutch children on each age level perform slightly better than Surinam and Turkish children.

Table 2. Means and standard deviations on the Auditory Discrimination Task

	D4	D6	D8	S4	S6	S8	T4	T6	T8
Mean	29.1	40.4	45.6	26.7	35.4	42.7	24.0	38.4	41.3
SD	13.9	5.4	3.7	12.5	9.3	5.3	16.5	10.8	8.0

Analysis of variance demonstrated that the main effects Ethnic group and Age both reached a level of significance (see Table 3). The interaction between the two effects appeared not to be significant. It can be concluded that the observed differences between ethnic groups on the Auditory Discrimination Task do not change as children get older.

Table 3. 2 × 2 ANOVA statistics on the Auditory Discrimination Task ($*p < .05$, $**p < .01$)

Source	Sum of squares	DF	Mean squares	F
Ethnic group	722.9	2	361.4	3.3*
Age	10095.4	2	5047.7	46.7**
E × A interaction	160.7	4	40.2	.4
Error	21508.9	199	108.1	

Further analysis distinguished between different patterns of phoneme discriminations. In Figures 3a, 3b and 3c the mean scores of the three ethnic groups are displayed as to the discrimination of vowels, consonants and phoneme distributions respectively.

For all groups the discrimination of vowels appears to be the easiest subtask, whereas the discrimination of consonants is the hardest one. A more detailed analysis of the difficulties on individual items yielded both interlingual and intralingual errors. The discrimination of voiced/unvoiced phoneme pairs turned out to be difficult for children of each ethnic group. On the other hand, young Surinam and Turkish children experience specific difficulties with the vowel contrasts /ı/-/i/, /ö/-/ü/, /a/-/o/, the consonants contrasts /v/-/w/, /n/-/ŋ/ and the insertion of /ə/.

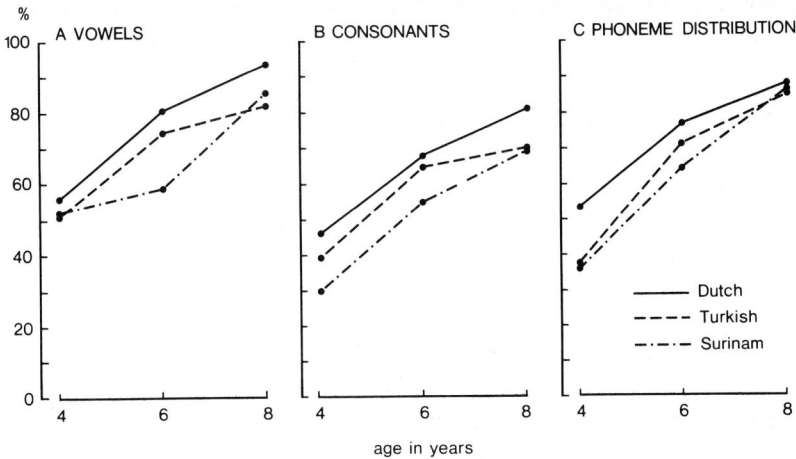

Figure 3. Percentages of correct scores on vowel discrimination (A), consonant discrimination (B) and phoneme distribution (C) of the Auditory Discrimination Task for three ethnic groups: Dutch, Surinam and Turkish

4.1.2. Word imitation

Table 4 presents the means and standard deviations on the Word Imitation Task. Except for the 4-year-olds no differences could be found between ethnic groups.

Table 4. Means and standard deviations on the Word Imitation Task

	D4	D6	D8	S4	S6	S8	T4	T6	T8
Mean	35.2	40.4	41.7	36.0	39.3	41.1	31.5	39.4	40.2
SD	10.1	2.9	2.5	3.9	3.3	3.3	11.7	3.7	3.6

Analysis of variance demonstrated no significance as to the main effect Ethnic group (see Table 5). The main effect Age, on the other hand, was significant. No significance was found as to the interaction between those main effects. The conclusion is that no significant differences in word imitation scores can be traced between ethnic groups at each age level.

It was determined whether differential score patterns could be found as to the imitation of CVC-patterns and CC-patterns. In Figure 4a and 4b it can be seen that for the youngsters in each ethnic group CC-patterns are relatively difficult, whereas in the course of time these patterns become even easier than CVC-patterns.

Table 5. 2 X 2 ANOVA statistics on the Word Imitation Task (**p < .01)

Source	Sum of squares	DF	Mean squares	F
Ethnic group	185.2	2	92.6	2.3
Age	2079.5	2	1039.7	25.7**
E X A interaction	107.8	4	26.9	.7
Error	8048.4	199	40.4	

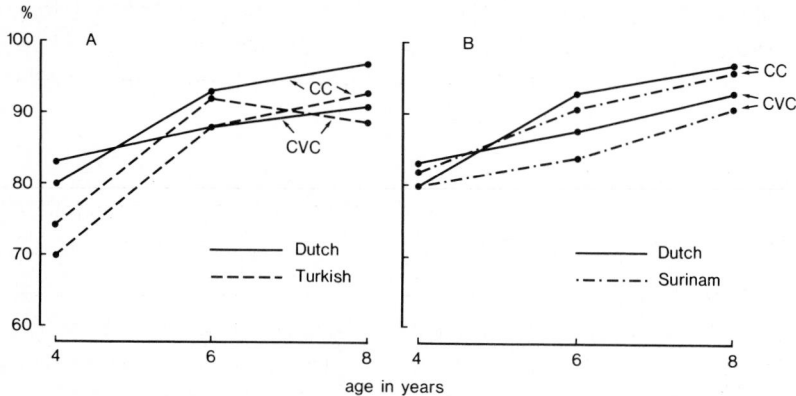

Figure 4. Percentages of correct scores on word imitation: CVC and CC patterns of Dutch and Turkish (A) and Dutch and Surinam (B) children.

Finally it was checked which phonemic patterns were difficult to imitate for each of the ethnic groups. The imitation of both /ɪl/ and /il/ proved to be problematic to both Turkish and Surinam children at each age level. Moreover, the pronounciation of /ŋ/ turned out to be difficult for the youngest group of Turkish children. Finally, complex word final clusters (/-ts/, /-rts/, /-rst/) proved to be problematic for the youngsters of each ethnic group. Thus both group-specific and group-universal error patterns were found.

4.2. Vocabulary

4.2.1. Receptive Vocabulary

Table 6 presents the means and standard deviations on the Receptive Vocabulary Task. As can be seen from this table, the scores of the Turkish children on receptive vocabulary are very low, compared to the scores of their Dutch peers.

Table 6. Means and standard deviations on the Receptive Vocabulary Task

	D4	D6	D8	S4	S6	S8	T4	T6	T8
Mean	47.4	84.0	99.2	53.1	77.8	91.9	21.1	48.1	68.6
SD	23.1	13.0	4.3	20.8	12.9	10.3	15.4	18.7	16.3

Surinam children obtain comparable scores, somewhat lower at the age of 6 and 8, than the Dutch children. The analysis of variance supports this finding in that the main effects Ethnic groups and Age level are both significant (see Table 7). The interaction between both main effects turned out not to be significant, so ethnic group differences in receptive vocabulary do not change very much in the course of time.

Table 7. 2 × 2 ANOVA statistics on the Receptive Vocabulary Task (**p < .01)

Source	Sum of squares	DF	Mean squares	F
Ethnic group	46321.5	2	23160.7	93.1**
Age	79562.6	2	39781.3	59.9**
E × A interaction	1108.1	4	277.0	1.1
Error	49507.6	199	248.8	

4.2.2. *Productive vocabulary*

In Table 8 the mean scores and standard deviations on the Productive Vocabulary Task are presented. Here again, the scores of the Turkish children are very low, compared with the scores of the Dutch children. Surinam children have somewhat lower scores compared to their Dutch classmates. In contradistinction to phonology, differences between the Turkish and the Dutch children seem to increase as time passes by. For productive vocabulary the score of D4 is quite as high as that of T8. For

Table 8. Means and standard deviations on the Productive Vocabulary Task

	D4	D6	D8	S4	S6	S8	T4	T6	T8
Mean	29.0	53.5	72.4	22.3	47.2	61.8	9.3	21.8	32.1
SD	10.6	11.8	9.9	15.7	10.5	13.6	9.1	10.9	12.1

the Surinam children, there are no such big differences from the Dutch reference group, but, as for the Turkish schildren, in productive vocabulary they tend to lay further behind. Many researchers report that bilingual children achieve low scores, especially in vocabulary, in each of their two languages.

The analysis of variance supports these findings in that the main effects Ethnic group and Age level are both significant, as was the interaction between those effects (see Table 9). This result can be interpreted as an increasing distance between the Turkish children and the other ethnic groups with the passage of the years.

Table 9. 2 × 2 ANOVA statistics on the Productive Vocabulary Task (**p < .01)

Source	Sum of squares	DF	Mean squares	F
Ethnic group	43722.9	2	21861.4	176.4**
Age	37493.5	2	18746.8	151.3**
E × A interaction	3371.4	4	842.8	6.8**
Error	24664.4	199	123.9	

4.2.3. Size of vocabulary

As mentioned in 3.2, the vocabulary tasks were constructed on the basis of a corpus of 6785 words, evaluated by Dutch elementary school teachers on the basis of the question whether a particular word had to be understood by 6-year-old native speakers of Dutch. So the question dealt with teacher norms about children's receptive vocabulary.

The socres on the Receptive Vocabulary Task correlate significantly with the teachers' evaluations for all groups, as can be seen from Table 10.

Table 10. Correlations between teachers' evaluations (Kohnstamm et al. 1981) and scores on the Receptive Vocabulary Task (Pearson, **p < .01)

	age 4	age 6	age 8	all
Dutch	.85**	.60**	.39**	
Surinam	.70**	.64**	.54**	.51**
Turkish	.78**	.82**	.70**	

Especially those children who have low scores (4-years-olds of all groups, and 6- and 8-year-olds of the Turkish) show high correlations. This indicates that the evaluations of the teachers hold for roughly the first 4000 words, whereas the children's knowledge of the following words shows much less variation. Indeed, all correlations are significant, but the explained variation for the target group (D6) is not so high. Some explanations are: a. the list is meant as a target list to be aimed at; because teachers were asked to indicate what six-year-olds *had to* know; b. the answer to the question had to be "yes" or "no", and did not relate to a percentual range of children: in such a dichotomic model much information is lost; c. the word had to be known given a particular context, whereas in our task there is much less contextual information, only the picture and the verbal stimulus. The correlations between teachers' evaluations and test scores for productive vocabulary are presented in Table 11.

Table 11. Correlations between teachers' evaluations (Kohnstamm et al. 1981) and scores for the Productive Vocabulary Task (Pearson, **p < .01)

	age 4	age 6	age 8	all
Dutch	.73**	.78**	.76**	
Surinam	.62**	.75**	.71**	.60**
Turkish	.63**	.73**	.80**	

For productive vocabulary, these correlations are significant too. The explained variation is somewhat higher than for receptive vocabulary, but again not so high.

On the basis of the scores of the children it is possible to give an indication of the number of words known by them. Because of the nature of the procedure (pictures, artificiality) and the status of the utilized corpus (based on judgements), the size of vocabulary of 6-year-olds is generally rough indication. The productive vocabulary of 6-year-olds is generally estimated at about 3000 words (see O'Rourke 1974), but the reported numbers have increased in the last 50 years, as is mentioned by Augst e.a. (1977) from 2500 to 5000. For 6-year-old Dutch children a productive vocabulary of 2500 à 3000 words is mentioned (see Geerts 1978).

Scores on the vocabulary tasks in this study indicate that D6 have a productive vocabulary of 3250 words, comparable with the numbers mentioned above. The size of the productive vocabulary of the different groups is given in Figure 5.

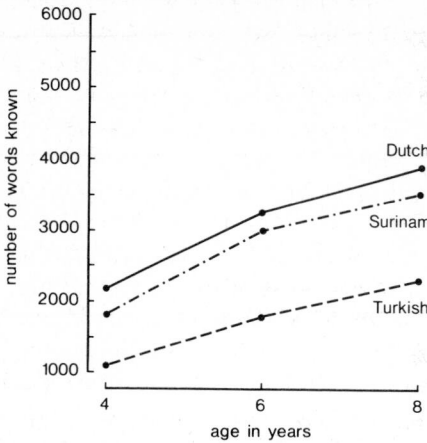

Figure 5. Productive vocabulary, number of words known

Figure 5 shows that Surinam children know fewer words than their Dutch classmates, the difference being about 350 words for each age group. Between Dutch and Turkish children there is an increasing gap of more than 1000 words: 1050, 1450 and 1600 words for the three age groups respectively. T8 children know hardly more words (2300) than D4 children (2150). The analysis of variance showed that this process of divergence is significant.

The size of the receptive vocabulary gives the same picture (see Figure 6).

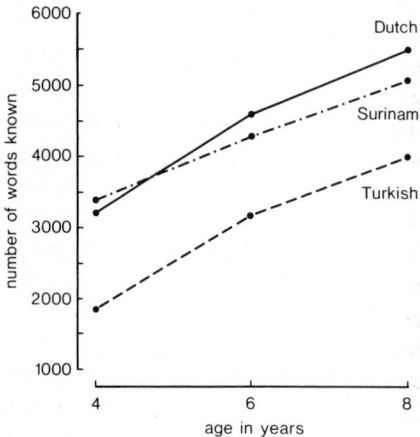

Figure 6. Receptive vocabulary, number of words

As can be seen from Figure 6, the Dutch children understand more words than their minority classmates, except for S4, which discrepancy may be due to the small group (n=7). Here again, the Dutch and Surinam children understand far more words than the Turkish children, but the difference between the Dutch and Turkish children remains the same: 1550, 1400 and 1500 words for the three age groups respectively.

So with respect to the size of the receptive and productive Dutch vocabulary, Turkish children are at least two, perhaps three or even four years behind, as compared to their Dutch age peers. This fact may be a major obstacle to doing well at school, because the meaning of words is the basis of understanding and being understood.

4.3. Morphology

In Table 12 means and standard deviations on the morphology subtasks are presented.

Table 12. Means and standard deviations on the morphology subtasks

		D4	D6	D8	S4	S6	S8	T4	T6	T8
plural	mean	9.3	11.5	13.8	6.6	8.1	13.5	1.9	4.5	8.6
	sd	3.6	2.3	1.4	6.1	5.4	1.9	2.9	4.3	3.6
past participle	mean	3.2	7.6	10.4	4.9	6.2	10.6	0.8	2.1	5.1
	sd	2.3	3.0	1.7	3.4	3.3	2.4	1.3	2.5	2.4
diminutive	mean	5.5	10.6	14.1	6.0	9.5	14.3	2.3	4.9	9.7
	sd	4.5	3.8	1.9	5.6	4.4	1.4	3.4	4.2	3.3
comparative	mean	7.2	12.4	13.8	5.7	10.9	13.4	1.5	5.9	9.5
	sd	5.3	1.7	1.1	6.2	3.5	0.9	3.3	4.7	3.9
superlative	mean	5.9	11.6	13.3	5.6	11.2	12.3	1.5	6.2	9.0
	sd	5.1	2.6	1.1	5.4	3.0	1.4	3.1	4.7	4.0
past tense	mean	1.1	4.3	8.7	1.7	3.6	8.3	0.1	0.6	1.9
	sd	2.0	3.4	2.7	2.2	3.4	2.8	0.4	1.5	2.1
total morphology	mean	32.2	57.9	73.9	30.4	49.5	72.4	8.0	24.2	43.9
	sd	17.0	11.7	7.2	25.3	18.9	8.3	10.9	15.9	14.2

As can be seen from Table 12, Dutch children score higher than their non-Dutch classmates on all six subtasks of morphology, except for the past participle, where S4 and S8 score somewhat higher. As for vocabulary, for morphology there are only slight differences between Dutch and Surinam children, whereas the Turkish children have overall low scores. In four subtasks T6 have a lower score than D4, in two subtasks they have the same score; T8 have considerable lower scores than D6 in all cases.

For a better insight into the productive ability of the children to form the most frequent alternants of some conjugations and inflections of the noun, adjective and verb, Table 13 shows a /+/ where in 3 or 4 out of 4 times a correct form was supplied, and a /-/ where it was not. As can be seen from Table 13, Dutch children in the beginning perform better than Surinam children, but at their 8th year Surinams have acquired the same level: the Dutch children have lost their head start over them. For the Turkish children, T8 do not even correctly obey the rules that are required by D6. So here again, the difference between Dutch and Turkish children is more than two years.

Table 13 also makes clear that the order in which the different groups acquire the rules of morphology, shows remarkable resemblances. Both L1 and L2 learners, having different L1 backgrounds, first acquire a rule to form a noun plural, then a rule to form the past particle; within the noun plural system, -( )*en* is the first rule, -*s* the second one, and irregular the last one. Although this is a cross-sectional study, our outcome indicates that the structure of L2-acquisition has a strongly universal character, whereas the tempo in which these rules are acquired, differs from group to group. For similar results in a longitudinal study see Vermeer (elsewhere in this Volume). The analysis of variance demonstrates that for morphology the main effects Ethnic group and Age both reach a level of significance (see Table 14). The interaction between the two effects appears not to be significant. It can be concluded that the differences between ethnic groups on the Morphology Task do not change as children get older.

4.4. Syntax

4.4.1. Sentence imitation

With regard to syntactic abilities of the children, the results on the Sentence Imitation Task show that Surinam children reproduce the syntactic elements and patterns in the same way as Dutch children, whereas the

Table 14. 2 × 2 ANOVA statistics on the Morphology Task (**p < .01)

Source	Sum of squares	DF	Mean squares	F
Ethnic group	41224.9	2	20612.5	106.4**
Age	52075.0	2	26037.5	134.4**
E × A interaction	785.9	4	196.5	1.0
Error	38555.1	199	193.7	

| | NOUN FORMATION | | | | | ADJECTIVE FORMATION | | | | | VERB FORMATION | | | | | |
| | plural | | | diminutive | | comparative | | | superlative | | past participle | | | past tense | | |
Alternants	-( )en	-s	irr	-(t)je -etje/ -p/kje	irr	-( )er	-der	irr	-(s)t	irr	-t/d	strong	irr	-te/de	strong	irr
Dutch 4	+	–	–	–	–	–	–	–	–	–	–	–	–	–	–	–
6	+	+	–	+	–	+	+	–	+	–	+	–	–	–	–	–
8	+	+	–	+	+	+	+	–	+	–	+	+	–	+	–	–
Surin. 4	–	–	–	–	–	–	–	–	–	–	–	–	–	–	–	–
6	–	–	–	+	–	+	–	–	+	–	–	–	–	–	–	–
8	+	+	–	+	+	+	+	–	+	–	+	+	–	+	–	–
Turk. 4	–	–	–	–	–	–	–	–	–	–	–	–	–	–	–	–
6	–	–	–	–	–	–	–	–	–	–	–	–	–	–	–	–
8	+	–	–	+	–	+	–	–	–	–	–	–	–	–	–	–

Table 13. Correct (+) and incorrect (–) conjugations and inflections of different alternants of noun plural/diminutive, adjective comparative/superlative, verb past participle/tense

124   *Ludo Verhoeven & Anne Vermeer*

Turkish children lay far behind. Table 15 presents the mean scores and standard deviations of the three ethnic groups.

Table 15. Means and standard deviations on the Sentence Imitation Task

	D4	D6	D8	S4	S6	S8	T4	T6	T8
Mean	47.6	74.3	82.5	45.7	72.7	81.2	22.9	55.1	69.3
SD	25.4	9.1	5.8	32.9	11.4	5.7	21.6	23.2	16.2

It can be seen that Dutch children perform better than the other ethnic groups, and that Surinam children do better than Turkish children. Analysis of variance supports this finding. The main effects Ethnic group and Age level were both significant (see Table 16). The interaction between these main effects was not significant, so differences between ethnic groups on the sentence imitation tasks do not change as children get older.

Table 16. 2 × 2 ANOVA statistics on the Sentence Imitation Task (**p < .01)

Source	Sum of squares	DF	Mean squares	F
Ethnic group	17212.6	2	8606.3	26.4**
Age	57657.6	2	28828.8	88.6**
E × A interactions	1089.1	4	272.3	0.8
Error	64780.3	199	325.5	

With respect to the different subcategories, the T8 group scores considerably lower than the D6 group, except for *Wh*-words, where D6 and T8 have the same scores. Overall, Turkish children make relatively fast progress in syntactic elements such as *WH*-words, but still have great difficulties with respect to syntactic patterns such as complex NP or VP clusters (*on my white paper, will have done*) and S-bar constructions (embedded clauses, subject/object clauses), as can be seen from Figures 7a and 7b. These figures display the relative difficulties of syntactic elements (E) on the one hand and syntactic patterns (P) on the other hand. It can be seen that all groups do better on the elements than on the patterns, and that the Turkish children have considerably lower scores than the other ethnic groups.

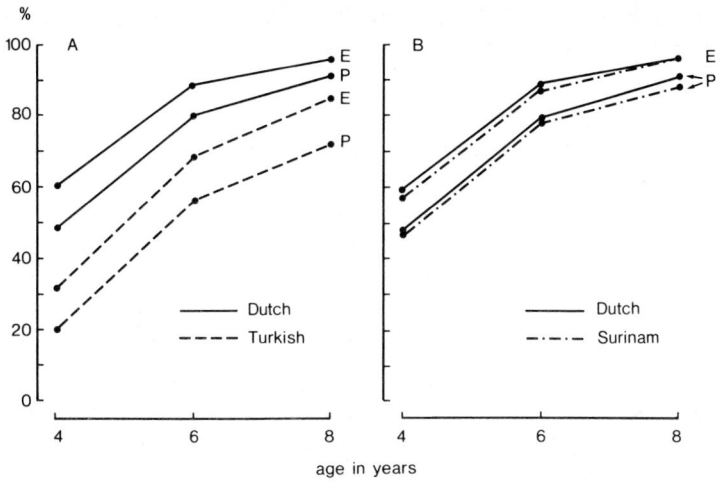

Figure 7. Percentages of correct scores on syntactic elements (E) and syntactic patterns (P) of the Sentence Imitation Task of Dutch and Turkish (A) and Dutch and Surinam children (B).

4.4.2. Sentence comprehension

Table 17 presents the mean scores and standard deviations of the three ethnic groups on the Sentence Comprehension Task.

Table 17. Means and standard deviations on the Sentence Comprehension Task

	D4	D6	D8	S4	S6	S8	T4	T6	T8
Mean	42.5	63.6	73.9	46.7	61.4	70.3	28.2	55.2	62.4
SD	18.5	10.6	4.8	21.9	6.8	5.6	20.2	10.4	13.0

It can be seen that Dutch children (except for D4) perform better than the other ethnic groups, and that Surinam children do better than Turkish children. Analysis of variance supports this finding in that the main effects Ethnic group and Age level both were significant (see Table 18). The interaction between both main effects turned out not to be significant. The conclusion is that ethnic group differences in sentence comprehension scores do not dramatically change with the passage of the years.

To get more insight into the sentence comprehension abilities of the children we traced how the three ethnic groups perform on the two sub-tasks. Figure 8a and 8b display the relative difficulty of both subtasks. All

Table 18. 2 × 2 ANOVA statistics on the Sentence Comprehension Task (**p < .01)

Source	Sum of squares	DF	Mean squares	F
Ethnic group	6210.4	2	3105.2	17.0**
Age	35679.7	2	17839.8	97.7**
E × A interaction	663.2	4	165.8	.9
Error	36351.9	199	182.7	

groups do better on the explicit meaning task than on the implicit meaning task.

Furthermore, if can be seen that on either task the Surinam children perform similar to their Dutch peers, whereas Turkish children obtain clearly lower scores on each of the tasks. Later, however, the relative distance between ethnic groups on both tasks get smaller. At the age of 8 Turkish children seem to have caught up with their peers, especially on the explicit meaning task.

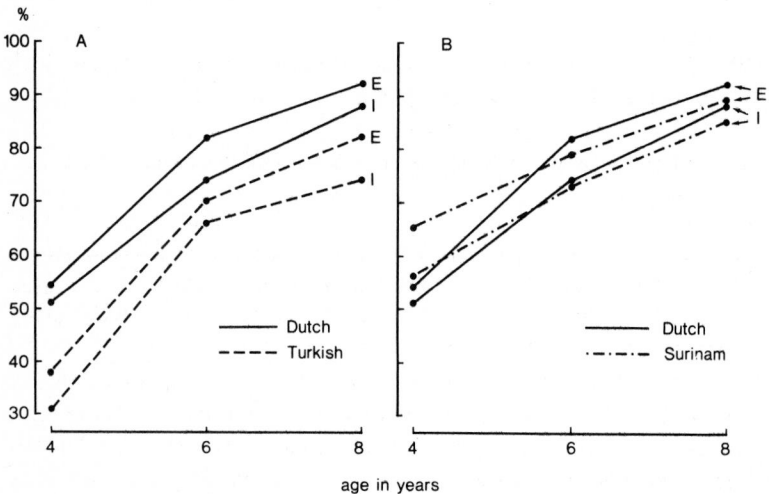

Figure 8. Sentence comprehension: explicit meaning (E) and implicit meaning (I)

4.5. Discourse comprehension

In Table 19 the mean scores and standard deviations on the Discourse Comprehension Task are presented. It can be seen that Dutch and Surinam children obtain comparable scores at each age level. The Turkish children, however, obtain lower scores than their Dutch and Surinam peers. Especially at the age of 4 the differences are dramatic.

Table 19. Means and standard deviations on the Discourse Comprehension Task

	D4	D6	D8	S4	S6	S8	T4	T6	T8
Mean	14.0	19.3	21.4	14.4	19.4	20.9	6.5	17.1	18.3
SD	6.9	3.2	2.1	6.9	2.0	2.0	6.6	2.9	4.0

Analysis of variance seems to support these findings. As can be seen in Table 20 the main effects Ethnic group and Age were both significant, as was the interaction between those effects. This result points to a diminishing distance between Turkish and other ethnic groups in the course of time.

Table 20. 2 × 2 ANOVA statistics on the Discourse Comprehension Task (**p < .01)

Source	Sum of squares	DF	Mean squares	F
Ethnic group	874.8	2	437.4	21.8**
Age	3275.5	2	1637.7	81.7**
E × A interaction	281.9	4	70.5	3.5**
Error	3986.9	199	20.0	

Again we looked for differential patterns in ethnic groups between text-explicit and text-implicit items. In Figures 9a and 9b the scores on both subtasks are graphically displayed. It can be seen that at the age of 4 text-explicit items were easier for each ethnic group. At a later age, however, no substantial differences in scores between the two subtasks could be found.

4.6. Factor analysis

Common factor analysis[3] shows that for both minority children and Dutch children three factors explain over 86 percent of the total amount of variance. For both groups a first factor already explains 70 percent of the variance. For the minority group the second and third factors explain 11 and 7 percent of variance respectively; for the Dutch group these percentages are 10 and 7 percent respectively. In Table 21 the factor structure matrices for both groups are displayed.

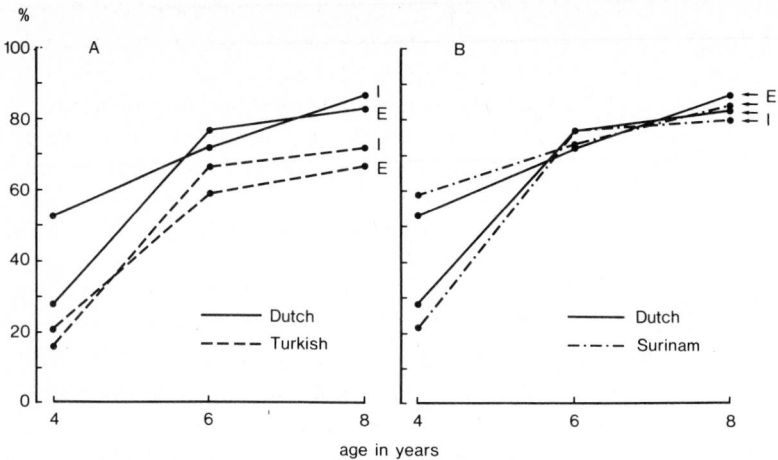

Figure 9. Discourse comprehension: text-explicit (E) and text-implicit (I) items

Table 21. Factor structure matrices for the minority group and the Dutch group

	Minority children			Dutch children		
	F1	F2	F3	F1	F2	F3
Word imitation	20	16	83	19	17	67
Auditory discrimination	27	44	50	33	47	37
Productive vocabulary	86	25	19	84	34	29
Receptive vocabulary	81	34	35	71	48	40
Morphology	81	37	20	68	50	34
Sentence imitation	68	46	29	54	61	15
Sentence comprehension	49	83	24	52	64	40
Text comprehension	55	55	39	38	58	51

A comparable factor structure matrix can be identified in both groups of children. Both structures can tentatively be interpreted in terms of the underlying linguistic levels in oral proficiency in Dutch as a first or a second language as postulated earlier (see paragraph 2). A first factor seems to be primarily related to the lexical level, as can be concluded from the high factor loadings on the tasks for vocabulary productive and receptive) and morphology. In addition, however, this factor seems to a lesser degree to be related as well to the levels that go beyond word level, i.e. syntax and text. The suggestion is that at these levels the first factor explains the lexico-semantic aspects. A second factor shows predominantly high loadings at the syntactic and textual level. As regards this factor it can be supposed that primarily structural aspects at these levels are accounted for. Finally, a third factor seems to be primarily related to the phonological level, as can be concluded from the high loadings on the Word Imitation Task and the Auditory Discrimination Task.

5. DISCUSSION

From the present study several conclusions can be drawn. Firstly, it appears that the rate of acquisition of Surinam children's Dutch corresponds more or less to that of native Dutch children from the same socio-economic background. Only in vocabulary (especially at the productive level) Surinam children seem to fall behind their Dutch peers. The same appears to be the case with morphology. However, with the passage of the years differences on the Morphology Task between Surinam and Dutch children tend to disappear.

The second conclusion is that Turkish children clearly lay behind in the acquisition of Dutch as compared to their Surinam and Dutch peers. Except for word imitation, substantial differences in Dutch language proficiency have been found between Turkish children on the one hand and Surinam and Dutch children on the other hand. Only on the Auditory Discrimination Task did these differences tend to disappear in the course of time. At the level of vocabulary, however, the differences get even larger as children grow older. Furthermore, the Turkish children demonstrate much larger standard deviations on each of the tasks than their Surinam and Dutch peers; this indicates that the inter-individual differences in the rate of acquisition of Dutch are relatively high within this ethnic group.

The third conclusion of this study is that from a structural point of view the acquisition process of Dutch seems to be highly comparable for learners of different ethnic groups. Only at the phonological level were found slight differences in acquisition patterns, due to different source languages. However, at the levels higher in the hierarchy of the linguistic system these patterns appear to be universal for both first and second language learners. At the level of vocabulary significant correlations were found between teachers' judgements of children's word knowledge and children's actual word knowledge. As regards morphology, the order of acquisition of rules appeared to be comparable to a high extent. The same conclusion applies to the level of syntax and the level of discourse. At both levels comprehension of explicit structure appeared to be easier than comprehension of implicit structures for each of the ethnic groups.

Furthermore, as regards the imitation of sentences, for all groups the reproduction of syntactic elements proved to be easier than the reproduction of syntactic patterns.

The conclusions so far can be interpreted as follows. Temporal similarities and differences can primarily be explained from the linguistic environments of the different ethnic groups. The fast acquisition process of Dutch by Surinam children can be explained from the fact that most Surinams have a more frequent contact with Dutch than Turkish children.

This could explain the fact that Turkish children make slower progress in their acquisition of Dutch. The high degree of structural correspondence in language acquisition features is in line with the outcome of earlier studies that suggest that in the process of first and second language acquisition universal strategies are predominant (see McLaughlin 1978).

Furthermore, the present study makes it clear that the concept of language proficiency as a pluralithic ability does make sense. From this concept different relative patterns of language development can be demonstrated. Relative patterns of differences in language acquisition can be observed between ethnic groups, whereas within groups interindividual profiles in language progress can be observed. The results between and within ethnic groups concerning Dutch proficiency give empirical evidence of the functioning of a linguistic system that recognizes different structural levels.

Naturalistic studies like the present one can show whether temporal and structural differences exist in the acquisition of Dutch between and within ethnic groups. However, in the present study this acquisition process was only cross-sectionally studied for two minority groups. Furthermore, only small samples of children within these groups were studied. These facts prevent the conclusions of this study from having wide applicability. More research is needed into a broader range of ethnic groups each containing a more or less representative sample of children.

Finally, it should be said that studies like the present one do not really *explain* the observed similarities and differences in language acquisition patterns between and within ethnic groups. To arrive at a deeper understanding of variation in the acquisition of Dutch within different minority groups, we need studies that take into account the precise linguistic environments of these groups. In such studies structural differences in the acquisition patterns of Dutch can be related to differential patterns of language input for ethnic minority groups.

NOTES

1. The ultimate goal of the research project reported here is to construct a diagnostic test to evaluate the acquisition of Dutch of ethnic minority children from 4 to 9 years old.
2. We like to thank Susan van der Beek, Marieke Boers, Linde van de Bosch, Willemijn Bronzwaer, Desirée Derksen, Raymond Godding, Hanneke van Gorp, Brigitte van Hilst, Louise van 't Hof, Els Klaassen, Monique Knaapen, Sjoukje van de Kolk, Lijsbeth Kraijenhoff, Heleen Maaskant, Dimf van Rozendaal, Arie Smulders, and Ineke Vugs, who participated in this project for their efforts in trying out and commenting upon the preliminary version of the test battery. All are students of the Department of Language & Literature of Tilburg University.
3. PA 2-Factor Analysis of SPSS was done, followed by a Varimax Rotation of the original factor structure matrix.

Cultural Biases in Second Language Testing of Children[*]

Anne Kerkhoff & Ton Vallen

1. INTRODUCTION

During the last decades many researchers have drawn attention to the importance of sociolinguistic factors operating on test situations. They have shown that both procedure and content of many tests are culturally or linguistically biased for at least some of the individuals being tested. Johnson (1981) for instance investigated the effect of both cultural origin and semantic and syntactic complexity of reading texts on reading comprehension of ESL-students. Her subjects were adult Iranian ESL-students, who were tested on reading comprehension by multiple-choice questions and recall questions. Two stories were used: one from Iranian folklore and one from American folklore. The reading texts were about Mullah Nasr-el-Din and about Buffalo Bill. Two versions of each test were used, different as regards the level of language complexity. The performance of the Iranian students on the different tests was compared with the performance of American students on the same tests. The results indicated that the cultural origin of the reading texts had more effect on the reading comprehension of the Iranian students than the level of semantic and syntactic complexity of the English language.

One of the implications which Johnson extracts from these results is that the culturally determined background of texts should be considered as a criterion for selecting materials for teaching and testing language skills. Cultural biases can seriously affect the validity of the test results.

In our study we investigated the effect of the cultural background of tests on the language performance of children belonging to different ethnic groups. We tested proficiency in Dutch of primary school children with different tests. The children belonged to three different ethnic groups: Dutch, Turkish and Moluccan. The results of the ethnic minority children were compared with the results of their Dutch classmates. Turks and

[*] We wish to thank those students of the Department of Language and Literature Tilburg, who took part in this study, and Pieter Nieuwint for his help in correcting the first draft of this article.

Moluccans were chosen because they form large ethnic minorities in Holland and because they differ in the amount of contact they have with Dutch language and culture. The Moluccans, who have lived in Holland for almost 30 years are supposed to have acculturated more into Dutch society than the Turks, who came to Holland in the late sixties or later. Both groups show less school success than Dutch children (Van Esch 1983, Vallen & Kerkhoff 1984). After primary school about 70% of Turkish and Moluccan children between 12 and 16 years of age attend 'Lower Vocational Education', which can be said to train for 'blue collar jobs', while only 30% attend 'General Secondary Education', training for 'white collar jobs' or in some cases for further studies at university level. For autochthonous Dutch children these percentages are precisely the reverse. Because the level of job one can get depends on the education one has received, it should be clear that these ethnic minority children are in a disadvantaged position. It is often suggested that minority children are disadvantaged because of the well-known link between ethnic group membership and low socio-economic status. Teachers however suggest that 'language difficulties' of minority children play an important role too. Teachers' opinions about the capabilities of children are crucial factors in the decision process about different types of secondary education. Of course teachers' ideas about the children's abilities are to a large extent based on the performance of children on tests. We tried to investigate whether the differences teachers notice between the performances of children belonging to different ethnic groups depend on the cultural background of the tests being used.

2. METHOD

Ninety-two subjects participated in the experiment. All children were 10 or 11 years of age and attended class 5 of elementary school in 5 different classrooms. All children had lived in Holland for five years or more. In three classes Turkish (n=21) and Dutch children (26 classmates) were tested, in two classes 21 Moluccan children and 24 Dutch classmates. Two groups of Dutch children were tested to make comparisons within classes possible. Each child completed two tests: one which took into account his own culture and one which reckoned with another culture. In Figure 1 a schematic illustration of the experiment is given.

The Turkish children and their Dutch classmates did one test which focused on Turkish culture (the TUT) and one which focused on Dutch culture (the NET). The Moluccan children and their Dutch classmates did one test dealing with aspects of Moluccan culture (the MOT) and the NET.

		NET	TUT	MOT
Dutch	(n=21)	X	X	
Turks	(n=26)	X	X	
Dutch	(n=24)	X		X
Moluccans	(n=21)	X		X

Figure 1: Design of the experiment.

The tests were administered during schooltime and instructions were given by the children's teachers. To control for possible repetition effects, the order in which the tests were taken was counterbalanced. Half of the children in each ethnic group did the NET first, half of them did the other test first (TUT or MOT). The results of the ethnic minority children on both tests were compared with the results of their Dutch classmates on the same tests.

Johnson (1981) tested reading comprehension with recall questions and multiple-choice questions. We decided to use another procedure because the scoring of recall protocols and the construction of multiple-choice questions are complicated and can raise important difficulties. We preferred to use a written cloze-procedure, which is often used as a measure of second language proficiency and which generally shows substantial reliability and validity coefficients (Oller 1979).

For several reasons cloze-tests have become less popular. The reliability of the tests is not as high as it once was supposed to be (Klein-Braley 1983, Farhady 1983), and it is not clear what precisely it is that a cloze-test requires of the individuals being tested. However, we had some important reasons in choosing the cloze-procedure. For our experiment we needed three tests to determine the level of Dutch language proficiency. The cultural origin of the tests had to be the only difference between them. Leaving aside the fact that it would be very difficult to find comparable Turkish and Moluccan-Malaysian tests, it may be clear that it wasn't possible to translate tests from the languages of the ethnic minority children. Many researchers, for instance Brière (1973) have warned against the practice of translating tests.

We decided to construct the three tests ourselves. Cloze-tests can be constructed, administered and scored relatively easily, and were therefore very suitable to our purposes.

We designed three texts of comparable level of complexity in Dutch. Several formulas were used to measure the syntactic and semantic complexity of the texts.

The first formula was that of Douma (Werkgroep 1982) who adapted Flesch's formula for the readability of English texts for Dutch. Two variables are used: word length and mean sentence length.

The second formula, that of Zondervan (1976), reckons with the percentage of 'different difficult words' and the number of auxiliaries. A word was regarded as difficult if it had a frequency less than 10 according to the Uit den Boogaart (1975) frequency count for written texts. These factors (word length, sentence length, frequency of words and amount of auxiliaries) can not be regarded as the only parameters of readability. Therefore we analysed the given-new structure of the three texts (according to Baten (1981), who borrowed this concept from Halliday (1976) and Chafe (1974)). All NPs in a text are taken into account for this analysis. Distinctions are made between four categories: given and new, defined and undefined. A particular NP is regarded as 'new' if it has not been introduced in the text before. It is 'given' if it has been introduced before. If the determiner is an indefinite article or a zero-marker, a NP is considered to be 'undefined', if it has a definite article it is 'defined'. Baten's hypothesis states that the more given and defined concepts a text contains, the easier it is. The more new and undefined concepts, the harder. The distribution of the NPs in our three texts over these four categories was about the same for each.

In this manner we aimed at three texts of a comparable degree of complexity in Dutch. The main difference between the texts was the story's topic. Each text consisted of a story in which a child talked about a festivity in which it had partaken at home. One story was about a typical Dutch festivity, a 12½ year wedding anniversary, one about a typical Moluccan wedding festivity, and one about a typical Turkish celebration; the Şekir bayrami. The first text formed the basis for NET, the second for MOT and the last for TUT.

Each text numbered approximately four hundred words. Every seventh word was deleted, until fifty-seven blanks had been obtained. In each test the first seven blanks were treated as examples, so each test consisted of fifty items. Within these fifty items the proportion of content words (nouns, adverbs and verbs) versus function words was 27:23, 27:23, 28:22 respectively.

Two different ways of scoring the cloze-test were used: the exact word method and the scoring for contextual appropriateness. Although research has shown that these methods strongly correlate (Oller 1979, Hinofotis 1980), we thought it necessary to use them both, and to check whether the correlations between these two methods were of equal strength for the different tests.

3. RESULTS

Test statistics were computed separately for the Turkish children and their classmates and for the Moluccan children and their classmates. First we will present the results for the Turkish/Dutch group, then the results for the Moluccan/Dutch group.

Turkish and Dutch children

For both tests reliability coefficients for the two scoring methods were computed by the Kuder-Richardson Formula 20. Results are presented in Table 1.

As can be seen in Table 1 reliability coefficients for the whole tests (raw data) are highest for NET. For NET and TUT acceptable scores result in higher reliabilities than exact scores.

By deleting those items which showed an item-total correlation of less than .30 we tried to increase the reliability of both tests. To 'clean' the NET we removed those items which both in the Turkish/Dutch and in the Moluccan/Dutch group showed an item-total correlation of less than .30. This revision of the data made the reliability of TUT considerably higher, so we decided to analyse further only the revised versions of NET and TUT. Adjusted reliability coefficients, calculated for the revised tests lengthened to 50 items using the Spearman-Brown formula (Ferguson 1981: 440), are presented in the last column of Table 1. For these revised tests exact scores correlate highly with acceptable scores. Cloze-exact correlates with cloze-acceptable for both NET and TUT at .97. Both correlations are significant at .01 level. It is a fact that errors of measurement tend to reduce the size of the correlation coefficient. Correction for attenuation resulted in coefficients even higher than 1.0.

Table 1: Reliability coefficients for NET and TUT (two ways of scoring).

	'Raw data'			'Revised data'			
	maximum score	N	KR20	maximum score	N	KR20	adjusted KR20 for revised data
NET exact	50	47	.93	44	47	.93	.94
NET acceptable	50	47	.95	44	47	.95	.96
TUT exact	50	47	.88	30	47	.91	.96
TUT acceptable	50	47	.91	36	47	.93	.95

In spite of the apparently higher reliability of the acceptable scores, the high correlation between exact and acceptable scoring methods made us decide to use only the exact scores on the two revised tests for comparing the results of Turkish and Dutch children. Using the exact-scores eliminates the element of subjectivity that characterizes the acceptable scoring method. It is often very hard to decide whether an alternative that does not correspond exactly to the original word is appropriate in the context. This is often the case with content words which are more or less culture-bound. Is it for instance correct when a child writes 'church' in a context in which a Moslem father and his son visit a place which in the original text is called 'Mosque'? Although most of these 'culturally defined' items disappeared by revising the tests, we decided to analyse the exact scores only.

Means and standard-deviations for Dutch and Turkish children are presented in Table 2. Results of t-tests for significance of the difference between the means are also presented.

Table 2: Mean correct scores (in percentages) and standard deviations for Dutch and Turkish children on NET and TUT.

	mean(N)	NET SD	N	mean(T)	TUT SD	N	N–T	df	t
Dutch	54.33	18.74	21	57.62	26.19	21	–3.29	20	–1.08
Turks	24.83	15.09	26	39.36	21.42	26	–14.53	25	–6.59**

** means significantly different at .01 level.

These results indicate that the cultural origin of the tests has no effect on the scores of the Dutch pupils, but a highly significant effect on the scores of their Turkish classmates: on TUT our Turkish subjects perform significantly better than on NET.

However, it is necessary to interpret these results with care. Despite our efforts to make NET and TUT comparable, with the exception of the cultural character of the tests, it is still possible that other, still unknown, factors have affected the results. Note, for instance, the fact that after the tests had been revised, NET consisted of 44 items and TUT of 30 items.

For that reason we computed z-scores for the two samples of test-scores (NET and TUT) and carried out an analysis of variance on these data. Mean z-scores are listed in Table 3.

Table 3: Mean z-scores on NET and TUT for Dutch and Turkish children, with Student's t.

	Mean z-scores Dutch(D)	mean z-scores Turks(T)	D–T	df	t
NET	.73	–.59	1.22	45	5.85**
TUT	.40	–.33	.73	45	2.63*

* means significantly different at .05 level.
** means significantly different at .01 level.

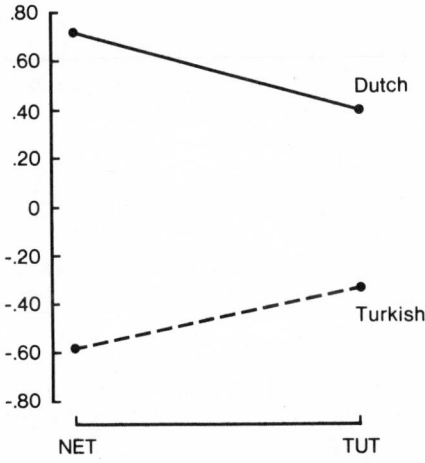

Figure 2: Mean z-scores on NET and TUT for Dutch and Turkish children.

The results of the analysis of variance (Table 4) show that the interaction between subjects and tests, as illustrated in Figure 2, is significant. It is interesting that the difference between Turkish children and their Dutch classmates on NET is larger than on TUT. Both differences are significant.

Moluccan and Dutch children
Table 5 shows the reliability coefficients of NET and MOT for Moluccan children and their classmates to be lower than those we have presented earlier for NET and TUT.

It is hard to explain the observed differences. Especially the very low reliability of MOT is striking. Perhaps careful inspection of the individual items (especially those which had to be deleted) can yield a plausible

Table 4: Analysis of variance: Dutch and Turks.

Source	Sum of squares	df	Mean square	F
Between subjects				
Ethnic group	24.43	1	24.43	18.25**
Subjects within ethnic group	60.25	45	1.34	
Within subjects				
Test	0	1	0	
Subjects × Test	2.08	1	2.08	17.33**
Residual	5.23	45	0.12	
Total	91.99	93		

** significant beyond the .001 level.

explanation. The correlation between exact and acceptable scores for the revised tests are highly significant, although not as high as the correlations for NET and TUT. Pearson's r between exact and acceptable scoring for NET was .92, for MOT .84. After correction for attenuation we again found correlations higher than 1.0.

Table 5: Reliability coefficients for NET and MOT (two ways of scoring).

	'Raw data'			'Revised data'			
	maximum score	N	KR20	maximum score	N	KR20	adjusted KR20 for revised data
NET exact	50	45	.83	44	45	.84	.86
NET acceptable	50	45	.83	44	45	.84	.86
MOT exact	50	45	.67	20	45	.77	.89
MOT acceptable	50	45	.77	29	45	.81	.88

In accordance with the analysis of the data obtained from Turkish children and their classmates, the analysis of the data obtained from Moluccan children and their classmates was carried out on the exact scores for the revised tests. Means, standard-deviations and Student's t are presented in Table 6.

Again we notice a difference in the effect of the cultural origin of the test on the scores of the two ethnic groups. Mean z-scores are listed in Table 7.

Table 6: Mean correct scores (in percentages) and standard-deviations for Dutch and Moluccans on NET and MOT.

	mean(N)	NET SD	N	mean(M)	MOT SD	N	N-M	df	t
Dutch	67.70	10.74	24	66.04	18.65	24	-1.66	23	.55
Moluccans	49.35	12.16	21	56.19	15.48	21	-6.84	20	-2.45**

** means significantly different at .01 level.

Table 7: Mean z-scores on NET and MOT for Dutch and Moluccan children, with Student's t.

	mean z-scores Dutch(D)	mean z-scores Moluccans(M)	D-M	df	t
NET	.59	-.67	1.26	43	5.38**
MOT	.26	-.30	.56	43	1.91

** means significantly different on .01 level.

Analysis of variance (Table 8) shows a significant interaction between the variables Subjects and Tests again (Figure 3).

Table 8: Analysis of variance: Dutch and Moluccans.

Source	Sum of squares	DF	Mean square	F
Between subjects				
Ethnic group	18.38	1	18.38	14.94**
Subjects within ethnic group	52.86	43	1.23	
Within subjects				
Test	0	1	0	
Subjects × Test	2.76	1	2.76	8.36**
Residual	14.01	43	0.33	
Total	88.01	89		

** significant beyond the .001 level.

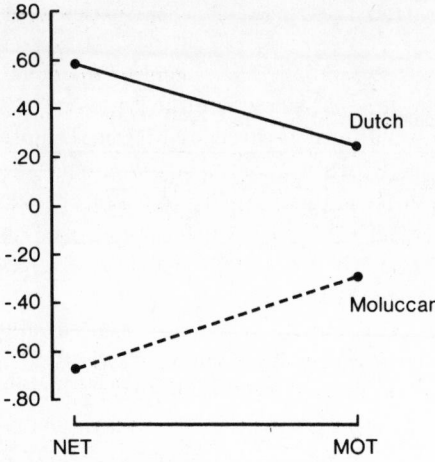

Figure 3: Mean z-scores on two tests (NET and MOT) for two ethnic groups (Dutch and Moluccan).

T-tests for the significances of the differences between the means of the Moluccan children and their Dutch classmates on the same tests show the difference between the means of the Dutch and Moluccan children to be significant for NET but not significant for MOT.

Finally the results of our subjects on NET, the test which was completed by all children, are presented in Table 9.

The means of the three ethnic groups were compared using Scheffé's method for multiple comparisons. As level of significance we used .10 level instead of .05 level, following Scheffé's recommendation (Ferguson 1981: 309).

As can be seen in Table 9, Dutch children performed significantly better on NET than Moluccan and Turkish children did. Moluccan children in their turn, performed significantly better than the Turkish children.

Table 9: Means and standard-deviations for the three ethnic groups on NET, incl. results of Scheffé's method of multiple-comparisons.

		mean	SD	Turks	Moluccans	Dutch
Turks	(n=26)	24.82	15.09	.	.	.
Moluccans	(n=21)	49.35	12.16	*	.	.
Dutch	(n=45)	61.46	16.30	*	*	.

* means significantly different at .10 level.

4. CONCLUSIONS

Before we discuss the results of our experiment with regard to the effect of the cultural origin of the tests, it is necessary to make some remarks concerning the reliability and the validity of the tests we utilized. Despite our efforts to construct three tests which were comparable in linguistic complexity, we found large differences in the reliability of the three tests. The difference between the reliability of NET when administered in different ethnic groups is remarkable. Of course the reliability of a test depends on the group of subjects being tested.

For the Turkish/Dutch group NET was more reliable than for the Moluccan/Dutch group. Our groups however were not very large and it is possible that these NET reliability differences wouldn't have occurred if the tests had been administered in larger groups. The very low reliability of MOT is striking. More than half of the MOT items showed an item-total correlation of less than .30. For TUT and NET these percentages were 40 and 12 respectively.

It does not seem possible that our method for constructing the tests caused the differences in the reliability. The texts were especially written to serve as bases for cloze-tests. In writing them we made sure that the readability of the texts was more or less the same. An equal number of content-words and function-words were deleted from each text. Furthermore, in the three texts the deletion rate was equal. This method for constructing cloze-tests is not in accordance with the principle of random selection of items which is generally favored for constructing cloze-tests. Some researchers, however, have warned against an overenthusiastic acceptance of this random procedure. They have shown that the difficulty of cloze-tests is variable, depending upon the words deleted. Even the same deletion procedure, starting deletions at different points in the texts, can result in differences in test difficulty. Alderson (1983) therefore recommends abandoning the random selection procedure in favour of a more rational selection of items. Our way of constructing cloze-tests, that is, trying to keep them comparable with respect to text complexity and number/kind of deleted words, can therefore hardly have caused the differences in reliability. And, as a matter of fact, compared with the results of a number of other studies our reliability coefficients are not that bad. Klein-Braley (1983) for instance, reexamined the question of the reliability of cloze-tests, and found much variation at this point too. Even her adjusted reliability coefficients for the tests lengthened to 50 items, do not reach the .90 level.

In accordance with Klein-Braley (1983) we computed the correlations between the different tests. Results are presented in Table 10.

Table 10: Correlation coefficients between different tests (revised versions, exact scoring method).

		N	Pearson's r	Pearson's r, corrected for attenuation
Dutch	(NET & TUT)	21	.86	1.00
Turks	(NET & TUT)	26	.87	1.00
Dutch	(NET & MOT)	24	.60	.92
Moluccans	(NET & MOT)	21	.60	.92

The high correlations (.86 and .87) between the scores of the Dutch and Turkish children on NET and TUT indicate that NET and TUT are parallel tests when completed by these two groups.

For NET and MOT these correlations, computed for Dutch and Moluccan children are much lower. They do not reach the .80 level which Nunally (1967) demands for parallel tests. Corrected for attenuation, however, these correlations reach the .80 level too.

Although the data concerning the reliability and validity of our tests indicate that our results have to be handled with care, some implications with regard to the effect of cultural origin of the tests on the performance of the subjects can be mentioned.

The results indicate that the differences in Dutch language proficiency of Dutch children and their ethnic minority classmates are actually not as large as teachers often presume. The great differences which are observed by teachers and testers can be caused by the fact that they are based on scores on tests like NET, which are not appropriate for ethnic minority children. On NET we also found significant differences in the mean scores of children belonging to different ethnic groups. Dutch children performed significantly better than did ethnic minority children. Moluccan children in their turn performed significantly better than did Turkish children. However, the results on TUT and MOT show that the differences between Dutch language proficiency of the Dutch children and their ethnic minority classmates are not as large as the results on NET indicate. The difference between Dutch and Turkish children on TUT is not as large as on NET, but it is still significant. The results on MOT show no difference at all in Dutch language proficiency of the Dutch and the Moluccan children.

The results on TUT and MOT are good reasons for doubting the validity of linguistic inferences concerning Dutch language proficiency of ethnic minority children made on the basis of scores on tests like NET. Unfortunately we are sure that most of the linguistic and instrumental inferences about Dutch proficiency of ethnic minority children in the Netherlands are based on such, culturally biased tests. The results of our study again show the urgent need for tests which are free of cultural biases.

8

Cognitive Academic Skills: an Attempt to Operationalize the Concept

Dorian de Haan

0. INTRODUCTION

In the debate about the relationship between language proficiency and school success, Bernstein (1962) postulated a dichotomy between so called 'restricted' and 'elaborated' codes for the language use of different socio-economic groups. Recently, this discussion has taken on new dimensions. Within the research field of second language acquisition and mother tongue and second language teaching, a dichotomy is hypothesized which seems to be cognate to the earlier distinction made by Bernstein. Differences in language proficiency are claimed to be not primarily a function of bilingualism, but of differences in the sociolinguistic backgrounds and the socio-economic position of the families to which bilingual children belong. Cummins (1979) provides the new terms. According to him, there is a difference between Basic Interpersonal Communicative Skills (BICS) and Cognitive Academic Language Proficiency (CALP). Although both concepts have an intuitive appeal, there has been hardly any operationalisation of the linguistic parameters of these skills until now.

The present paper is an attempt to set up a classification scheme for analysing spoken and written texts [2] of bilingual Surinam and monolingual Dutch children. The emphasis will be on the CALP dimension of the dichotomy. After a brief outline of the research project (1), I will describe some relevant aspects of Bernstein's and Cummins' concepts (2). Then I will go into three categories which seem to be important in specifying the concept of CALP: objectivation (3), explicitness (4) and integration (5). In discussing these categories, I will give some possible operationalisations of the concept by analyzing texts produced by children within the research project.

1. THE RESEARCH PROJECT

It is a general feeling among policy makers and teachers in the Netherlands that Surinam children do not have great difficulties with the Dutch language: in Surinam Dutch is the official language and medium of instruction in school. Compared to children of foreign workers and refugees, for Surinam children there are few state-supported measures and specific teaching programs aimed at sustaining the acquisition of Dutch. However, many Surinam children have other home languages than Dutch: Sranan Tongo and other Creole varieties, Sarnami Hindi, Surinam Javanese, Hakka (a Chinese language variety), and in incidental cases Indian languages. Little is known about the extent to which these language varieties are used. Since the greater part of the migration from Surinam to the Netherlands occurred around Surinam's declaration of independence in 1975, most Surinam children have already lived for some years in the Netherlands and express themselves reasonably well in Dutch nowadays. Speaking in Cummins' terms, most of them seem to have acquired Basic Interpersonal Communicative Skills. Nevertheless, their school results, allowing for specific school, class and ethnic group, are worse than those of Dutch children (Van Esch 1983). It is possible that their communicative skills in Dutch are just a "linguistic facade" (Cummins 1978).

The central question in this research project is: what kind of problems are Surinam children confronted with in acquiring sufficient Cognitive Academic Language Proficiency to follow the school curriculum successfully? In more concrete terms:

- What does the Dutch language use of Surinam children look like in the school situation?
- Which problems do Surinam children experience as a consequence of the language used by teachers and in curriculum materials?
- Are there any differences between Surinam and Dutch children in the extent to which they experience these difficulties?
- Are there any differences between Surinam children related to dominance of language?

The subjects in this study are 30 Surinam children from Creole (i.e. Sranan Tongo speaking) and Hindustani (i.e. Sarnami Hindi speaking) backgrounds and 14 indigenous Dutch children. The focus is on the interaction of school language and children's language. To gain a better insight into relevant school factors, a small number of schools has been selected with large Surinam populations. The study covers four schools, one class (6th grade) per school. Two schools have a majority of Hindustani children (The Hague) and two schools contain mostly Creole children (Amsterdam). Dutch children form a minority in all four schools. Table 1 shows the number of children per school. The children are matched for socio-economic class (SES 1-3) and, as far as the Surinam children are

Table 1. Number of subjects per school

Children	Classroom population			Selection			School population		
	Surinam	Dutch	total class	Hindustani	Creole	Dutch	Surinam	Dutch	Other
The Hague school 1	17[1]	3	24	8	-	3	76.6%	7.6%	15%
The Hague school 2	11[2]	3	23	8	-	3	17 %	30.4%	51%
Amsterdam school 1	17[3]	4	28	-	10	4	64 %	22 %	14%
Amsterdam school 2	10[4]	4	23	-	4	4	48 %	26 %	26%

(1) All Surinam children are from Hindustani backgrounds
(2) 9 Children are Hindustani, 2 children have Javanese backgrounds
(3) 10 Creole children, 4 Hindustani, 2 Chinese, 1 mixed background
(4) 4 Creole children, 3 Hindustani, 1 Chinese, 2 mixed backgrounds

concerned, for at least some proficiency in one of the Surinam languages. Schools differ in type of curriculum and in the total population of Surinam children.

Most data are collected in situations or activities in school in which 'CALP' is at stake. In addition, material is being collected in informal (school) situations in which 'BICS' predominate. The bulk of the data is formed by spontaneous language use that is being transcribed for analysis; the number of language tests utilized was necessarily limited because of characteristics of the home languages (there does not exist a written standard form) and cultural biases. At this moment data collection is not yet complete. The following has to be viewed as a search for units of analysis of spoken and written texts produced by children. Where possible some illustration will be given from data already collected.

2. DICHOTOMIES OF LANGUAGE SKILLS

Bernstein has tried to gain an insight into the way in which language use in socialisation influences social identity and social position of children. Initially (1959, 1962) he postulated a distinction between 'linguistic codes'. Differences between a 'restricted' and an 'elaborated code' were formulated in terms of the degree of complexity of grammatical structures, the degree of use of categories like adverbs, adjectives and connectives, and the degree of predictability and explicitness of expressions. In later years, Bernstein (1971) has retracted or differentiated his hypotheses about the relationship between social class and the use of a specific code, and about the linguistic and psychological aspects of the two codes. He now uses the term 'sociolinguistic code', referring to the way in which experiences take shape in meanings in language and communicative styles within the family. The meanings and communicative styles influence specific lexical and grammatical choices. The dichotomy of codes remains a theoretical construct; empirical research within this framework does not support the dichotomy. Instead of distinguishing two separate codes it is more adequate to think of differences in the *extent* to which speakers develop "particularistic" and "universalistic meanings" (Bernstein 1971). A second objection against the (code) theory is that there is no one-to-one relation between meaning and syntactic structure of sentences. An analysis of the linguistic realization of meaning structures has to focus on semantic patterns related to the task speakers are asked to perform. Nevertheless, Bernstein's work and the discussion that has followed have led to a deeper insight into differences in language use in socialization.

Cummins also proposes a dichotomy in his distinction between BICS and

CALP. This dichotomy however, is of a different nature than Bernstein's. BICS are loosely defined as 'accent', 'oral fluency', 'sociolinguistic competence' and 'basic competence in a Chomskian sense' (Cummins 1980). By CALP is meant "the ability to make effective use of the cognitive functions of the language, i.e. to use language effectively as an instrument of thought" (Cummins 1978: 397). Empirical evidence for Cummins' dichotomy mainly concerns correlations of dimensions of language proficiency with IQ. Those language skills that do have a clear correlation with IQ supposedly measure the CALP dimension. They are mainly reading and writing skills. Cummins (1980: 177) defines CALP as: "those aspects of language proficiency which are closely related to the development of literacy skills in L1 and L2". However, he gives hardly any further specification of "those aspects".

Cummins is oriented towards the situation of minority children who have to learn a second language. Bernstein is directed towards the situation of monolingual children acquiring their mother tongue. Acquisition of the linguistic structures of the mother tongue or the second language is not viewed as a main problem. Differences between children would arise in the way in which language is used. And that is where Bernstein's concept of codes and Cummins' concept of CALP comes in. At the level of acquisition of an 'elaborated code' or of 'CALP' parallels can be found between the two theories. Both authors write about 'decontextualization', i.e. the use of language "taken out of the context of the immediate interpersonal situation" (Cummins 1979: 238). Quoting Olson (1977) Cummins emphasizes the importance of "an autonomous representation of meaning" and "no cues other than linguistic ones" (Cummins 1979: 238). Bernstein's concepts of "particularistic" and "universalistic meanings" are defined in terms of the degree of contextboundedness. While Cummins (1979: 240) defines the problem for ethnic minority children who are educated in their weaker second language as "semi-literacy" (i.e. "less than native-like levels of literacy in both languages"), Bernstein never mentions literacy related skills in characterizing his concept of codes.

In analyzing spoken and written texts, it is useful to distinguish between form and meaning of language. This is precisely what many researchers have failed to do. Either they do not differentiate between form and meaning, or if they do, they focus too much on one of the two aspects. The advocates of the 'deficit' hypothesis were mainly preoccupied with language functions and meaning: what children do with words. A verbal deficit is defined as a shortcoming in the transmission of information, in describing, explaining or analyzing content matter (Bereiter & Engelmann 1966). By stating that the standard language was the only medium for acquiring these functions and 'logical' meanings, the deficit theory missed fundamental insights into the existence and the form of different language varieties. The 'variability' concept was a response to incorrect statements about the superiority of the standard variety (Labov 1969), but did not pay enough attention to statements about meanings expressed in language. Huls (1982: 35) writes: "concerning essential aspects of the ideas as developed by Bernstein the variability concept offers no alternative". According to Huls, Bernstein's approach of the concept 'language' can be characterized by such notions as 'functional', 'interactional', 'semantic', whereas syntactic and phonological aspects of language are often the object of investigation within the variability concept.

3. CATEGORIES OF "COGNITIVE ACADEMIC LANGUAGE PROFICIENCY"

My attempt to operationalize the concept of 'Cognitive Academic Language Proficiency' is to a great extent an attempt to make this concept usable for analyzing spoken and written texts produced by primary school children. In the following three paragraphs I will first distinguish meaning and form and then relate them. Three categories will be discussed which seem to be important tools in specifying the concept of CALP. I will use the term *objectivation* - instead of decontextualisation - to indicate monitoring [3] aspects of meaning, *explicitness* to refer to monitoring aspects of forms of language use, and *integration* to indicate monitoring aspects of both meaning and form in order to develop thematic cohesion. The concept of objectivation refers to the awareness that signification in school language is based upon the mutual defining relations of linguistic elements within different meaning systems. Being explicit presupposes children to be conscious of the demands of the context in which language is used in transmitting meaning. The concept of integration covers the skill to deliberate adjustment of meaning and form in structuring a text. These terms give an indication of my orientation: it will be for the most part towards the CALP pole of the dichotomy [4]. The main question concerns what a child that masters basic communicative skills in a language has to acquire, in order to master skills related to the CALP-dimension.

3.1. *Objectivation: monitoring meaning*

The meaning of words, sentences or texts is *always* created within a specific context; every context has a constitutive effect on the meaning of linguistic elements being used. "The question is", as Walkerdine (1982: 130) puts it: "what, in specific concrete cases, do children take to be the context?". The term "decontextualisation" is a misleading one, because it suggests that there is a difference between language with and without context. Children do not make a shift from context to no context at all, but they change their orientation from the physical context to a context of words. For all children, to learn at home is to learn in the context of social practices in which what is said is an important factor in signifying objects or actions. Families vary in the type of language they use and in the extent to which language figures in regulating behavior and in socializing children. These differences are important in the transition from home to school. In the course of the school curriculum the children's learning process will make less and less an appeal to daily experience and is increasingly embedded in more abstract symbolic activities. Children learn *to talk about school topics* and they learn *another modality* of language use, i.e. they learn to read and write.

School topics
Talking about school topics enables a child to generalise everyday knowledge, and it confronts a child with new meaning systems. The generalized concepts are increasingly related to *language* experience and less and less to experience with perceptual objects and actions. Children can imagine objects and actions when they use words like 'toys', 'tools' or 'purchases', because they have experience with those concepts in everyday life. But words from geography- or history-bound language like 'trade', 'raw material', 'period', mainly make an appeal to experience with language. To acquire concepts related to subject matter in school, children even have to ignore their experiences and learn new meaning systems.

Jakobson's terms 'metaphor' and 'metonymy' are helpful here (see Walkerdine 1982). Following De Saussure, who introduced the concepts of 'paradigmatic' and 'syntagmatic' relations, Jakobson distinguishes two different relations in the language system as well. 'Metaphor' concerns the relations between linguistic elements which bear systematic resemblance, and refers to *selection* of linguistic elements. 'Metonomy' refers to the relations between the linguistic elements as they are *combined* within sentences or texts. School language employs to a great extent the same lexical-syntactic elements as everyday language. But the interpretation of the same symbols changes with the context of the meaning system in which they occur. [5] E.g., a symbol as 'human being' has different connotations in biology and history, the connotation of 'liquid' in chemistry is different from the concept of 'water' in everyday experience. At the other hand school subject matter has its own specific words.

Children have to learn to recognize language elements in school practice as metaphors for different meaning systems. And that is where the problem begins. Tannen (1980) observes that children "approach school tasks as real-world problems, rather than decontextualized tasks". Walkerdine

(1982: 140) gives the following example of a child crossing the border from England to Scotland while saying: "This can't be Scotland, because there's nobody wearing a kilt". In its reasoning the child shows that he has not yet mastered the concept of 'border' as it is used in geography. It is still a perceptual phenomenon, and not a 'scientific' one.

It is not only a different orientation to content words that is demanded; children also have to make a shift in using function words that are related to causality, disjunction, condition etc. Wells (1981: 250) points to the following difference: "There is hardly a 4-year-old who does not understand correctly what his father means when he says: "If you don't eat up your cabbage, you will have to go to bed without any pudding". The children in Wells' study used the *if-then* construction themselves before entering school. But it takes years before they can solve problems when the *if-then* construction focusses only on the meaning in the sentence rather than on situational aspects.

Reading and writing
By the time they are five or six years old, children have acquired the phonological structures of their mother tongue. Perrera (1984) shows that, although knowledge of syntactic features is elaborated, there are several structures left to be acquired. The process of acquisition of meaning structures continues, too, in an intensive way. This is the proces of "mastering the conventions both for putting more and more of the meaning into the verbal utterance for reconstructing the intended meaning of the sentence per se" (Olson 1977: 261). Learning to read and write stimulates that process; children are taught to use language in a different way. Reading and writing about school topics have a distancing function. They teach children to reflect on meanings expressed in language – on words, rather than situations.

    It will be clear that a distinction between 'concrete' and 'abstract' words would be too vague here. Generalizing is a basic element of language competence and closely related to culture-specific conditions. [6] Vygotsky's distinction between "spontaneous" and "scientific" concepts [7] is more precise: Vygotsky (1962: 113) formulates the difference in terms of the awareness of a *system* of meanings. Children have to become conscious of relationships of generality between concepts in the different meaning systems of subject matter in school.

In my research project spoken and written texts of Surinam and Dutch children, teachers and curriculum materials will be analyzed on variables which are related to the characteristics of school language. Units of analysis are among others:

- The use by children, teachers and curriculum material of metaphors (number of T-units in which metaphors are used related to the length of the text). The category of metaphors which will be analyzed are the words that are specific for a school subject, i.e. terms like 'trade', 'industry', 'period' etc. Those words often can be found in the index of curriculum books. Teachers select them as keywords of a text and explain them in the transmission of subject matter.
- The way of and consistency in using these metaphors within the structure of the text: the focus is on the conformity with the rules for combination of these words within the meaning system of the specific school subject.

Of course we must bear in mind that children do not only learn the metaphors by heart, but also the sentences in which they appear. So it is expected to be a difficult task to distinguish clear-cut examples of texts which unambiguously give evidence of mastery of the meaning system.

Minority children for whom the language of the school is the weaker second language, will have four tasks to master: they have to acquire new language forms (phonology, morphology, syntax), new words (symbols), new concepts (semantic structures) and a new style of using language (the literate style).[8]

The following illustration of selection and manipulation of metaphors is derived from a conversation where the child is asked to comment upon a geography text (Werkgroep Van Dongen).
In the following translation from Dutch, rough English equivalent are given for the errors and idioms used by the children.

```
 1 Interviewer: On which means used people to exist?
 2 Simla: People used to exist on agriculture, fishery and trade.
 3 I:   Do you know what it means: agriculture, fishery and
 4      trade?
 5 S:   (...) And trade is er, to trade with each other, for example
 6      exporting and importing.
 7 I:   O.K. Splendid.
 8 I:   Why is it becoming a good time for the towns near the
 9      coast?
10 S:   It is becoming a good time er, the towns near the coast, because,
11      voyages of discovery were undertaken, seas were conquered and from
12      countries far away all kind of industry is brought in (literally
13      from the geography text itself, except the end "all kind of goods
14      were brought in").
15 (...) Text: How did it come about that in the 19th century the towns
16      were expanded?
17 S:   It came about because, er, all kinds of machines have been
18      invented and er, industry starts up, and, yes, then the country needs
19      more raw material from other countries, and er, that's it.
```

20 I: What does it mean – the towns expand?
21 S: Towns expand, er, they need something from other countries and
22   they expand.
23 I: But what does 'expand' mean?
24 S: One country needs something from the other country, so then they're
25   in contact with each other.
26 I: Yes, expand, do you know what expand means?
27 S: Yes, expanded, yes, yes.
28 I: What does it mean when you say – the towns expand?
29 S: The town er, gets, that er, hi er, that ge-, the town expands
30   er, the people of the, of the town, they've got more
31   contact with other people now
32 I: No, that's not quite right. (Explanation follows).
33   What has that got to do with those machines and that industry do
34   you think?
35 S: Eh, those machines, if they didn't have machines, then er, they
36   had to do it with their hands, with a lot of people, would need a lot
37   of people and that would take a long time. The industry, er, industry,
38   mm, aahm, industry means that er, that er, to export and import with
39   other countries.
40 I: Yes, yes. But you just said the same about trade.
41 S: Yes.
42 I: But it is not the same, trade and industry.
43 S: No? (pause)
44   Industry that comes into your country.
45 I: Yes, but what is it when you sai: Holland has a lot of industry.
46 S: Holland has a lot of thin-, er, many things to er, to ask from
47   other countries.
48 I: No, that's trade, that has to do with trade.
49 S: Oh. (laughs)
50 I: (Explanation)

Simla has not yet acquired the concepts behind the metaphors 'trade' and 'industry', and the boundaries between them are diffuse; the concepts mean roughly the same to her. The metonymy rules of 'trade' seem to be applied to the term 'industry': "all kind of industry is brought in" (line 12), "industry that comes into your country" (line 44). It is important to look at the way these words are presented to the children. Unfortunately we can only analyse the geography books and not the usage of the terms by teachers from the beginning. But it seems clear that children like Simla are severely hindered in understanding the text by not being aware of the concepts involved.

3.2. *Making things explicit: monitoring forms*

There is no absolute difference between explicit and implicit language use. The hearer and speaker always have to supply information. However, there *is* a difference between the demands oral speech and written text pose for the language user. Before discussing different ways of expressing meaning, it is again important to ask: what is the context of the language used? I will limit myself to the main features of the means for being explicit which differentiate "oral" and "literate styles." [8] In doing so I distinguish three aspects of context: aspects of the situation, aspects of the linguistic channel and aspects of conceptual structures.

Situational aspects of context

As stated before, a language user adapts her or his language to the demands of a context: conversation about objects or activities which are visible in the language-use situation will have a greater amount of exophorical references than conversations about objects or activities which cannot be perceived. Deictic elements (definite articles, demonstratives, pronouns, proper names, adverbs of time and location, etc.) often refer to aspects of a specific physical context; features of participants, action, time and location are clear. Writing demands that these features be made explicit by language. Exophorical referential procedures are allowed for in speech, but not in written texts. However, there are differences between children to the degree in which they rely on relevant parameters of the situation in expressing meanings. Hawkins (1973) shows that working class and middle class children use different styles. An orientation to be explicit about situational aspects may facilitate the acquisition of a literate style.

Aspects of the linguistic channel

In speech, being explicit is done partly in another way than in writing, and partly it is not necessary to be explicit at all. In oral discourse a lot of information is not made explicit in the words actually spoken. There are 'contextualisation cues' like dialect-, code- or style-switching, the nature of conversational openings, closings, sequencing strategies, on the grounds of which "people make decisions about how to interpret a given utterance based on their definition of what is happening at the time of interaction" (Gumperz 1982: 130). There is a 'cooperative principle' in conversations; a tacit contract between participants specifies when particular meanings of words in a conversation differ from conventional meanings (Grice 1975). Information in oral speech is partly encoded by prosodic and paralinguistic cues; in written text it has to be done with words. Collins and Michaels (1980) show that similar relations can be expressed in an 'oral' and 'literate' style by different means. Some children rely more on "rhythm and cadence" to signal relations and others confine themselves more to lexical and syntactic devices. These authors indicate that "in the transition from oral to written language prosodic cues are lost (..) a child who relies heavily on these cues (..) may be at a disadvantage in making the transition to literacy" (Collins & Michaels 1980: 153). Learning to write is learning to be explicit by means of linguistic elements.

Aspects of the conceptual system involved

The difference between "spontaneous" and "scientific" frames of reference is also relevant when talking about language forms. Children become conversant with the school register by grasping the explicit definitions of meanings and of the mutual defining value of words within the meaning systems. In language acquisition in the school setting, the relationship between language and reality is reversed. Instead of deriving meaning from reality, words now create reality. Explicit theoretical statements become the basis for constructing meaning. But the need for stating things explicitly is here also a relative phenomenon, dependent on the extent to which language-users (conversation partners, writers and their audience) know each other's words. Both in oral and in literate styles a certain amount of shared knowledge is assumed to be present. Grice's strategies for efficient communication centre around this reciprocal knowledge of the world. The extent to which people are obliged to be explicit depends on this knowledge. The school register may be not explicit enough for some children; it may be that curriculum writers and teachers do not know the worlds of those children.

In this research project spoken and written texts of Surinam and Dutch children and their teachers will be analyzed on the three aspects mentioned above. A specification of the skill of being explicit may include the following units of analysis:

- Selection by the children of linguistic means to put into words the obligatory information (amount of exophorical referential procedures).
- The introduction and use of new concepts in curriculum material and teacher-pupil interaction in terms of the means employed to relate new concepts to children's language (frequency of occurence of explicit definitions, amount of synonyms, superordinates and hyponyms).

Bilingual children for whom the language in school is the weaker one, who have to take greater pains to acquire the forms and formulations of the school language than monolingual children do, can spend less time on the obligatory rules at the metalinguistic level. Three texts in which three Surinam children (Aida, Shirley and Simla) give a resumé of a text from the geography book serve as an inllustration. The text is about the use of fertilizer in agriculture and how it is made from nitrogen.

1 *Aida*: When you wanted to keep alive, those people always needed food,
2 animals. But the farmers did it, because some farmers were poor, and

3 then they could not .. upgrow the ground, so, there were, not so many
4 fruits could grow there. And nitergen, comes fro- from the air, but
5 the plants don't mind, because they, because them have from the root.
6 Er, I don't know any more.

7 *Shirley*: Er, um animals and, animals and plants need a lot of food
8 and people too, and espe-, especially when you, because we, we liv',
9 li', we the Dutch and so on, but also are other Surinam and of that
10 agriculture, and like, they go, we too, like, from corn, and berries and
11 brambles and vegetables all come from the ground, and that nee-, needs
12 a lot of food, and when you put a little plant outdoors, also needs food,
13 you must also all the time give water, and I think that's the most
14 important thing, because if you don't like that a plant or a flower,
15 because, they had, like they has to have a lot of oxygen like us and
16 they live like us too only with them don't eat so much like us, so,
17 so, so, 'n, 'n, I should think much better if they gave a lot of food,
18 because if we eat berries and so on, we have to wash it well first,
19 because, because people could have spit or something and, like, put
20 poison on, then if you, when my mother makes things like, or buys
21 vegetables she also looks if it's good, because she is not going to put
22 it in the pot just like that, because otherwise you get, because sometimes
23 there's worms in it and, when you, and when you haven't got any more
24 food, like, or you-re, er, you chokes, so then, look wha-, what you
25 also straight away so, then go, then you feel very funny, also if you
26 fall into a swoon like, then, then you think you are somewhere else,
27 but it's not really true either, but, as well, when you are going to
28 swim ... (..)."

29 *Simla*: Some people think that er, water is already enough for fl,
30 for flowers and plants, but that's not true, because er, on er, on er
31 a, on a field, a farmer also needs artificial manure, you can er hear
32 that straight away, Er, and, what was it about? (Recorder off, she
33 thinks it over). The farmers soon twigged it, that er, the field, yes,
34 that he didn't just have to plant the same er fruit or vegetables,
35 because, er, yes, after, after years, before or behind, the farmer has,
36 the farmers have worn out the ground, and then, er ... Wow! Er yeah, er,
37 then the vegetation was, less coming up. Later they discovered that the
38 artificial manure were also needed for the gr, plants and flowers,
39 therefore, er, ni, nitrogen was er, come from the manure, and it, it
40 was in the air as well, but the plants didn't so much good get out of it,
41 well and, la-, and then the people have discovered that er, was in the
42 air, and have they made grains and er, and er, manure out of and they
43 have, that er, they sow on the ground, on the ground of the countryside,
44 and er, if they didn't do that the flowers and plants wouldn't get
45 bigger, and the, the colour green would get a little er, pale, and yes,
46 er ...

Aida sticks very close to the text: indexical expressions like "those people"
(line 1) "the farmers" (line 2) "did *it*" (line 2), "the plants don't care"
(line 5) "them have - from the root" (line 5), are considered as exo-

phorical references, where referents are in the book. She may suppose that the investigator has also read the text, although that is not what actually happened in the research setting. Meanings are not made explicit. Shirley's resumé has only the book as starting point, and from the sentence "when you put a little plant outdoors" (lines 11/12), her exophorical referents concern matters of her own life. She abandons the frame of the geography text in talking about plants and vegetables, choke (in Dutch the word for nitrogen is 'stikstof', choke is 'stikken' which permits an association with spitting, fall into a swoon) and food. She associates freely. From the start she tries to bring her own life in ("we the Dutch and so on, but also are other Surinam" (lines 8/9), and she seems eager to tell a lot.

Simla's text contains few referents that do not have an antecedent within the text. The sentence "The farmer *soon* twigged it ..." (line 29) presupposes an indication of time she does not give, and "later *they* have discovered" (line 33) is ambiguous in relation to the antecedent (farmers, or people not introduced).

3.3.   Integration: monitoring meaning and form in order to develop thematic cohesion

It is important to look not only at meaning expressed in particular words or sentences, but also at meaning expressed in an entire text. When Olson states "the meaning is in the text" (1977: 277), his orientation is towards the autonomous representation of meaning in sentences.

To specify Olson's view I have to refer to the definition of 'text' mentioned earlier (see note [2]). According to Halliday & Hasan (1976) a text is constituted by related sentences, and these relations are brought about by two elements: the concept of cohesion (the presence of semantic relations in terms of ties) and the concept of register (the presence of semantic relations in terms of the connections between the concepts involved). The register portion is in Olson's terminology interpreted as, or limited to, registers in which meaning is constituted by the 'logical' relations within and between linguistic elements. Whereas the crucial distinguishing feature in Halliday & Hasan's terms is 'relatedness', for Olson a 'text' is arrived at by the 'autonomy' criterion. Olson formulates a sharp contrast between oral and written language; the focus is on two counterparts, and little attention is paid to the nature of the words which are inserted in both styles. In addition Olson does not account for the way children have to acquire in school a style in which meaning is fully intrinsic to language. In the following I will first go into the language involved in "oral" and "literate styles" from the viewpoint of 'integration' of texts, and then into the practices in which styles have to be acquired.

Acquiring language to understand and produce cohesive devices of the literate style

Halliday & Hasan (1976: 26) define cohesion of a text as "the set of meaning relations that is general to all classes of texts, that distinguishes text from non-text and interrelates the substantive meanings of the text with each other". I will use the term 'integration' to indicate the activity of creating cohesion.

Cohesive devices are to be found in everyday speech as well as in written language. Differences are related to the feedback the speaker or writer gets on the transmission of meaning. Speech is characterized by, as Cook-Gumperz & Gumperz (1981) put it, 'multi-modality' or multi-level signalling by which different aspects of the meaning structure can be transmitted at the same time. Collins & Michaels (1980) show how intonation patterns are processed along with lexical and syntactic options in shaping the structure of a narrative. Cohesion in written text and in 'literate style' is characterized by more than one-level signalling : meanings do not so much rely on prosodic cues but are mainly organised in a sequential way and depend on lexicalization and syntax. Collins & Michaels (1980) show how a specific use of intra-clausal complements, inter-clausal structures and connectives functions in referring back at a later point in the narrative. Hasan & Halliday distinguish grammatical cohesion (reference, substitution, ellipsis), lexical cohesion (repetition, synonyms, superordination, for example) and cohesion by connectives.

To use and understand cohesive devices of the school register children have to acquire knowledge of specific vocabulary, concepts and structures. The degree of acquisition of the school-register *vocabulary* determines a child's potential for creating cohesion in school texts: the relation between clauses, sentences and parts of the text is often implicated by the use of synonyms, hyponyms, antonyms etc. It is essential to recognize these words as related to their antecedents in reading. Additionally, children are required to have language experience in specific lexico-syntactic elements which are acquired late in language development. Relations such as disjunction, condition, causality, concession etc., expressed by words specific to written text (Perera 1984), can cause serious problems for children in integrating text items in reading or writing. *Conceptual* knowledge facilitates the recognition or construction of a meaning structure: knowing what the text is about, knowing the arguments, leaves room for concentration on the relations imparted. Knowledge of how written texts are *structured* facilitates performing the cognitive task of organizing a written text as a coherent meaning structure (Kok, Boonman & Beukhof 1980). Research into the connection between child languages and the demands of school language particularly in higher grades of primary school classrooms, shows that for many children such a connection does not exist.

Practices in the classroom for acquiring cohesive devices of the literate style

Language acquisition in school not only differs from language acquisition outside school in the *way* but also in the *why*: in school, children have to acquire in any case the labels, even if they don't understand the concepts. Acquisition of knowledge in school is for many children learning to reproduce subject matter or to reproduce the right words. Edwards (1976: 153) calls this process "hunting the label". It is very difficult for many teachers to build fully upon the existing knowledge of the children in their evaluation.

Concepts are often transmitted and learned incompletely, because there is a gap between frames of reference. Teachers intend more than pupils infer (Kusters & Bonset 1980). For children a lot of 'knowledge' consists of fragments. The meanings that are offered sink in as reduced language. Sharp (1980: 147) calls this process 'cognitive impairment': "school knowledge is experienced as reifed, fragmented, and disparate collections of unproblematic facts". According to her, the school does not just fall short on the level of transmitting relevant meanings within coherent meaning systems, but aside from that, the school does not bring about an orientation toward the frames within which knowledge emerges and is evaluated to be important. To evaluate the acquisition of children's skill in integrating texts, it is essential to account for the conflicts between the meaning structures of the school and those of the children themselves.

In this research project a specification of the skill at integrating texts includes the following units of analysis:

- Linguistic means for relating clauses and sentences (repetition of lexical elements, use of synonyms e.g., anaphorical referential procedures, connectives, etc. (Collins & Michaels 1980, Halliday & Hasan 1976, Kusters & Bonset 1980, Noordman & Vonk 1981, Ochs 1979).
- Ratio of amount of episodes within a text to length of episode (in terms of number of T-units). A high number of short episodes may indicate low coherence (for the concept of episode, see note [2]).

Integration in school texts will be an extremely difficult task to perform for minority children who are taught in their weaker language. They are supposed to express both the meaning structure of the school register and the syntactic-lexical structures of the literate style which are related to it. Integration is a skill that combines prerequisite skills for objectivation and making things explicit, and in acquiring this skill the difficulties inherent in objectivation and explicitness exacerbate each other.

Aida's earlier presented text contains three episodes, which are all within the frame of the geography text. Boundaries between episodes may be determined by the absence of explicit cohesive devices between parts of the text. In Aida's case the first episode (lines 1-2) is about people who need food. The references in the second episode (lines 2-4) are exophorical, so they cannot function as ties, as items that relate this sentence with the preceding one; the second episode is about the 'upgrowing' of the ground; the third one (lines 4-6) about nitrogen contains no ties with the second or first episode. The entire text has seven T-units.

In Shirley's text the (10) elliptical sentences which are not interpretable are not counted as T-units. On 3 episodes (lines 1-16, 17-21, 23-25) she has more and longer T-units (15) than Aida has. But this figure is misleading. Only the first episode is within the frame of the geography register, and within this episode only three of the nine T-units; the other episodes are about experiences of 'us', plants and food.

The text of Simla is composed of one episode with lexical repetitions ('farmer', 'artificial manure', 'flowers and plants') and synonyms ('the vegetation') as ties. The 14 T-units are within the frame of the geography text. So Simla's text is the most cohesive one.

The texts of all three children start with a topic sentence, but Aida's sentence does not function as such: there is no explicit connection with what follows. All texts contain anaphorical references. The connectives in the texts will be analyzed according to their functioning as cohesive devices. Aida for example uses 'but' (lines 2 and 4), the function as adversative connection however is not clear. 'Because' (line 5) is ambiguous: the preceding sentence does not offer a clue for the causal relationship. Simla's connectives all function as ties; in Shirley's text most of the connectives are cohesive.

4. FINAL REMARKS

The evidence Cummins supplies to sustain his hypothesis about the interdependence of the acquisition of CALP in the mother tongue (L1) and the second language (L2) makes him conclude that "if optimal development of a minority language child's cognitive and academic potential is a goal, then the school program must aim to promote an additive form of bilingualism involving literacy in both L1 and L2" (Cummins 1979: 247). Cummins' view is that the acquisition of CALP by minority children is conditional on mother tongue teaching. However, there is obviously no guarantee that mother tongue teaching is sufficient in reaching that goal:

monolingual children from low socio-economic backgrounds also have difficulties in acquiring CALP. The statement of Olson (1977) that "a mother tongue is not the same as the language of prose texts" is very relevant here.

Research data indicate that a match between linguistic experience in childrens' homes and the linguistic demands in the classroom is fundamental for their progress in school (Wells 1978). Middleclass children have better results in literacy, whether they are taught in their mother tongue or in a second language (Swain 1981). According to Wells (1981), almost all children attain a basic level of literacy. Differences emerge when higher levels of reading are at stake. The core of the teaching of reading and writing is supposedly "practice makes perfect". It seems that this does not work for minority children. There is no satisfying theory about the fundamental aspects of what to teach and how to teach in a systematic way (Bol 1978). It looks as if, first of all, the teaching of processing and producing information has to be improved, in order to enable minority children to reach the level at which they can use literacy to develop the cognitive functions related to it. A research design concerned with the acquisition of CALP by minority children must take into account not only spoken and written texts produced by the children, but also the relevant features of the contexts in which the children are supposed to acquire those skills.

NOTES

1. I would like to thank Guus Extra, Ton Vallen, Anne Vermeer, David Ingleby, Elly Singer, and Valerie Walkerdine for their comments on an earlier version of this text.
2. For a definition of 'text' I refer to Halliday & Hasan (1976: 25): "a unit of situational-semantic organisation: a continuum of meaning in context constituted around the semantic relation of cohesion". The units of analysis in this project are based on different textual activities: interviews, classroom conversations, essays etc. These texts can be split up into episodes: elements within the text which stand by themselves but which are more or less connected with a series of other elements by the frame of the activity. 'Ties', pairs of cohesively related elements, relate the items of a text within an episode.
3. The concept of monitoring is defined and worked out by Hagen (1981: 198): "a cognitive strategy directed towards controlling language production for optimal communication (..)". Monitoring is a form of linguistic awareness, to be distinguished from reflection. Reflection can be considered as more explicit, conscious linguistic awareness, with the goal of analysing language products, while monitoring is of instrumental nature. According to Hagen (1984: 90): Reflection on language is "outside language use, while monitoring is expressed inside language use" as part of communication.

4. To determine Basic Interpersonal Communication Skills an error analysis will be made and quantitative measures will be used (mean length of utterance, syntactic complexity measures) for the texts within an everyday context.

5. For example, for the well informed reader the word "metaphor" in this sentence invokes quite different meanings from its everyday use.

6. Williams (1970: 395) states: "The point to be made is that abstractions and relations are so typically tied to the milieu and requirements of social structures that one cannot fully sense them without being a linguistic member of that structure (or else an ethnographer) and certainly will be hard-pressed to comprehend or communicate them under conditions of cross-class speech".

7. In recent publications within the tradition of Soviet psychology (Davidov and others), the terms 'empirical' and 'theoretical' concept are preferred, roughly indicating language referring to perceptions and experiences, versus language within which meanings are derived from a theory respectively. But these terms have been criticised for drawing the dividing-lines too absolutely.

8. Akinnaso (1982) gives an overview of differences between spoken and written language. These differences do not necessarily coincide with those of an oral and a literate *style*. The term literate style here does not simply indicate syntactic and lexical characteristics of written language use. Collins & Michaels (1980) use the terms "oral" and "literate *discourse* style". They use them in a heuristic way to label differences between children in transmitting meaning in narratives. They define a style in which specific linguistic – instead of prosodic or paralinguistic – devices are used in constituting thematic cohesion of a text as a "literate" style; these devices bear "closer resemblance to the oral style of middle class, literate adults." I also use the terms heuristically, in analysing the use of language forms and meanings which are supposed to be characteristic of the school register.

9

Educational Settings, Teaching Methods and Second Language Proficiency of Turkish and Moroccan Children

Kees de Bot, Alex Buster & Anne-Mieke Janssen-van Dieten

1. INTRODUCTION

In the last two decades emigration from Mediterranean countries to Western European countries has increased considerably. Due to changing economic and political circumstances, migration of male foreign workers has turned into more or less permanent emigration of families from these countries. In the Netherlands the resultant increase of the proportion of immigrant children in schools has led to serious problems, for pupils as well as teachers, that have not been solved as yet. The Dutch Administration was rather late in recognizing that simple ad hoc solutions would be insufficient in the long run. Dutch schools and teachers were in fact neither trained nor prepared to deal with large numbers of immigrant children in the classroom. The schooling of immigrant children has not been organized uniformly, nor has it been guided by the government, so that many different educational settings are found in schools with immigrant children (Van Esch 1982).

After establishing what the various educational settings had in common, the aim of the present study was to analyse the ways in which educational settings influence the acquisition of Dutch as a second language by immigrant children.

2. IMMIGRANT CHILDREN IN DUTCH SCHOOLS

The majority of educational settings in Dutch schools fit in with one of the following models:
1. The children are admitted to regular schooling according to age.
   In addition they attend classes in Dutch given by a special teacher. This set-up is comparable with what is generally known as 'immersion' or 'submersion', except that in the Netherlands six or more different background languages in one class are by no means exceptional.
2. The children are placed in preparatory classes before they are admitted to the regular school system. Next to the acquisition of Dutch, the emphasis in these classes is on getting used to Dutch schools. The

children are not placed according to age but according to their respective proficiency levels of Dutch.

In the aforementioned models the children may attend additional classes in their first language. Generally, there are no institutionalized contacts between the teachers of Dutch and the teachers of Turkish and Moroccan.

3. The children are placed in a special program in which for the first few years part of the teaching is done in the first language. These transitional programs aim at gradual integration into the regular Dutch school system.

Initially the purpose of the study was to assess the effectiveness of the models under discussion as well as of the various approaches to teaching Dutch as a second language (Buster 1981)*. However, it appeared that many educational settings comprised a combination of aspects suggestive of different models. Therefore it was decided to change the design in such a way that educational setting would not be treated as the independent variable, but a number of aspects of educational setting would be included as independent variables in the design.

The present study started from circumstances different from those of the well-known research on the effectiveness of second language programs for children in the US and Canada (Mc Laughlin 1978, 133-145). These projects focused on comparing well-defined programs and on assessing their relative merits. In the present project the educational system is investigated as it is: there are no presupposed models, but only a limited number of potentially relevant parameters.

3. APPROACHES TO TEACHING DUTCH AS A SECOND LANGUAGE

Research into the most efficient way to teach and/or learn a second language has always been one of the major goals of applied linguistic research. In the last few decades research focused on issues such as the effectiveness of language laboratories (Keating 1963, Smith 1970), and inductive vs. deductive rule learning (Levin 1972, Von Elek & Oskarsson 1975).

A more recent controversy concerns the role of grammar in second language teaching (for an overview see Van Els et al. 1984, chapter 12).

* This project was sponsored by the Dutch Foundation for Educational Research (SVO). The authors wish to thank Adri Elsen for his correction of the English manuscript.

Recent literature in the field of applied linguistics suggests that communicative teaching in 'in', while teaching grammar, or even mentioning it, is 'out'. In our study we broadly distinguished between grammar-oriented approaches and communication-oriented approaches to second language teaching. In a grammar-oriented approach, emphasis is either implicitly or explicitly on certain *form* characteristics of the language. Form characteristics play an important role in structuring language teaching, particularly when the grammatical complexity of the language materials used increases. In a communicative approach, *function* rather than form is the most important feature. In such an approach it is more important that the learners' utterances are communicatively adequate than that they are grammatically correct.

The distinction between 'grammatical' and 'communicative' is not very explicit, but must be considered a continuum ranging from more form-oriented to more content-oriented. In literature on communicative language teaching, 'linguistic competence' is regarded as one of the main elements of 'communicative competence'.

In the present study we did not aim at an explicit comparison of grammar-oriented teaching versus communication-oriented teaching. Instead, a number of aspects of language teaching have been considered that might be suggestive of a preference for either of the approaches. This does not rule out 'inconsistent' behaviour of a given teacher: she may show a 'grammatical' preference for one aspect and a 'communicative' one for another.

4. AIM OF THE PROJECT

The aim of our project can be formulated as follows: to what extent do differences in educational setting and differences in L2 (i.e. Dutch) teaching methods lead to differences in L2 proficiency in the case of Turkish and Moroccan children.

5. DESIGN

After a study of the variety of educational settings 3 different groups of pupils were selected to participate in the experiment:
1. 6/7-year-old first graders who had no previous second language training in primary school;
2. 9/10-year-old third graders who had had 2 years of second language training in primary school;
3. 12/16-year-old children who had been placed in transitional classes

preparing them for regular secondary education. They either came directly from their home countries, or had already attended Dutch primary schools for some time, but still lacked the L2 proficiency required to function adequately in the regular Dutch school system.

Children of two different nationalities were tested, i.e. Turkish and Moroccan. They had been selected because they constitute the main ethnic minority groups at Dutch schools.

Given the different backgrounds of the target groups, it is clear that the present study cannot be termed cross-sectional. In fact three parallel studies have been carried out. The research design comprised a pretest and a posttest for second language proficiency. L2 proficiency as measured by the posttest was treated as the dependent variable, the pretest score was treated as covariate, and differences in educational setting and language teaching approach were treated as independent variables. For the independent variables a multiple indicator approach was used.

In our statistical analyses the experimental unit consisted of individual children's performances.

6. TESTS AND INSTRUMENTS

6.1. *Language proficiency tests*

Given the size and aim of the project, as well as the size of staff and amount of time available, the language tests used had to meet a number of requirements:
- Efficiency was important: group testing would be preferable to individual testing, and the criteria for scoring would have to be objective;
- A wide range of proficiency levels had to be covered;
- The tests had to be age-independent;
- The tests had to be as culture-fair as possible.

Most research into second language acquisition in the Netherlands is concerned with the development of a limited number of specific linguistic (mainly syntactical) aspects (Verhoeven & Extra 1983, Lalleman 1983).

Because the majority of the tests used in these experiments could not be used in the present experiment, we had to construct tests ourselves. In recent literature on language testing (Oller 1979, Farhady 1979, Vollmer & Sang 1980), it is often discussed whether language proficiency is a multidimensional skill or a uni-dimensional skill. Results from empirical research do not overwhelmingly support either of these views. For our research we decided not to concentrate on a number of specific linguistic aspects, but to test general proficiency. Following the 'unitary competence hypothesis', indirect integrative tests seemed preferable to direct discrete-point tests. Such a preference is in line with Oller's remarks in his overview of research in this field: 'There is considerable evidence to show that in a wide range of studies with a substantial variety of tests and a diverse selection of subject populations, discrete-point tests do not correlate as well with each other as they do with integrative tests. Moreover, integrative tests of very different types (e.g. cloze versus dictation) correlate even more highly with each other than they do with language tests which discrete-point theory would identify as being more similar' (1979: 60).

Group 1: Sentence imitation test

For the youngest group no written tests could be used, because the children had only just started learning to read and write. In the literature on testing there is little information on the use of indirect integrative tests with young second language learners. Cracker (1971, in Oller 1979) found that this procedure is sensitive to variations in language proficiency in the case of children who cannot or who have just started to learn to read or write. Unfortunately, detailed descriptions of tests and procedures used were not presented. Two types of tests appeared to be applicable: sentence imitation tests and oral cloze tests.

Sentence imitation tests have been used widely in research on first and second language development (Fraser et al. 1963, Slobin 1973, Naiman 1974, Swain et al. 1975) Naiman's 1974 research indicates that sentence imitation is more than just a perceptual motor skill. His main conclusion is that sentence imitation can be a useful tool for tapping the competence of the second language learner (Naiman 1974: 33). In a pilot study, a number of sentence imitation tests were tried out. Based on the results of the pilot study, a test consisting of a series of sentences that formed a simple story was selected. We decided to use what is called a 'verbatim' score, which means that each individual word in a sentence was scored as correct/ incorrect. Furthermore, errors on sentence level (inversion, addition of words) were scored separately.

Group 2: Cloze test

For the second group a written test could be used. The obvious choice for an indirect, integrative test was the cloze test. It is generally considered to be a useful instrument for measuring second language proficiency, and its psychometric record is fairly impressive (Wijnstra 1977, Oller 1979, Mullen 1979, Hinofotis 1980). Again, a number of cloze tests have been compared in a pilot study. It appeared that the children had some problems in understanding the task. The children did not seem to be accustomed to blank filling excercises, which held for the Dutch pupils as well. Adequate instructions for the test leaders had to be set up.

The cloze tests used in the pilot studies could be scored in two ways. In the pilot study the correlation between 'exact' scores and 'acceptable' scores was .96. We decided to use the exact scores procedure because it is more efficient.

One of the tests that had been constructed turned out to be adequate for our purposes.

Group 3: Editing test

At the Nijmegen Institute of Applied Linguistics some research into editing tests has been carried out. This procedure was developed fairly recently and is in a way the opposite of a cloze test. In the latter, words have been left out of a text and the blanks have to be filled in. In the former, superfluous words have been added to a text and have to be removed by the testee.

Davies (1975) was among the first to use the principle of the editing test in what he called a 'speed-reading-test'. Bowen (1978) and Mullen (1979) carried out research into this procedure and reported high reliability coefficients and a promising concurrent validity. An existing editing test could be used for our third target group (Janssen-van Dieten & Van der Linden 1983). No piloting was considered necessary, because the test had already been used for the same population.

In our design, the same tests were adopted as pretests and posttests. Given the lapse of time between the administration of the two tests (about 6 months), a retest-bias was very unlikely to occur, and even if it occurred, it was to be preferred to the bias arising from using different tests.

6.2. Attitude scales

Attitude is an essential factor in second language acquisition (Gardner & Lambert 1972, Van Els et al. 1984: 115-121). The outcome of research into the relationship between attitude and acquisition of young children is somewhat ambiguous. As compared with adult learners, attitude seems to play a less prominent role with young second language learners. It is held that attitudes are generally less developed and less stable in young children than in adults (Genesee & Hamayan 1980, Day 1983). Two aspects of attitude have been considered in our study: attitude towards Dutch society and attitude towards the vernacular culture. Because of the efficiency constraints, which have already been mentioned with respect to the language tests, we opted for an attitude test that could be administered groupwise. The same test was used for all age groups. The test we used was an adapted version of Zirkel & Greene's (1976) Cultural Attitude Scales (CAS). In CAS, attitudes are measured by presenting children with graphic illustrations of dress, sports, foods and other symbols from everyday life. The child reacts to these pictures by marking one of five faces on a happy-sad Likert scale. Three different scales had been developed: a Dutch scale, a Turkish scale and a Moroccan scale. Turkish children did the Dutch version and the Turkish version, Moroccan children did the Dutch version and the Moroccan version.

Previous research by Zirkel and Greene (Greene & Zirkel 1973, Zirkel & Greene 1974, 1976) had shown that these cultural attitude scales were sufficiently reliable but, as with most attitude scales, the validity was less well-established.

6.3. *Other learner characteristics*

In order to collect detailed information on each individual child, we devised a questionnaire that had to be filled in by the teachers.
The following aspects were included:
- amount of time spent in Dutch nursery school;
- length of residence (for group 3);
- previous primary school education in Turkey or Morocco (for group 3);
- education in the vernacular language and culture;
- absence from school;
- classification of the father's job;
- level of education of the parents;
- language spoken at home;
- nationality of the parents;
- attendance at Dutch schools of elder brothers and sisters;
- proportion of immigrant population in the district of residence;
- socio-demographic characteristics of the district of residence (public libraries, community centres, play grounds);
- teacher's rating of the level of proficiency in Dutch.
Besides, the children were asked to name their six best friends. This was expected to give some indications of language contacts and language acquisition out of school.

6.4. *Teacher characteristics*

As indicated earlier, most teachers working with immigrant children were not trained for this kind of teaching, simply because no such training was and is available to date, except for some in-service training and some guidance by educational services. Because the teachers were expected to vary a lot, information about individual teachers was needed. In the questionnaire teachers were also asked to give information about their careers and educational backgrounds.

Finally, we tested the teachers' attitudes towards teaching immigrant children by having them react to a number of statements about immigrant children in Dutch schools.

6.5. *School characteristics*

Information on school characteristics was provided by the headmasters of all the schools participating in the experiment.
The questionnaire dealt with the following aspects:
- What procedure is adopted when immigrant children enter either the first or any of the ensuing forms of the school;
- What criteria are used in placing immigrant children (age and/or level of proficiency in Dutch);
- Are there any special courses for immigrant children, particularly additional Dutch classes;
- To what extent do immigrant children participate in the regular Dutch curriculum;
- Does the school employ teachers who have been appointed exclusively for teaching immigrant children;
- Number of children at school, proportion of Dutch children;
- Attention paid to immigrant children in staff meetings;
- Facilities provided by the local or national authorities; educational guidance.

For the third group, additional information was needed about the type of school the transitional class was attached to, the proportion of lessons attended jointly by Dutch and immigrant children, and about the number of lessons and the proportion of teachers working exclusively with immigrant children.

6.6. *Approaches to teaching Dutch as a second language*

In research on language teaching one can distinguish between the contribution of the learner and the contribution of the instructional program, i.e., what is taught and how it is taught. The present study focused on the latter, which comprises the following factors: educational setting, and both the what and the how of teaching within the setting. Therefore, we had to develop an instrument that would enable us to include these factors in a quantitative analysis.

The best procedure would have been to carry out observations in the schools to be studied. Limited financial resources made us adopt an alternative procedure, i.e. asking the teachers what they teach and how they teach it. Additionally, some informal observations in school were planned.

On the basis of relevant literature and an analysis of specific teaching methods for Dutch as a second language, a number of aspects had been selected that could indicate either a grammatical or a communicative approach to teaching.

The following aspects were included in the teachers' questionnaire:

- Relative emphasis on the respective linguistic skills: listening, speaking, reading, writing;
- Instructional materials used in the classroom. This included existing text books as well as materials prepared by the teacher;
- Gradation of instructional materials;
- Didactic procedures;
- Presentation of grammatical rules;
- Reactions to speech errors;
- Grouping of Dutch and Turkish/Moroccan children during classroom activities.

A detailed description of the development of the questionnaire is outside the scope of the present article.

7. SELECTION OF SCHOOLS AND PUPILS

In the selection of schools two criteria had been adopted: a proportionate number of Turkish/Moroccan children and supposed differences in educational setting between the schools.

Because a large number of testees was required, schools with relatively small numbers of immigrant children were not included in the sample.

For the first two groups, 30 schools were selected from different parts of the Netherlands. Eventually, data from 27 schools were used. For the third group 20 schools were selected, and data from 19 schools were used. 10 of them were attached to schools for vocational training, 9 were attached to other types of schools for secondary education.

In 1981 there were 22,988 Turkish children and 13,608 Moroccan children in Dutch primary schools, i.e. some 3% of the total attendance. In secondary schools there were 10,471 Turkish pupils and 4,995 Moroccan pupils i.e. 1.5% of the total number. These two groups were by far the largest groups of immigrant children in Dutch schools (Onderwijsverslag 1983).

A sample from the total population was drawn on the basis of the criteria for selection of schools mentioned before. The sample consisted of the following numbers of children:

Table 1. Number of children per group.

	Turkish	Moroccan	Schools
Group 1	197	69	27
Group 2	243	74	} 19
Group 3	177	67	
	617	210	

The total number of children tested was about 10% larger than the numbers presented in Table 1. One of the well-known drawbacks of pretest-posttest designs is the 'mortality' effect: informants are lost in the lapse of time between pretest and posttest.

8. PROCEDURE

In the study three stages can be distinguished with respect to the collection of data:
A. September/October 1981: Selection of schools on the basis of criteria mentioned earlier;
B. November/December 1981: Pretesting of language proficiency and obtaining information on other learner characteristics;
C. June 1982: Posttesting of language proficiency and obtaining information on school characteristics and teacher characteristics.

In view of the large number of children to be tested, testing periods were rather long. Test administration had been organized in such a way that the time lag between pretest and posttest was more or less equal for all children.

9. RESULTS

9.1. *Language proficiency*

Reliability coefficients (standardised α) for the language proficiency tests are presented in Table 2.

Scores on the language tests were also compared with teachers' ratings of language proficiency for each child. Correlation coefficients between ratings and test scores are presented in Table 3.

Table 2. Reliability coefficients of language proficiency.

	pretest	posttest
Group 1 (Sentence imitations)	.97	.96
Group 2 (Cloze test)	.91	.89
Group 3 (Editing test)	.96	.95

Table 3. Correlation between teachers' ratings of language proficiency and test scores.

	pretest scores	posttest scores
Teachers' Ratings group 1	.57	.53
Teachers' Ratings group 2	.38	.34
Teachers' Ratings group 3	.54	.51

Because the same test had been used for pretest and posttest, scores on the two tests correlated. The correlations between pretest and posttest for the three groups were .76, .74 and .82, all significant at the 1% level.

Given this fairly high correlation between pretest and posttest, it was of crucial importance that children improved between the respective administrations. Scores for pretest and posttest are given in Table 4.

Table 4. Pretest and posttest scores.

	pretest	posttest
Group 1 (max. 143)	85.1 (SD 26.1)	100.3 (SD 22.2)
Group 2 (max. 44)	11.9 (SD 7.9)	15.7 (SD 7.5)
Group 3 (max. 47)	15.9 (SD 12.2)	24.3 (SD 12.8)

9.2. *Cultural attitude scales (CAS)*

In order to optimize the explanatory power of the analysis, optimal attitude scales have been developed for each of the groups. This means that the original scales, which had been used for all ages and nationalities, were adapted statistically for the respective age groups and nationalities with the aim to obtain high reliability coefficients. Accordingly, different items were deleted for each group on the basis of (low) item-rest-correlation. The resultant reliability coefficients for each group are presented in Tables 5 to 7.

CAS-scores for the oldest groups have been compared with scores on an additional questionnaire for measuring the attitude towards Dutch on the one hand and vernacular language and culture on the other (Migchielsen 1983: 54-55). We found a weak, though significant relation (r = .15 to

Table 5. Reliability coefficients for Dutch CAS.

	Turkish children	Moroccan children
Group 1	.75	.72
Group 2	.72	.74
Group 3	.81	.81

Table 6. Reliability coefficients for Turkish CAS.

	Turkish children
Group 1	.81
Group 2	.87
Group 3	.91

Table 7. Reliability coefficients for Moroccan CAS.

	Moroccan children
Group 1	.91
Group 2	.94
Group 3	.91

.40) as far as attitude to the Dutch language was concerned. Correlations for Dutch culture were not significant.

Unlike the validity of the language proficiency tests, the validity of the attitude tests could not be established.

9.3. *Teachers' attitudes towards teaching immigrant children*

The teachers' attitude test consisted of 26 statements about teaching immigrant children (e.g. 'Immigrant children are politer than Dutch children'; 'It is impossible to explain to immigrant children what you want them to do'). Teachers could react to these statements using a 7-point scale ranging from complete agreement to complete disagreement. A principal components analysis yielded two components. These two scales could be summarized as 'Immigrant children tend to isolate themselves' and 'The presence of immigrant children at school is a disadvantage to Dutch children'. Reliability coefficients for the scales were .79 and .69 respectively. Teachers generally tend to disagree with these overall statements. Interestingly, teachers who work exclusively with immigrant children (like most teachers of group 3) are more likely to disagree than teachers who teach Dutch children as well.

9.4. *Educational setting and approaches to language teaching*

In order to obtain a manageable number of parameters for the main analyses, a limited number of factors based on data from schools, teachers and pupils have been arranged.

For educational setting a number of aspects have been selected. The rather intricate and elaborate analysis of the data of the teachers' and headmasters' questionnaires, described in Buster et al. (1984), led to the selection of the following factors:

(A) Preparatory classes: does it make a difference whether children attend preparatory classes before entering Dutch schools (for groups 1 and 2);

(B) Criteria for placement of children in Dutch schools: does it make a difference whether children are placed either according to age or according to language proficiency level;

(C) Joint lessons: what is the influence of the proportion of lessons attended by Dutch as well as Turkish/Moroccan children;

(D) Special teachers: Are there any differences that can be accounted for because the teachers exclusively teach immigrant children, instead of teaching Dutch children as well (group 3).

With respect to approaches to language teaching, various aspects of the teachers' questionnaire have been combined and reduced in such a way that 3 factors could be used in the analyses:

(E) Selection of instructional materials: the selection can be either more grammar-oriented or more communication-oriented;

(F) Gradation of instructional materials: gradation can also be more grammar-oriented or communication-oriented;

(G) Teachers' reactions to errors.

9.5. *Main analyses: Educational settings and approaches to language teaching*

First we looked for variance restricted to the respective factors, i.e. interaction between factors was not taken into consideration.

In the analyses of variance the dependent variable comprised the posttest scores and the pretest scores were treated as covariate.

The analysis shows that none of the factors we investigated contributes substantially to the increase of proficiency in Dutch. In fact, only 2% of the variance can be accounted for in the analysis (Table 8).

For the first group a grammatical gradation led to higher proficiency scores, while for the second group less correction led to higher scores.

Given the fact that the pretest was administered in November/December, i.e. 2-3 months after the start of the first term, an analysis similar to

Table 8. Main analysis of posttest scores.

	Group 1 (N = 247)		Group 2 (N = 309)		Group 3 (N= 232)	
	% var.	p.	% var.	p.	% var.	p.
Variance explained	78%	.000	65%	.000	72%	.000
Covariate pretest scores	76%	.000	63%	.000	70%	.000
Factors:						
A Preparatory classes	–	ns	–	ns		
B Criteria for placement	–	ns	–	ns	–	ns
C Joint lessons					–	ns
D Special teachers					–	ns
E Selection of instructional materials	–	ns	–	ns	–	ns
F Gradation of instructional materials	1%	.001	–	ns	–	ns
G Reactions to errors	–	ns	1%	0.30	–	ns

the one adopted for the posttest scores could be used for the pretest scores.

Results are presented in Table 9:

Table 9. Main analysis of pretest scores.

	Group 1		Group 2		Group 3	
	% var.	p.	% var.	p.	% var.	p.
A Preparatory classes	3%	.009	2%	.016		
B Criteria for placement	–	ns	1%	.053		
C Joint lessons					–	ns
D Special teachers					–	ns
E Selection of instruc- tional materials	–	ns	–	ns	–	ns
F Gradation of instruc- tional materials	3%	.017	–	ns	2%	ns
G Reactions to errors	–	ns	2%	ns	3%	ns

The analysis indicated the following significant tendencies: preparatory classes have a positive effect on language proficiency. The same can be said about a grammatical gradation for group 1, and for the use of language proficiency as a criterium for placement in the case of group 2.

The picture presented by these two main analyses is a rather sobering one. A possible explanation could have been that the procedure we used to reduce the number of factors in the main analyses obscured rather than elucidated the importance of certain aspects. Therefore, we carried out an explorative analysis of all the variables on which data were available. Table 10 presents the results of unifactorial analyses of variance with posttest scores as covariate. This means, that in each analysis only *one* variable has been treated.

The explorative analysis yielded the following factors:
- For group 1: Moroccan children appeared to do somewhat better than Turkish children (3); The following aspects positively influenced language acquisition: out-of-school contacts with Dutch language (9 & 10), vernacular language and culture education (11), special attention at staff meetings (14) and educational guidance (15).
- For group 2: Girls appeared to be slightly better than boys (4) and a larger proportion of Dutch pupils in the class is associated with higher proficiency scores (13).
- For group 3: none of the variables reached the 5% level of significance.

182   *Kees de Bot, Alex Buster & Anne-Mieke Janssen-van Dieten*

Table 10. Explorative analysis of posttest scores.

	Group 1		Group 2		Group 3	
	% var.	p.	% var.	p.	% var.	p.
Learner characteristics						
1. Attitude Dutch	–	ns	–	ns	–	ns
2. Attitude Turkish/Moroc.	–	ns	–	ns	–	ns
3. Nationality	1%	.007	–	ns	–	ns
4. Sex	–	ns	1%	ns		
5. Dutch nursery school	–	ns	–	ns		
6. Dutch primary school (and/or preparatory cl.)			–	ns	–	ns
7. Age	–	ns	–	ns	–	ns
8. Length of residence					–	ns
9. Social-demographic characteristics of residential districts	1%	.041	–	ns	–	ns
10. Number of elder brothers or sisters in Dutch schools	1%	.011	–	ns	–	ns
11. Vernacular Language and Culture Education	1%	.011	–	ns	–	ns
12. Dutch friends	–	ns	–	ns	–	ns
School characteristics						
(groups 1 & 2)						
13. Proportion of Dutch pupils in Class	–	ns	–	ns		
14. Special attention paid to t/m children at staff-meetings	3%	.013	–	ns		
15. Educational guidance	2%	.019	–	ns		
(group 3)						
16. School type					–	ns
17. Proportion of girls at school					–	ns
18. Proportion of 'group 3'-pupils in entire school population					–	ns
19. Language proficiency as placement criterium					–	ns
Teacher characteristics						
20. Sex	–	ns	–	ns	–	ns
21. Function in school	–	ns	–	ns	–	ns
22. Proportion of Dutch pupils in class	–	ns	–	ns	–	ns

Table 10. Explorative analysis of posttest scores.

	Group 1		Group 2		Group 3	
	% var.	p.	% var.	p.	% var.	p.
23. Self-assessment of expertise	–	ns	–	ns	–	ns
24. Importance of nationality in formation of groups in class	–	ns	–	ns	–	ns
25. Attitude towards teaching immigrant children	–	ns	–	ns	–	ns
26. Number of years of experience in teaching immigrant children	–	ns	–	ns	–	ns

Again, the pretest scores could be analyzed in the same way.
Significant results are presented in Table 11:

Table 11. Explorative analysis of pretest scores.

	Group 1		Group 2		Group 3	
	% var;	p.	% var.	p.	% var.	p.
a. Attitude Turkish ch. towards Dutch culture	4%	.029	–	ns	6%	.007
b. Attitude Turkish ch. towards Turkish culture	–	ns	–	ns	4%	.045
c. Attitude Moroccan ch. towards Dutch culture	–	ns	–	ns	15%	.006
d. Attitude Moroccan ch. towards Moroccan culture	–	ns	9%	.045	–	ns
e. Dutch nursery school	12%	.000	5%	.001		
f. Dutch primary school			13%	.000	10%	.000
g. Age	–	ns	4%	.009	–	ns
h. Length of residence					11%	.000
i. Dutch friends	–	ns	6%	.000	4%	.004
j. School type					6%	.003
k. Proportion of Dutch pupils in class	–	ns	4%	.007		
l. Self-assessment of expertise	–	ns	–	ns	4%	.009
m. Attitude towards teaching immigrant children	–	ns	8%	.000	4%	.026

Potential factors resulting from these analyses were:
- For group 1: a positive attitude towards Dutch culture (**A**) and at-

tendance at Dutch nursery school (E) appeared to result in a higher proficiency in Dutch.

- For group 2: the attitude of Moroccan children towards their vernacular culture (D), attendance at Dutch nursery school and primary school (E & F), age (i.e. variation within the group) (G), Dutch friends (I) and (higher) proportion of Dutch pupils appear to influence language proficiency positively.
- For group 3: apart from the teachers' attitudes (M), all the significant results had been anticipated.

For groups 2 and 3 there is a tendency towards an inverse relation between proficiency and teachers' attitudes: less positive attitudes are associated with higher proficiency scores.

It should be stressed here, that the explorative analyses have no explanatory power whatsoever. Variables may overlap considerably – e.g. attendance at primary school (F) and Dutch friends (I) – which can lead to significant results for both variables.

10. DISCUSSION AND CONCLUSION

In a number of respects the present study can be compared with earlier attempts to assess the influence of language teaching characteristics on language learning (Keating 1963, Smith 1970, Hauptman 1971, Levin 1972, Ekstrand 1984).

In all of these projects language teaching approaches and educational settings were compared by looking at the relative merits of approaches and settings.

The main differences between these projects lie in the design used: some projects used quasi-experimental designs (Smith 1970, Hauptman 1971, Levin 1972), while others applied reversed treatment designs (Keating 1963, Ekstrand 1984). In the former, predefined treatments were compared, whereas treatments as they occurred in 'real life' were studied in the latter.

The major objections that have been raised against quasi-experimentation are:

- teachers might have to teach in ways that they actually dislike, which has detrimental effects on motivation;
- teaching behaviour has to be defined and prescribed in great detail and extensive observations are necessary in order to prevent variation between teachers within a given treatment;
- it appears to be extremely difficult to make a quantitative and measurable distinction between treatments that are readily distinguishable on a common sense basis.

Therefore a reversed treatment design was chosen for the present study.

Our results show that systematic differences in educational settings and in approaches to language teaching do not lead to significant differences in second language proficiency. Such an outcome is not very surprising in the light of earlier attempts to assess the impact of education on learning. In his discussion of the Pennsylvania project (Smith 1970), that aimed at assessing the merits of the audiolingual method and the language laboratory, Carroll (1969: 235) estimates that variations in teaching strategies account for approximately 3% to 5% of the total variance. Findings in other projects point in the same direction.

What *is* surprising in our results, however, is that there is hardly any effect of out-of-school language contact and social environment. Since there are substantial differences between children and schools in this respect, it cannot be accounted for by a lack of variability.

Our results can be interpreted in a number of ways. First of all, one could doubt the validity of the instruments and tests we used. The questionable validity of the attitude scales has already been mentioned. As far as language proficiency is concerned, it seems justified to have some doubts about the cloze test used for the second group. Apparently, this test was rather difficult. However, it would seem that there is little evidence to question any of the other tests. The potential contribution of a large number of variables has been examined. The fact that only a limited number of these individual variables appear to have some influence on proficiency is, indirectly, a validation of the results of the main analyses since these variables have been combined to form the instructional/educational factors in the main analyses.

Secondly, it may have been the case that the wrong type of variables had been concentrated on. In recent educational research (e.g. Smets 1981), it is suggested that process variables rather than product variables should be looked at. Most of the variables in the present study, such as 'proportion of Dutch pupils' and 'teachers' educational background', are typically product variables. Process variables, like interaction processes in the classroom, were not included in our study. In addition, some relevant factors are simply too complicated to be measured. Notions like 'school climate', which refer to a large number of aspects of school as a social institution rather than as an educational plant, fell outside the scope of our project.

The results might also have been influenced by the exclusion of two potentially important factors: first language proficiency and non-verbal intelligence. We could not test first language skills because no appropriate tests were available, and we did not have time to construct them. Even if we had, there would have been the problem of what should be regarded as 'first' language, especially in the case of Moroccan children.

Intelligence has not been tested because, apart from a general reluctance to use intelligence-tests in this kind of research, there are no IQ-tests available that have established norms and standards for this particular group. Furthermore, comparable studies that included intelligence in the design (Hauptman 1971 and Ekstrand 1984) arrive at contradictory conclusions about its impact.

Finally, it may have been the case, that *un*systematic variations between schools, teachers and pupils have resulted in language proficiency improvements. Direct interactions between learner needs and school/teacher-activities may have led to such an individual variation that no general trends could be brought to light in the statistical analyses. This possibility, already mentioned by Cummins (1979), is supported by our impressions from incidental observations done in the course of the study and by the fact that schools appear to differ as far as mean proficiency scores are concerned. Further research on the micro- rather than the meso-educational level may support such a claim in the future.

10

Referral of Ethnic Minority Children to Special Education

Johan Wijnstra

1. INTRODUCTION

In the Netherlands, as well as in other Western European countries, there has been an influx of ethnic minority groups during the last decades: people from former colonial territories (mainly Surinam and the Dutch Antilles) and migrant workers from countries around the Mediterranean (mainly Turkey and Morocco in the Dutch case). This paper deals with the referral of minority children to special education, a problem that has only recently been recognized in the Netherlands. It has been observed that minority children are underrepresented in schools for the learning disabled (LD), while children of Surinamese and Antillian origin are overrepresented in schools for the educable mentallly retarded (EMR). Similar cases in Europe can be found in Great Britain and West Germany (see Schröder 1979; Tomlinson 1981). In the USA the overrepresentation of black students in EMR programs has received considerable attention in recent years (see Heller et al. 1982).

In 1982 the Dutch government requested the assistance of the National Institute for Educational Measurements (CITO) with respect to this problem and supplied funds to initiate a research project. Although the ultimate goal is the development of adequate procedures and assessment instruments, we started with an exploratory study as it was not very clear what the reasons for referral and the criteria for admission to special education were (special education is organized in self-contained schools in the Netherlands). The main question in the study was why some children of Surinamese, Turkish, and Moroccan origin were placed in EMR schools, while others, with comparable achievement levels, were not. For reasons of comparison, a sample of Dutch children with similar (low) levels of academic achievement also participated. The study was conducted in the city of Rotterdam, one of the cities in Holland with a large concentration of ethnic minority groups.

The main question addressed in this paper is whether EMR and low achieving regular education (RE) children from these ethnic groups show any differences on six subtests of an intelligence test and five subtests of a

Dutch language proficiency test. Before the research methods and the results are presented, a short description of the educational situation in Rotterdam is given to provide a context for the study.

2. ETHNIC MINORITY CHILDREN IN ROTTERDAM ELEMENTARY SCHOOLS

Today one out of every three to four children in Rotterdam is a child of (parents of) non-Dutch origin. In kindergarten the percentage has been higher than 30 since 1982 (of a total of about 12 000 children), while in elementary education the percentage increased by more than ten points during the last five years to 28.5. In the same period the total number of children in elementary schools dropped from almost 45 000 to less than 35 000. The distribution of ethnic minority children among schools is very uneven. Some schools have a minority enrollment of over 90%, while others have almost no children of non-Dutch origin. With the proportionate increase of minority children in elementary education, the schools for LD and EMR children also experienced an increase, although this was more dramatic in EMR schools than in LD schools. The percentage in EMR schools is currently 37.9. In 1979 it was 16.5 which is almost equal to the percentage in regular education in that year. The percentage in LD schools in 1979 was still as low as 5.3. The 1984 figure is 10.9%.

The category of children of non-Dutch origin includes children of very different backgrounds, including (the smaller part) children from countries belonging to the European Community. Figures 1, 2, and 3 show the development of the numbers of children of Moroccan, Turkish, and Surinamese and Antillian origin during the last five years as a percentage of the total number of children in regular education and special education (EMR and LD, only) at the elementary level (as no data are available for special education in the years 1980 and 1981, dashed lines are drawn between 1979 and 1982).

It appears that the percentage of Moroccan children in LD schools is negligible, while in EMR schools it is constantly at a somewhat lower level than in regular education (Figure 1). The percentage of Turkish children in LD schools is also low, but has increased somewhat since 1982. In EMR schools the percentages in 1983 and 1984 are at the same level as in regular education and one might wonder how this will continue (Figure 2). Compared to the children of Turkish and Moroccan origin, the percentage of Surinamese and Antillian children in LD schools is high, although lower than in regular education, and very high in EMR schools, with a sharp increase during the last five years (Figure 3). Unfortunately, the percentages of Surinamese and Antillian children in special education

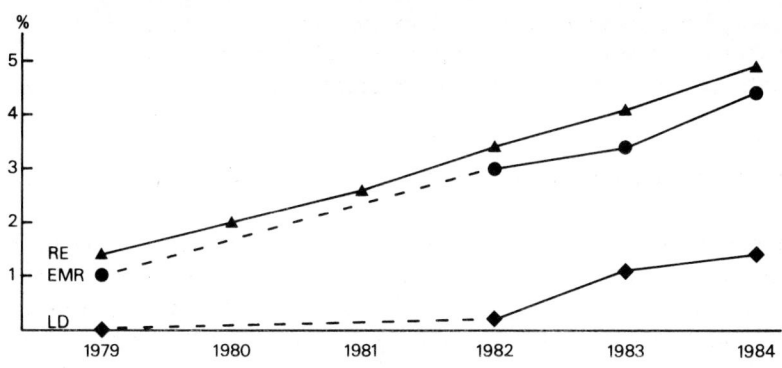

Figure 1. Percentage of children of Moroccan origin in Roterdam elementary schools (1979–1984).

are not completely comparable to those in regular education as in this latter type only foreign-born children have been included in the statistics (up to now the majority), while presumably in special education Dutch-born children of parents of Surinamese and Antillian origin were also

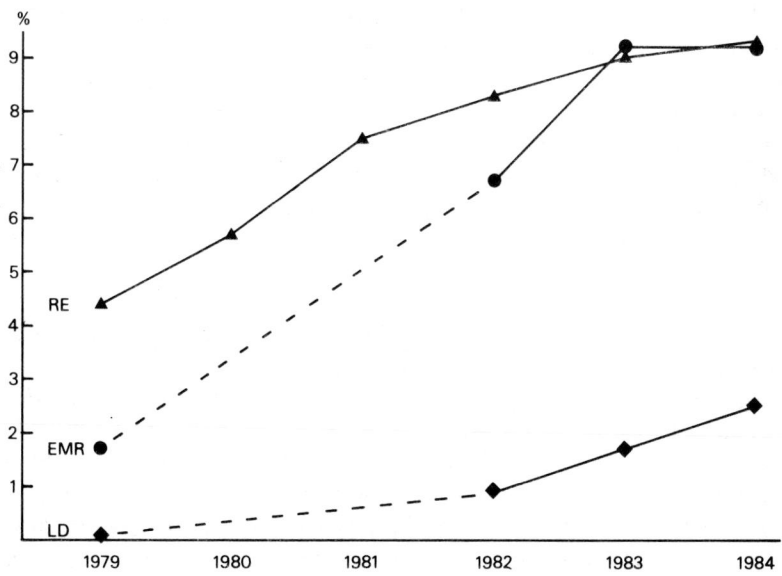

Figure 2. Percentage of children of Turkish origin in Rotterdam elementary schools (1979–1984).

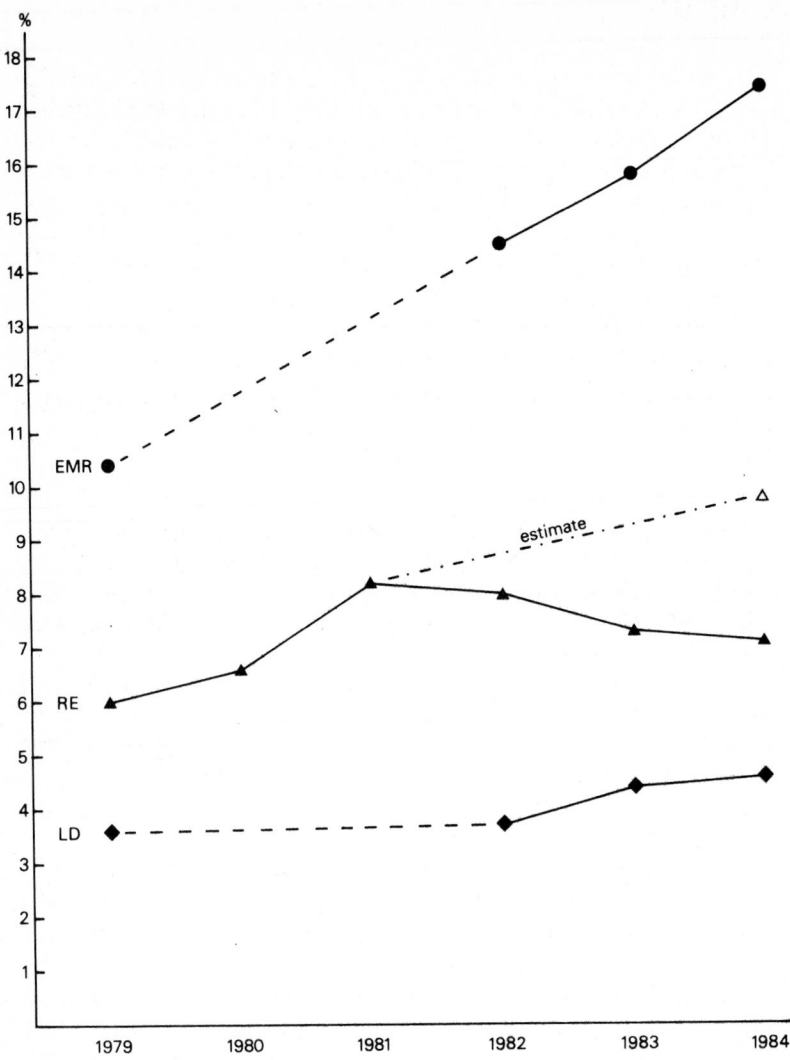

Figure 3. Percentage of children of Surinamese and Antillian origin in Rotterdam elementary schools (1979-1984).

counted. Therefore, in Figure 3 an estimate of the percentage of foreign and Dutch-born children in regular education in 1984 has been included (based on an inventory in the schools participating in the project). Although the definition of Surinamese and Antillian origin might cause some problems in comparisons, the trend is quite clear. Children of Surinamese and Antillian origin are overrepresented in EMR schools.

3. METHOD

The study started in spring 1983 with a stepwise Dutch reading and mathematics achievement screening in all nine Rotterdam EMR schools. Children classified as non-readers and/or who had not yet reached a minimal level of numeracy (teacher ratings) were excluded and assigned the level code 1. The reading and mathematics level of all other children under the age of twelve was classified by means of tests. Children were given a higher level test only if at least 70% of the items of the preceding one had been answered correctly. The top level (5) roughly corresponds with the level which is reached by the modal child by the end of grade 2. Only ten children out of a total of 313 Dutch, Surinamese, Turkish, and Moroccan children received classifications for reading and/or mathematics higher than 5. Of the remaining children 202 were of Dutch origin, 54 of Surinamese, and 47 of Turkish or Moroccan origin.

The same stepwise procedure was carried out in a sample of 56 elementary schools that had agreed to participate in the project. The sample of schools was stratified by percentage of minority enrollment. Each teacher in grades 2 – 5 selected two or three of the children with the lowest level of achievement, while the non-readers and the children who had not yeat reached the stage of initial mathematics were identified in grade 1. Out of a total of about 800 children, 243 under the age of twelve were identified with achievement classifications comparable to the EMR children, keeping age constant. Of thes 243 children, 83 were of Dutch origin (1.6% of the total number of Dutch children in these schools), 33 of Surinamese origin (3.7% of the corresponding total number), and 127 of Turkish or Moroccan origin (7.1% of the total number).

From these pools of EMR and RE pupils, about 50 from each ethnic group were selected for participation in the main part of the study which was carried out in the school year 1983/84. When less than 50 children were identified, all available children were included in the sample.

In the fall of 1983 all children in the sample were individually given the short form of a newly revised Dutch intelligence test (six subtests: closure, exclusion, verbal meaning, quantity, discs, and learning names; Bleichrodt et al. 1984), and five subtests from a specific oral language proficiency test (vocabulary – active, syntax – receptive, morphology – active, syntax – active, and implicit meaning; Van Bon 1982).

The raw scores on these tests (number of items correct, unless otherwise indicated) were used as independent variables in stepwise linear discriminant analyses for each ethnic group, the dependent variable being school type. The project was planned to compare within each ethnic group EMR and RE samples of comparable composition on the variables sex, age, length of residence in the Netherlands (if applicable), reading and mathematics level. Therefore, these control variables were entered into the discriminant analyses prior to the independent variables to correct for differences in the independent variables associated with possible differences in these control variables. In the computer program, the so-called jackknifed classification option was chosen (see Jennrich & Sampson 1981). Each individual is classified into a school type group on the basis of the linear discriminant function which has been computed from all the data except the case being classified.

4. RESULTS

The means and standard deviations on the control and independent variables for each school type per ethnic group are presented in Table 1. If the EMR and RE children had been completely comparable on the control variables, the discriminant functions resulting from the analyses on these variables would have produced 50% correct classifications for each ethnic group. Mainly because of differences in achievement level for reading and mathematics, or age, the total percentage of correct classifications varies between about 60 and 70. The highest percentage correct for a school type is 78.0 in the case of the Turkish and Moroccan RE children, the lowest being 53.1 for the Surinamese RE children.

The independent variables were only entered into the discriminant function, a canonical variable (CV in Table 1), if significant differences remained between school types on these variables in an analysis of covariance, using the variables already entered into the canonical variable as covariates. In the case of the Turkish and Moroccan children no such variables were identified. For the children of Surinamese origin only two of the language proficiency subtests were included in the canonical variable resulting in an increase in the total percentage of correctly classified children of only 3.6 (69.9 - 66.3). Of the Dutch children 15.2% more were correctly classified after the inclusion of three independent variables in the discriminant function (77.8 - 62.6).

Although the discriminant functions result in a statistically significant improvement in the number of correctly classified children in each ethnic group (compared with chance level, which is 50%), the contribution of the independent variables varies from negligible to very moderate. This means that, keeping the control variables constant, in each ethnic group the EMR and RE children only differ slightly on these variables and that there is a very considerable degree of overlap.

Table 1. Means and standard deviations per school type for each ethnic group, and percentages correct of the jackknifed classifications resulting from the discriminant analyses

	Dutch children					Surinamese children					Turkish and Moroccan children				
	EMR (n = 48)		RE (n = 51)			EMR (n = 51)		RE (n = 32)			EMR (n = 46)		RE (n = 50)		
	M	s	M	s	CV	M	s	M	s	CV	M	s	M	s	CV
control variables															
sex	1.40	0.49	1.37	0.49	+	1.41	0.50	1.50	0.51	+	1.46	0.50	1.52	0.50	+
age in months	117.90	14.76	117.90	14.45	+	122.08	13.89	111.16	19.41	+	118.07	16.10	114.30	17.11	+
residence in Holland	not applicable		not applicable		−	62.25	30.91	52.59	40.31	+	76.85	33.28	68.96	30.88	+
reading level	2.88	1.44	3.59	1.28	+	3.31	1.46	2.81	1.65	+	2.00	1.23	2.60	1.31	+
mathematics level	2.65	1.47	3.14	1.33	+	2.67	1.23	2.72	1.67	+	1.89	1.27	2.28	1.29	+
percentage of children correctly classified	58.3		66.7			74.5		53.1			60.9		78.0		
(jackknifed procedure)	62.6					66.3					69.8				
independent variables															
closure	32.25	7.21	34.59	5.97	−	33.61	6.02	30.94	6.45	−	28.46	7.12	26.54	6.89	−
exclusion	27.65	7.36	30.29	7.22	−	30.27	6.14	28.31	6.61	−	28.20	7.21	26.74	8.01	−
verbal meaning	34.90	6.17	39.29	6.06	−	32.47	6.63	32.81	7.88	−	22.76	6.96	24.96	8.34	−
quantity	34.06	12.53	43.08	9.99	+	37.20	13.37	37.09	13.88	−	34.15	11.45	38.48	11.20	−
discs (seconds)	336.08	103.21	272.06	103.64	+	340.47	118.32	368.56	140.93	−	393.43	142.27	347.72	94.05	−
learning names	8.96	3.71	11.51	4.05	−	8.33	3.82	9.31	3.13	−	5.91	2.83	7.22	3.80	−
vocabulary (active)	28.33	8.42	36.00	7.61	+	23.86	8.44	24.53	9.42	−	14.17	6.50	14.16	8.29	−
syntax (receptive)	31.73	4.67	33.88	2.41	−	31.33	3.37	31.44	4.06	−	27.98	4.21	29.56	4.42	−
morphology (active)	20.23	6.44	25.94	6.04	+	14.04	6.91	16.31	9.13	+	5.52	4.61	6.30	6.64	−
syntax (active)	17.73	5.22	21.37	2.78	−	16.59	5.27	17.66	5.60	−	10.74	6.15	11.60	7.57	−
implicit meaning	19.77	4.38	22.80	4.35	−	20.24	4.29	18.25	4.88	+	17.72	4.52	17.28	4.40	−
percentage of children correctly classified	77.1		78.4			76.5		59.4			60.9		78.0		
(jackknifed procedure)	77.8					69.9					69.8				

5. DISCUSSION

The EMR as well as the RE children in this study are all low achievers compared with their age mates. The very fact that RE children with achievement levels (almost) as low as EMR children from the same ethnic group could be identified implies that low achievement is certainly not a sufficient condition for referral and EMR placement, although it is a necessary condition by definition. From this data it appears that the skills tapped by some subtests from a traditional intelligence test and a language proficiency test do not make so much difference. Almost the same situation was found by Ysseldyke et al. (1982) in a comparison of LD children with low achieving RE children. The classroom teachers, the gate-keepers who take the initiative for referral, must look at other characteristics of their pupils as well. One such characteristic might be ethnic group. From the percentages of children placed in EMR schools and the percentages identified in regular education with achievement levels in the EMR range, it can be inferred that schools are more reluctant to refer Turkish and Moroccan children to special education than children of Surinamese (and Antillian) origin. While several other interesting differences between ethnic groups can be observed in the data presented in the preceding section, these will be disregarded here.

From interviews with a few teachers it also appeared that severe learning difficulties are seldom the sole reason for referral for EMR or LD placement. Several other reasons, not associated with ethnic group per se, were mentioned such as low levels of adaptivity, poor work habits, low levels of concentration, deficient fine motor skills, problematic social relations with peers and teachers, etc. Subsequently, a questionnaire was developed for the RE children's present teachers and the former RE teachers of the children now placed in EMR schools. The questionnaire requested the teachers to indicate whether the children belong (belonged) to the two or three most noticeable pupils on several behavior aspects in their present (former) class. The results are shown in Table 2.

Unfortunately, it was not possible to contact a rather large number of the EMR children's former RE teachers (more than 50%). Nevertheless, the trend in the answers for each of the ethnic groups is quite clear. Although it is admitted that a great many of the RE children show learning difficulties, in the eyes of their teachers they combine this characteristic to a much lesser degree with other problems than the children classified EMR. The mean number of problems perceived for the EMR children is about twice as high as for the RE children in each of the ethnic groups and the answer patterns are very similar. Although there might be some distortion in the answers of the EMR children's former RE teachers because

Table 2. Percentages of problems per ethnic group as perceived by former and present RE teachers for EMR and RE children, respectively, and means and standard deviations of the numbers of problems perceived.

Type of problem	Dutch children		Surinamese children		Turkish/Moroccan children	
	EMR	RE	EMR	RE	EMR	RE
learning difficulties (reading, mathematics or prerequisite skills)	100	85	100	68	100	79
language proficiency	87	46	95	63	100	77
fine motor skills	80	33	68	11	53	19
work habits	91	71	91	50	89	43
adaptivity	70	16	62	7	45	19
social relations with peers	78	28	50	15	63	21
social relations with teacher	39	8	27	7	30	15
number of children	23	41	22	28	20	48
mean number of problems	5.26	2.83	4.77	2.18	4.70	2.71
standard deviation	1.32	1.55	1.27	1.42	1.26	1.69

of the time lag, from this data it appears that the combination of problems leads teachers to the referral of children for placement in special education (the choice between EMR and LD placement is usually left to psychologists). This finding will be further explored in subsequent analyses, within as well as between ethnic groups.

11

Text Comprehension of Bilingual Turkish Children in Dutch Primary and Secondary Schools

Cees Galema & Hilde Hacquebord

1. INTRODUCTION

Bilingual children from ethnic minority groups in the Netherlands are less successful in secondary schools than are Dutch children of the same age. This situation is not unique to the Netherlands; it is also a widespread phenomenon in other countries with ethnic minority groups. During the last few years there has been an increase of minority children in the different types of secondary schools. Most of these children have been in Holland for more than five years, have attended Dutch primary schools and have a fairly high communicative proficiency in Dutch. In primary schools they have generally had a lot of extra lessons in Dutch especially in the initial period. These extra lessons aimed at 'aanspreekbaarheid' ("addressability") in Dutch. However, this term has never been operationalized in a satisfactory way. It roughly refers to the following: children master the second language sufficiently well enough to participate in verbal interaction with their Dutch teachers and peers, and to participate in lessons in the Dutch language. Yet they are relatively unsuccessful in secondary schools.

In Holland a comprehensive school system like those in the United States and Sweden does not exist. Instead, the secondary school system contains different types of schools. Some of these types (e.g. LBO: junior secondary vocational education) prepare mainly for manual and low commercial professions, whereas another type (MAVO: junior general secondary education) contains general lower secondary schooling. A third type (HAVO: senior general secondary education) prepares for 'higher' professions and a fourth type contains pre-university education (Atheneum/Gymnasium).

In particular Moroccan and Turkish children are overrepresented in the lower types of schools, especially in LBO, as can be seen in Table 1, taken from Schakel-Bulletin (1983):

Table 1: Ethnic minorities in Dutch educational system (1-1-1982)

School type		total number	% minorities	Turkish	Moroccan	Other
Infant school	(4–6)	21698	5.4	8125	6212	4539
Primary school	(6–12)	56355	4.4	22988	13608	12067
LBO	(12–16)	16575	4.1	7680	3760	3044
AVO	(12–16/17)	13923	1.7	2991	1235	6624

Table 2: LBO or AVO recommendations for ethnic minority children by teachers (in %). (The percentages only relate to the children who participated in Van Esch's study in 1983)

Recomm.	Source country:						total ethnic min.	total Dutch
	Turkey	Morocco	Sur./Ant.	Moluccan	S. Europe	3rd World		
LBO	70.8	73.9	51.9	47.4	49.4	38.5	60.7	34.3
AVO	29.2	26.1	49.1	52.6	50.6	61.5	39.3	65.7
Abs. total (= 100%)	432	134	264	78	89	78	1075	225707

Table 2 (see Van Esch 1983) demonstrates that relatively many Turkish and Moroccan children are recommended by their teachers to continue their school careers in LBO after leaving primary school.

What is causing this relatively low level of school success? Teachers often suppose that this relative lack of success could be caused by the limited reading ability of these pupils in the second language (L2).

Texts play an important role in education. A considerable part of the contents of school learning appears in the form of texts. A limited text comprehension level will have negative consequences for success at school. Cummins' theoretical framework can be relevant with regard to the relation between success at school and text comprehension level. Cummins distinguishes between two different aspects of language proficiency. He states that basic aspects of language proficiency, the so-called BICS (basic interpersonal comminucative skills, involving phonological, syntactic and semantic skills which most native speakers have largely acquired by the age of 6) are mastered by L2 learning children within a few years. On the other hand, the development of more complex aspects of language proficiency (the so-called CALP, cognitive academic language proficiency, involving literacy-related language skills such as reading comprehension, writing ability and vocabulary/concept knowledge) will take a much longer time (Cummins 1979).

More recently Cummins (1981) has refined his theoretical framework. Now communicative competence is conceptualized along two continuums:

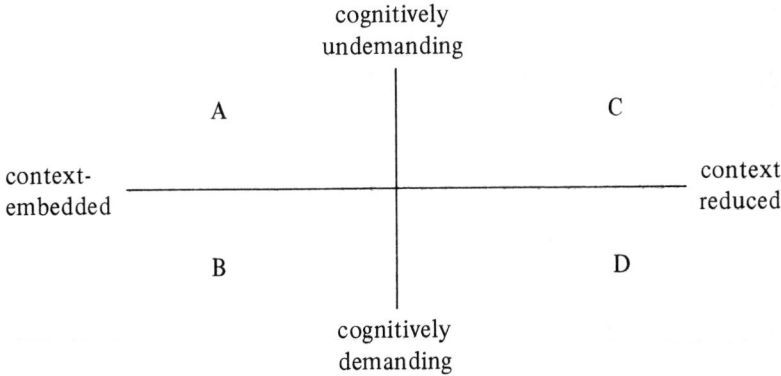

The horizontal continuum relates to the range of contextual support available for expressing or receiving meaning. The extremes of this continuum are described in terms of "context-embedded" versus "context-reduced" communication. The vertical continuum relates to communicative competence in terms of degree of cognitive involvement in a task

or activity. The upper parts of the vertical continuum consist of communicative tasks and activities in which the linguistic tools have become
largely automatized and thus require little active cognitive involvement
for appropriate performance. With regard to this framework Cummins
supposes that arriving at commonly accepted age/grade norms in context-
reduced domains of L2 proficiency takes a lot of time for ethnic minority
children.

Another aspect of Cummins' framework is his 'interdependance hypothesis'. This hypothesis states that literacy-related aspects of a bilingual's
proficiency in L1 and L2 are common or interdependant across languages
(Cummins 1979).

What is the relevance of Cummins' framework with regard to the earlier
mentioned teacher assumptions that the relatively low level of success of
bilingual children at school is caused by the limited/restricted L2 reading
comprehension? In Cummins' terms, reading comprehension is a rather
cognitively demanding task with little or no nonverbal contextual support.
Therefore, L2 reading comprehension may be problematic for bilingual
children over a long period of time.

The restricted L2 reading comprehension of bilingual children can also
be explained by theories concerning the reading process. Most authors
(e.g. Goodman 1970, Westhoff 1981) consider the reading process as a
hypothesis-forming and hypothesis-testing process, in which readers make
use of redundancy in texts. A good reader makes use of redundancies by
identifying only some key elements in a given text, while formulating and
testing hypotheses on the basis of these key elements. It will take more
effort to reach comprehension, when the degree of redundancy has been
reduced. The redundancy of a text relates to both structural aspects
(morphology, syntax, textual relations) and functional aspects (vocabulary, conceptual knowledge). Text redundancy might be lower for bilingual children because of their lower confidence with structural and/or
functional aspects of the second language.

The relative lack of success of bilingual children within the Dutch secondary
school system (see Bouwmeester 1979, Van Esch 1983), the previously
discussed teacher assumptions, and theories or models concerning reading
processes and text comprehension (in particular the framework of Cummins) led us to study the comprehension of L2 texts of bilingual children
at secondary school level. In the Netherlands hardly any research on L2
reading comprehension by bilingual children at secondary school level has
been done; Verhoeven (in this volume) is doing a study on initial L2
reading-comprehension at primary school level.

We set up our research project in order to come to grips with two main questions:
1. Do differences in text comprehension exist between bilingual children and their native Dutch peers at the same school levels?
2. Do differences in development of text comprehension exist between both groups?
The project will combine a longitudinal and a cross-sectional design in sofar as the development of text comprehension of subjects from different school levels will be followed for several years.

In this paper we present some results of the pilot study of our project. In this study we collected quantitative data on the reading comprehension of both bilinguals and monolingual native Dutch pupils of the same grades. Furthermore, we collected data on possible intervening factors such as vocabulary in L2 with regard to infrequently used Dutch words, reading comprehension in L1, non-verbal intelligence and some learner characteristics such as duration of education (in years) in the home country and duration of education in Holland. Different types of schools were taken into account. We also wanted to know more about the role of school achievement or school aptitude in reading comprehension.

These data were collected in order to make the first comparisons between bilingual and native Dutch pupils as to reading comprehension and to investigate the relationships between the earlier mentioned factors. Moreover, we selected subjects from different grades in order to gain insight into the developmental process of pupils. For this reason the research design of the pilot study is cross-sectional. Cross-sectional research cannot demonstrate the actual development of pupils over time, because different groups that are only partly comparable are taken into account. The pilot study can only provide some hints and tentative conclusions concerning the development of reading skills. In the next section (2) the method of our pilot study will be described; section (3) will offer some results and discussion.

2. METHOD

2.1. Subjects

Bilingual children were selected from one ethnic minority group in the Netherlands, namely the Turkish group. We concentrated on a particular group for several reasons:
1. Since every ethnic minority group is expected to have its own linguistic and non-linguistic characteristics, participation of different groups in the

project would imply an extra parameter and lead to a design that was too complex.

2. The Turkish group is extensive and relatively homogeneous; most children have Turkish as their first language, most of them are children of unskilled workers (Van Esch 1983).

3. The Turkish group has the highest proportion of pupils in lower secondary schooltypes, compared with other ethnic minority groups (Van Esch 1983).

Only Turkish pupils who had lived in Holland for at least four years were selected. These subjects were selected from four different secondary schooltypes:

1. LBO, preparing for manual and low commercial professions,
2. IBO, a school for retarded children, however with goals comparable to those of the LBO,
3. MAVO, an 'intermediate' type for general secondary schooling,
4. an additional group was formed of pupils from the primary school 6th grade with a teacher's recommendation to IBO, LBO and MAVO.

Three different grades were investigated: 6th grade primary school, first and second grade secondary school. In all cases, Dutch criterion groups were randomly selected from at least two different classrooms. Table 3 gives the numbers of participating children for every type of school and grade.

Table 3: Turkish and Dutch subjects from different school types and grades

Primary school 6th grade	Turkish 30				Dutch 16	
Secondary school	IBO		LBO		MAVO	
	Turkish	Dutch	Turkish	Dutch	Turkish	Dutch
first grade	17	11	20	16	16	20
second grade			24	12	21	17

Seven secondary schools and eight primary schools participated in the project. All schools were located in Hengelo and Enschede, in the eastern part of Holland. All Turkish pupils got extra tuition in Dutch as a second language.

2.2. Tests

All subjects participated in a Dutch text comprehension test, a Dutch vocabulary test, and a non-verbal intelligence test (Raven1938). Moreover, the Turkish subjects participated in a test of text comprehension in Turkish.

(a) *Text comprehension in Dutch*

The test consisted of 5 different texts of about 175 words each. Each text was followed by a number of statements about which the subjects, after reading the passage, had to give a true/false judgement.

The texts were chosen on the basis of the following criteria:

1. passages from geography text books frequently used in the first year of secondary schools; in this way the degree of difficulty of the passages is linked up with the degree of difficulty of textbooks the subjects are often confronted with at school.

2. increasing degree of difficulty. In order to rankorder these texts we asked about 30 teachers of bilingual children in secondary schools to compare 12 texts in pairs. In this way we got a rank order which was approximately the same as the rank order obtained by a linguistic analysis of the texts. We analysed the texts on variables such as length of T-unit, degree of subordination, number of afstract words, ratio given/new information and number of words probably known by the subjects (on the basis of their teachers' judgments all words in the texts were scaled from 'most probably known' to 'most probably unknown' by the subjects).

As said before, five texts increasing in degree of difficulty were selected for the test. Each text is followed by about 15 statements. either asking for literal comprehension, inference statements or an overall comprehension of the texts.

(b) *Dutch vocabulary*

We developed a vocabulary test consisting of 50 multiple choice items. Also in this case, the words were chosen from geography schoolbooks frequently used in the 12 texts we mentioned earlier.

The words were selected on the basis of the following criteria:

1. not belonging to the 2000 most frequently used words in Dutch as these words will be known by the pupils.

2. not belonging to a typical geography jargon; the teachers we mentioned before selected these words belonging to the learning contents of the first year of secondary school. Teachers indicated that they explain the meaning of these words to all pupils.

After removing the words mentioned in 1. and 2. we made a selection of 50 words from the rest of the texts.

(c) *Nonverbal intelligence*

We used the Standard Progressive Matrices, Sets A–E, developed by J.C. Raven (1938).

(d) *Text comprehension in Turkish*
This test consisted of 3 different texts with an average length of about 150 words each; again each text was followed by statements. The procedure was the same as in the text comprehension tasks for Dutch.

The texts were selected from schoolbooks frequently used in Turkey. The first text was taken from a primary school 3rd grade schoolbook, the second one from a 5th grade book and the third one from a first year secondary school textbook. In this way the texts were scaled from easy to difficult.

The test was developed in cooperation with Drs. Koopman and his students of the Turkish Department of Leyden University.

3. RESULTS AND DISCUSSION

In this section the following results will be presented:
1. mean scores and standard deviations for both language groups in the different grades of the different school types concerning text comprehension in Dutch, Dutch vocabulary and non-verbal intelligence;
2. mean scores and standard deviations for the Turkish groups concerning text comprehension in Turkish;
3. correlations between the variables (see also Appendices I and II). Comparisons are made by two-tailed T-tests.

(a) *Text comprehension in Dutch*

Table 4: Means and standard deviations for text comprehension in Dutch

	Turkish			Dutch					
Educ. level	Max.=70			Max.=70					
and form	n	mean	sd	n	mean	sd	T	df	p
BO-6	30	47.50	7.13	16	53.00	7.71	−2.42	44	*0.020*
IBO-1	17	42.94	5.11	11	46.91	6.32	−1.83	26	0.079
LBO-1	20	48.25	6.21	16	48.25	6.07	0	34	1.00
LBO-2	24	50.17	7.32	12	52.75	4.07	−1.13	34	0.265
MAVO-1	16	50.13	11.79	20	52.15	10.49	−.54	34	0.589
MAVO-2	21	58.24	4.11	17	58.41	5.62	−.11	36	0.913

Table 4 shows that the primary school level is the only level at which the difference between the two groups is significant; at some school levels the native criterion group has a higher mean score, but the difference is never significant (IBO1, LBO2, MAVO1). At other levels the mean scores are about the same (LBO1, MAVO2). The test seems to be a reliable instrument with respect to the correlation between the test scores and grade, type of school and report mark for Dutch. (see Appendix I).

(b) *Dutch vocabulary*

Table 5: Means and standard deviations for Dutch vocabulary

	Turkish			Dutch					
Educ. level	Max.=50			Max.=50					
and form	n	mean	sd	n	mean	sd	T	df	p
BO-6	29	25.72	8.51	16	37.00	4.75	−4.88	43	*.000*
IBO-1	15	18.80	6.55	10	27.90	5.65	−3.59	23	*.002*
LBO-1	20	26.30	6.51	16	29.75	8.06	−1.42	34	.164
LBO-2	24	28.79	6.99	12	35.92	7.27	−2.85	34	*.007*
MAVO-1	16	31.31	5.84	19	37.05	7.85	−2.41	33	*.021*
MAVO-2	21	37.71	4.03	17	40.12	3.84	−1.87	36	.070

In four out of six cases the Dutch subjects have a significant higher mean score on Dutch vocabulary: at primary school level, IBO1, LBO2 and MAVO1. The test seems to be a reliable instrument with respect to the correlations between the test scores and grade, type of school and report mark for Dutch (see Appendix I).

(c) *Nonverbal intelligence*

Table 6: Means and standard deviations for nonverbal IQ

	Turkish			Dutch					
Educ. level	Max.=60			Max.=60					
and form	n	mean	sd	n	mean	sd	T	df	p
BO-6	29	39.38	4.53	15	41.73	7.98	−1.25	42	.217
IBO-1	13	28.54	14.56	10	31.20	8.90	−.51	21	.617
LBO-1	20	37.65	4.87	16	38.31	4.53	−.42	34	.676
LBO-2	7	43.29	5.12	12	40.33	5.60	1.14	17	.269
MAVO-1	15	38.40	11.51	19	41.21	6.52	−.90	32	.375
MAVO-2	10	41.10	7.30	17	43.82	12.40	−.63	25	.534

Table 6 shows differences between Turkish and Dutch children which are in no case significant. At most school levels the native Dutch group however has a higher mean score than the Turkish group; only the Turkish LBO2 group has a higher score on nonverbal IQ.

(d) *Text comprehension in Turkish*

Table 7: Means and standard deviations for text comprehension in Turkish

Educ. level	Max.=29		
and form	n	mean	sd
BO-6	20	17.80	3.32
IBO-1	14	15.57	2.74
LBO-1	20	17.00	4.95
LBO-2	23	19.17	3.58
MAVO-1	17	16.88	4.24
MAVO-2	22	17.82	5.58

Table 7 shows the results for the different school levels on the text comprehension test in Turkish. A correlation exists between text comprehension in Turkish and text comprehension in Dutch (.27) which is not very strong, but significant at .001. A correlation is also found between text comprehension in Turkish and Dutch vocabulary (.18, p = .026). A third – negative – correlation exists between text comprehension in Turkish and length of stay in the Netherlands (-.16), significant at .038 (see Appendix II); a shorter stay in Holland implies a longer stay in Turkey and – in most cases – more schooling in Turkish.

Two conflicting tendencies seem to influence the results. On the one hand we find a negative influence of length of stay in Holland on text comprehension in Turkish, on the other hand one may conclude from the positive correlation between text comprehension in L1 and L2 that there is a transfer of comprehension skills from one language into the other, possibly from L1 to L2.

Cummins' interdependence hypothesis cannot be accepted or rejected on the basis of the results reported here. A more refined analysis which also takes more variables into account is needed.

We selected subjects from the first and second year of secondary school. In particular first year pupils have just passed the selection moment of entrance to different secondary school types. Therefore, a comparison between test results of different school levels is interesting. The mean scores on text comprehension of the Dutch reference group as well as the mean scores of the Turkish group at primary school level are relatively high (53.0, 47.5; see Table 4). The Turkish groups have higher scores as the school level is higher (BO-6, LBO-1/2, MAVO-1/2). This is not the case with the Dutch groups: the native groups IBO-1, LBO-1/2, MAVO-1 have lower scores than the primary school group; only the MAVO-2 Dutch group has a higher mean score than the primary school group. Results of the Dutch vocabulary test show the same pattern (see Table 5).

This pattern of lower scores in spite of higher ages may be caused by the fact that Dutch children at primary school level consist of a differentiated group with respect to verbal competance, whereas at IBO/LBO level children with relatively low verbal competence will be dominant. However, the cross-sectional design of our pilot study puts severe limits on group comparability. Results of longitudinal research are needed to get a more precise picture of development over time.

What about Cummins' framework which we mentioned before?

The Dutch comprehension test as well as the Dutch vocabulary test can be considered literacy-related CALP-skills. Both tests are context-reduced and cognitively demanding. Within the text comprehension test, comprehension has to be reached without external contextual support, whereas true/false statements are cognitively demanding tasks (often it is necessary to combine information from different parts of the passage). The vocabulary test is considered a CALP-test because of the selection of infrequently used Dutch words, a context-free presentation of the words and the multiple choice procedure. The vocabulary test shows significant differences between Dutch and Turkish subjects; however, no such differences have been found for the text comprehension test. These results suggest that one has to differentiate between different aspects of CALP.

In section 1 of this paper we referred to the reading process as a hypo-thesis-forming and hypothesis-testing process. In this view, the relatively poor reading results of bilingual children may be caused by relatively less familiarity with morphosyntactical and lexical aspects of a text. The same view may explain our results too. Although bilingual pupils have a smaller academic L2 vocabulary than their native peers, they do not show a significantly lower text comprehension level: bilingual pupils seem to make optimal use of the – for them relatively smaller – redundancy of a text on the basis of adequate hypothesis-forming and hypothesis-testing strategies. They may compensate for their smaller vocabulary by global "top-down" text comprehension strategies based on foreknowledge and context-related hypothesis. In order to find answers to such questions, we will make a detailed, longitudinal analysis of the L2 reading process of Turkish children.

Appendix I

	Dutch vocabulary	ed. level	form	report mark Dutch
Dutch text comprehension	.5182 (277) p = .001	.2351 (285) p = .001	.1947 (285) p = .001	.2285 (198) p = .002
Dutch vocabulary		.3551 (277) p = .001	.2192 (277) p = .001	.2084 (192) p = .002

Pearson correlation coefficients for Dutch text comprehension and Dutch vocabulary

Appendix II

	ed. level	form	length of stay in Holland	length of ed. in Turkey	age
Turkish text comprehension	.058 (117) p = .474	.0793 (131) p = .184	−.1555 (131) p = .038	.0308 (111) p = .374	.9111 (131) p = .151

	length of ed. in Holland	report mark Dutch	Dutch text comprehension	Dutch vocabulary
Turkish text comprehension	−.0670 (117) p = .236	−.0326 (131) p = .356	.2707 (128) p = .001	.1756 (124) p = .026

Pearson correlation coefficients for Turkish text comprehension

12

Spatial Reference in L2 Dutch of Turkish and Moroccan Adult Learners: The Initial Stages*

Peter Broeder, Josée Coenen, Guus Extra, Roeland van Hout & Rachid Zerrouk

0. INTRODUCTION

In 1982 an international project is initiated under the auspices of the European Science Foundation (Strasbourg), directed towards the study of second language acquisition by adult immigrants in Great-Britain, Germany, the Netherlands, France and Sweden. Factors which influence the structure/ order and speed/success of L2 acquisition by adults are studied from a crosslinguistic and comparative perspective. Source and target languages are combined in the following way:

L_2	English	German	Dutch	French	Swedish
L_1	Punjabi	Italian	Turkish	Arabic	Spanish	Finnish

The project is set up as a longitudinal multiple case study. For each source language at least four informants are followed during approximately 2½ years in their spontaneous acquisition of one of these five target languages. Data collection is organized in three cycles of about nine months each. An extensive description of the goals of the project, the design, the linguistic topics of analysis, the data collection procedures, and the informant selection criteria is given in a Field Manual. There are two versions of this FM, both of which have been edited by Perdue. The first edition is published by the ESF (Strasbourg 1982), the second one by Newbury House (Rowley Mass. 1984).

One of the main topics of investigation within the ESF project is referential development (see Perdue 1982: 167-202). Verbal communication requires reference to people, space and time. These three classical referential domains have been studied from (cross)linguistic, psychological

---

* We want to thank Ergün, Mahmut, Fatima and Mohamed for providing us with the raw data for this paper and Pieter Nieuwint for his help in correcting the first draft. Appendix 1 gives a Dutch/English word list of realized/intended spatial expressions in our informants' use of L2 Dutch, referred to in this paper. A slightly adapted version of this paper appeared earlier in Extra & Mittner (1984).

and developmental points of view. In many studies they are conceived as "semantic fields", although this concept is much more transparent in studies on color terms or kinship terms than in any other domain of the lexicon. Personal, spatial or temporal reference often occur in specific deictic ways. The term *deixis* refers to those aspects of communication whose interpretation depends on knowledge of the context. Although any interpretation is always dependent on context, for some words dependence is inherent (e.g. *I/you, here/there, now/then*). Rauh (1983), Jarvella & Klein (1982), Lyons (1977: 636-724) and Miller & Johnson-Laird (1976: 57-79, 301-321, 374-468) discuss a variety of deictic categories for referring to people, space and time; Tanz (1980) and Clark (1978) give a developmental perspective on specific deictic contrasts, whereas Weissenborg & Klein (1982) and Traugott (1978) offer cross-linguistic evidence in the domain of deixis from widely different languages.

Every language has numerous devices for expressing these basic types of personal, spatial and temporal reference and all language learners must necessarily acquire the specific linguistic means existing for this purpose in the target language. For his immediate communicative needs, the learner has to exploit optimally the limited resources which he has at his disposal at the outset. Gradually he will expand this small set to a wider range of resources. This report will focus on the *initial* stages of spatial reference in L2 Dutch, spoken by two Turkish and two Moroccan adults who – at the start of the project – spoke only a few L2 words.

In many Indo-European languages spatial entities and relations can basically be expressed by four types of linguistic devices: simple adverbs, prepositional phrases, verbs, and subordinate clauses. All of these devices can express two types of spatial relations: location and motion/direction (see Dervillez-Bastuji 1982: 297-324 for a semantic description of this spatial opposition). These entities can refer to position at a given point versus movement towards or from a given point. Leaving aside subordinate clauses, linguistic means and referential functions in Dutch can be classified in the following way (see also Perdue 1982: 179-191):

Table 1. Linguistic means in Dutch for spatial reference (exemplified survey).

		REFERENTIAL FUNCTIONS		
		location	direction towards ($\rightarrow \bullet$)	direction from ($\bullet \rightarrow$)
LINGUISTIC MEANS	verbs	zitten, zijn wonen	gaan (naar) rijden (naar)	komen (uit) vertrekken (uit)
	adverbs	hier/daar binnen/buiten beneden/boven links/rechts voor/achter thuis	hier/daarheen naar binnen/buiten naar beneden/boven naar l/r, l/r-af naar voren/achteren naar huis	hier/daarvandaan van binnen/buiten van beneden/boven van links/rechts van voren/achteren van huis
	preposit. phrases	in/op + NP voor/achter+NP	naar + NP NP + in	uit + NP van + NP NP + uit

With respect to local adverbs and prepositions, Dervillez-Bastuji (1982: 335-350) discusses a more thorough typology by distinguishing between four basic dimensions: interiority (*binnen* vs. *buiten*), verticality (*boven* vs. *beneden/onder*), perspectivity (*voor* vs. *achter*) and laterality (*rechts* vs. *links*).

The main purpose of our report is twofold:
● to describe procedures that can be used for analyzing *spontaneous* L2 data referring to space *in a longitudinal perspective*;
● to present and discuss *first results,* taken from selected informants and data.

Our concept of space relates to both perceptual and geographical space, more abstract spatial reference being left aside (see Perdue 1982: 179-181).

1. SELECTION OF INFORMANTS

We will focus on initial stages of spatial reference in L2 Dutch, spoken by two Turkish and two Moroccan informants who live in the Tilburg area. Basic sociobiographical characteristics of these four informants are presented in Table 2.

Table 2. Basic sociobiographical characteristics of pilot informants (dated November 1984).

	ERGÜN	MAHMUT	FATIMA	MOHAMED
Sex	male	male	female	male
Born: – date	31-08-1964	10-11-1962	15-04-1956	06-06-1961
– place	Ankara	Temürlü	Kenitra	Casablanca
Abode in SC	Ankara	Ankara	Kenitra	Casablanca
Schooling in SC: – type	prim.school	prim.school	prim.school	sec.school
– nr of yrs	5 yrs	5 yrs	2 yrs	2 yrs
Employment in SC	motor mechanic	motor mechanic	house wife/ needle woman	none
Arrival date in NL	oct. 1981	dec. 1981	sept. 1981	feb. 1982
Schooling in NL: – type	Educ.center	none	comm.center	none
– period	01-82/06-82		10-82/now	
– hrs/week	part-time		2 hrs/week	
Employment in NL: – type	fact.worker	fact.worker	kitchen-aid	fact.worker
– period	08-82/02-83	03-82/12-83 05-84/now	03-83/now	03-82/07-82 03-83/now
Civil status: single/married – if married, when and to whom – if children, nr. and year of birth	single	married 1981; L1 1; 1982	married 1981; L1 1; 1983	single
Housing in NL: with whom	Turkish family	wife	husband	parents
Session 1: date	21-09-1982	20-09-1982	05-10-1982	18-10-1982
Estimated L2 level at session 1	very limited	almost zero	almost zero	almost zero
Skill in other languages	none	none	none	a little French

2. DATA SELECTION

In the Dutch part of the ESF project each of the three intended data collection cycles consists of 9 sessions. Successive sessions take place with an interval of 25-35 days. The first cycle has the format of Table 3.

The main part of our report will focus on the least experimental, most spontaneous data gathered in this first cycle, i.e. on the (more or less structured) verbal interaction between a native speaker of Dutch (mostly Josée Coenen) and an informant. Three types of data are involved:
• loosely structured *conversations* between native speaker and informant;
• pre-structured *play-scenes,* in which both native speaker and informant take previously agreed roles;
• watching/commenting on *film-scenes,* taken from silent movies and supported by previously prepared checklists of relevant questions.

The data for pilot analysis have been italicized in Table 3. As will be clear from this table, only two experiments on spatial reference (during sessions 2 and 5) have yet been taken into account in this paper. Spontaneous data have been selected from *each* of the nine sessions involved, in order to get a *developmental* perspective on spatial reference by L2 learners. In all cases, pilot data analysis has been based on paper transcripts. At this moment, the transcribed data are gradually stored into a computer (see also 5).

All data selected for pilot analysis have been checked for the linguistic means for referring to location and direction described earlier. Analysis took place at the utterance level (indicated in the transcripts by T-units) at the same time taking into account the verbal and situational context of these utterances. The use of L1 elements and self-repairs were also part of the pilot analysis.

The following L2 data were not included:
• *direct imitations* of the native speaker (full or partial imitations of the preceding utterance), e.g.

Josée:	*dus jij moet die rollen in un doos stoppen?*
Mahmut:	*doos stoppen*
Josée:	*altijd thuis*
Mahmut:	*altijd thuis*

• *elliptic utterances* without a verb, meant as an immediate or direct response to what the native speaker has said, or as a continuation of the learner's own L2 use, e.g.

Josée:	*je moeder die was nog in Turkije*
Ergün:	*nee hier*

Table 3. Overall framework for the first 9-month cycle of data collection (* means: informant being interviewed by project-external Dutchman).

Session	Main topics of conversation	Additional activities
1 Audio	• socio-biographical information • (search for) work; educational activities • incidents in personal life	2 experiments: • L2 production of N/V • L2 → L1 translation of N/V
2 Audio	additional information about session 1 topics	2 experiments: • interpr. spatial relation terms • interpr. home related nouns
3 Video	Watching/commenting on 5 film fragments about a Dutch amateur racing cyclist and his coach	2 play-scenes: • transferring money by post • applying for a bakery job
4 Audio	• language use in source/target country (with use of map) • incidents in personal life • (search for) work	none
5 Audio	• watching/commenting on informant's family pictures in photo album/series • elaborating on kinship relations	2 experiments: • producing verbs of position • producing verbs of motion
6 Video	Watching/commenting on fragments of 2 silent movies: • Harold Lloyd (at the station) • Charlie Chaplin (the clochard)	2 play-scenes: • obs/repeating ash-tray theft • applying for housing accom-modation (*)
7 Audio	• discrimination • cultural differences between source/target country	self-confrontation of select-ed play scenes (taken from session 6)
8 Audio	going on holiday to source country (*)	none
9 Video	watching/commenting on fragment of Harold Lloyd silent movie (a new car)	2 play-scenes: • applying for family reunion • giving route directions

- utterances in which *the verb does not refer to space,* but has a different referential function; for the present, spatial adverbs and prepositional phrases in such utterances were also left out of account;
- *direct speech without grammatical subject,* e.g. *hij kom* (he said: "come"); this type of L2 data is particularly prominent in the ash-tray play-scene (session 6) and in the giving of route directions (session 9).

It is not easy to define clearly which spatial verbs should be taken into account as relevant data. Miller & Johnson-Laird (1976: 526-558) discuss several classificatory properties of verbs of motion in English; Levelt et al. (1977) do the same for Dutch. Some spatial verbs imply both *direction* and *motion*, whereas other verbs refer to just one of these spatial dimensions – or none, compare:

+ direction, + motion: *gaan/komen, zetten/leggen, vallen/gooien*
+ direction, - motion: *kijken naar*
- direction, + motion: *spelen, dansen, wassen* (expressing action)
- direction, - motion: *kopen/verkopen* (expressing change of situation)

Our pilot analysis will focus on local verbs (expressing being somewhere) and directional verbs (expressing coming/going somewhere).

3. DATA STORAGE

Every relevant occurrence in the selected data on spatial reference has been coded in a special record. All records have been stored in the ICL computer of Tilburg University. Per informant the following number of records is available: Ergün 357, Mahmut 328, Fatima 180, and Mohamed 249. A specification of the first 38 records of Ergün is given in Appendix 2. The upper row (numbered 1-12) specifies the following information:

1	informant (1=Ergün, 2=Mahmut, 3=Fatima, 4=Mohamed)
2	cycle (passim 1, for the present)
3	session number (1-9)
4	data type (1=conversation, 2=play-scene, 3=film-scene)
5	transcript line (001-999)

6	grammatical subject (0-2)
7	spatial verb (0-5)
8	spatial complex(es) (0-5)

9	realized verb in lemmatized form (infinitive), without possible particle
10	intended verb (if deviant from 9, according to L2 standard form)
11	realized spatial complex
12	intended spatial complex (if deviant from 11, according to L2 standard form)

The following algorithm has been used to code the information, given in the columns 6-8.

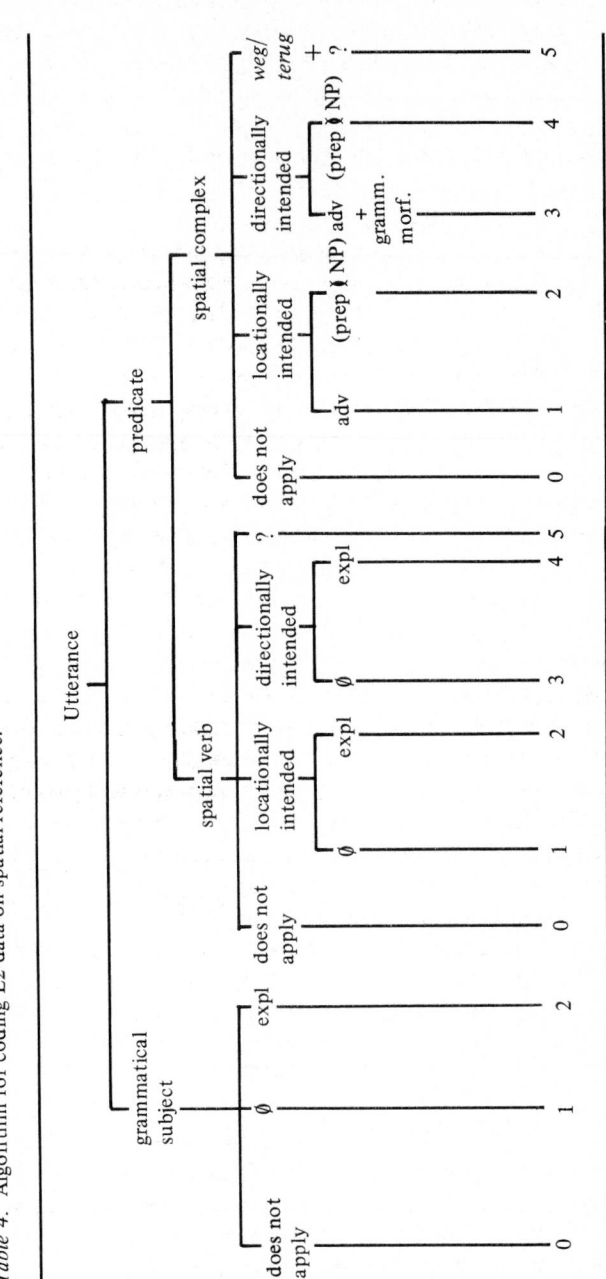

Table 4. Algorithm for coding L2 data on spatial reference.

It must be noted that this algorithm is not sensitive to word order characteristics, e.g.

- with respect to the sequencing of grammatical subject - spatial verb -
  spatial complex;
- with respect to word order characteristics within prepositional phrases,
  e.g. prep + NP or NP + prep (but see 4.3.).

Explanation of terminal symbols in the algorithm

grammatical subject
0: mostly indicates elliptic utterances (not yet analyzed)
1: indicates absence of obligatory grammatical subject
2: indicates presence of obligatory grammatical subject

spatial verb
0: mostly indicates elliptic utterances (not yet analyzed)
1: indicates absence of obligatory local verb
2: indicates presence of obligatory local verb
3: indicates absence of obligatory directional verb
4: indicates presence of obligatory directional verb
5: neither from the utterance, nor from its verbal/situational context can
   it be deduced whether reference to position or direction is intended,
   e.g. *hij weg, zij Turkije*

spatial complex
0: indicates that spatial verbs do not always necessitate reference to a
   spatial complex, e.g. *hij komt volgende week, hij zit goed*
1: including spatial adverbs like *hier/binnen/thuis* with directional verb
   komen, e.g.

   positional verb + adv: *hij is/woont hier/thuis*
   directional verb + adv: *hij komt hier/thuis*

2/4: the parentheses in the algorithm indicate that the L2 learner may realize prepositional phrases in the following ways:

Rule block		Examples
Prep.phrase	→ ∅ + NP	*Turkije*
	→ prep + NP	*naar Turkije*
	→ NP + "prep"	*Turkije naar*
	→ "prep" + ∅	*naar*

3: directional adverbs may be realized by the learner with or without an obligatory grammatical morpheme, which can be an unbound function word (*naar*) or a bound suffix (*-heen, -af*);

5: adverbs/particles *terug* and *weg*: their referential function depends on the meaning of the verb, e.g. *hij is terug* vs. *hij komt terug*, or *hij is weg* vs. *hij gaat weg*; spatial complexes are also coded 5, if neither from the utterance nor from its verbal/situational context can it be deduced whether reference to position or direction is intended, e.g. *hij Turkije* (see also code indicator 5 sub spatial verb).

4. DATA ANALYSIS

With the aid of a special computer program (Query, available at the Computer Center of Tilburg University), various samples could be drawn from the data base as described in section 3.

In Table 1 we distinguished between three types of linguistic means in Dutch (spatial verbs, adverbs and prepositional groups) for referring to location and direction. Learners of Dutch will acquire these linguistic means for both referential functions along specific developmental lines. In this process of acquisition they make use of *operating principles* (hence-forward OPs) which will be modified over time. Slobin (1973) is an early account of such principles in first language acquisition.

In this section, we will discuss hypotheses and data with respect to the utilization of spatial verbs (4.1.), spatial adverbs (4.2.) and spatial pre-positional phrases (4.3.) over time.

4.1. *Spatial verbs*

Language learners may initially leave spatial verbs implied ("unmarked"), which in a later stage will be referred to explicitly, e.g.

early L2 use	*late L2 use*
hij weg	hij is weg
hij terug	hij komt terug
hij Marokko	hij is in Marokko
hij Turkije	hij gaat naar Turkije

With respect to both locally and directionally intended verbs, we hypo-thesize the following order of acquisition:

OP1: leave verbs implied in referring to space
OP2: try a few spatially intended verbs which may be generalized
to a large number of contents
OP3: expand this small set of spatially intended verbs

OP1 will result in *zero-marking* of verbs, whereas OP2 will result in an overgeneralized use of "primary" spatial verbs. We will present data on locally and directionally intended verbs respectively.

Local verbs

Table 5 shows the distribution of utterances with implied versus explicitly used verbs of location, for all informants over time (sessions 1-9).

Table 5. Utterances with implied versus explicitly used verbs of location.

		1	2	3	4	5	6	7	8	9	Ntot
ERGÜN	impl	1	2	3	6	6	2	2	8	6	36
	expl	2	2	9	13	12	5	2	42	7	94
MAHMUT	impl	2	–	17	17	5	7	26	36	19	129
	expl	–	–	4	5	4	13	10	4	5	45
FATIMA	impl	–	3	–	–	3	1	8	10	3	28
	expl	2	–	5	1	5	7	8	5	4	36
MOHAMED	impl	3	–	2	9	5	–	5	16	–	40
	expl	1	1	4	7	11	9	–	18	5	56

The same information is given in Figure 1 (in %), with successive repetition of data at three intervals (I1=1+2+3, I2=2+3+4, ... I7=7+8+9).

Fig. 1 Degree of explicitness of local verb marking over time (in %)

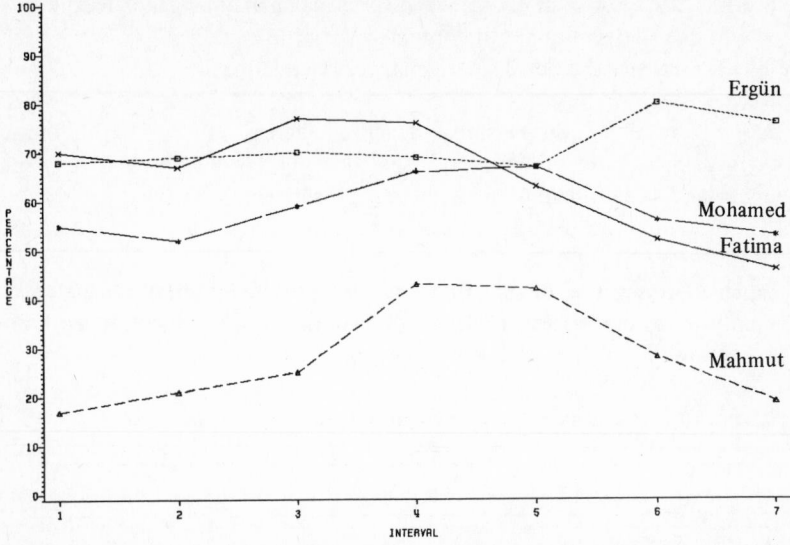

There is a more striking difference between informants than within informants over time: except for Ergün, we do not observe a developmental pattern from implied to explicit use of local verbs. Especially Mahmut strongly holds to OP1, even at the end of the first cycle of data collection.

Table 6 shows the explicitly realized local verbs (types plus tokens) which have been used by the informants during sessions 1-9.

Table 6. Local verbs of 4 informants during sessions 1-9 (types + tokens).

		1	2	3	4	5	6	7	8	9	N tokens
ERGÜN	blijven	2	1	8	13	12	2	2	23	5	68
	liggen	–	–	1	–	–	–	–	–	–	1
	wonen	–	–	–	–	–	1	–	–	–	1
	zitten	–	1	–	–	–	1	–	1	1	4
	zijn	–	–	–	–	–	1	–	18	1	20
MAHMUT	staan	–	–	–	–	–	–	–	–	1	1
	wonen	–	–	–	–	–	1	–	3	1	5
	zitten	–	–	4	4	4	11	10	1	2	36
	zijn	–	–	–	1	–	1	–	–	1	3
FATIMA	blijven	–	–	–	–	1	–	–	1	–	2
	staan	–	–	–	–	–	1	–	–	–	1
	wonen	–	–	–	–	–	3	2	2	3	10
	zitten	2	–	5	1	3	3	6	2	1	23

Table 6 continued Local verbs of 4 informants during sessions 1-9 (types + tokens).

		1	2	3	4	5	6	7	8	9	N tokens
MOHAMED	blijven	1	1	2	-	1	1	-	-	1	7
	passer	-	-	-	-	-	-	-	1	-	1
	staan	-	-	-	-	6	1	-	-	2	9
	wonen	-	-	1	5	2	4	-	4	1	17
	zitten	-	-	1	-	-	-	-	-	-	1
	zijn	-	-	-	2	2	3	-	13	1	21

In all cases, the repertoire of local verbs remains limited during these initial stages of language learning. If this first cycle is taken as a whole, the following order of frequency emerges.

Table 7. Order of frequency for local verbs (N ⩾ 2).

	Ergün	Mahmut	Fatima	Mohamed
blijven	1	-	3	4
staan	-	-	-	3
wonen	-	2	2	2
zitten	3	1	1	-
zijn	2	3	-	1

The informants show different preferential patterns in their utilization of these primary local verbs. With respect to *blijven, staan, zitten* and *zijn* we find the evidence presented in Table 8 for the second operating principle (OP2).

Table 8. Intended meanings of primary local verbs.

utilized verb	intended meaning	ER	MA	FA	MO	examples
blijven	*blijven*	17	–	2	7	misschien ik hier blijven
	logeren	4	–	–	–	auto hier blijven
	staan	4	–	–	–	die zus blijf hier *Kibris*
	wonen	40	–	–	–	zes zeventig blijven school
	zitten	1	–	–	–	ik ben hier blijven
	zijn	2	–	–	–	
staan	*staan*	–	1	1	4	en dan hier achter de weg staan strand
	liggen	–	–	–	1	die oma is bij hem staan
	zitten	–	–	–	1	hier staan een gemeente van *Boulis*
	zijn	–	–	–	3	
zitten	*zitten*	–	12	3	1	meisje kwaad he; hier zitten
	blijven	–	1	5	–	die kadootje daar zitten he
	liggen	3	3	–	–	dansen drinken zitten
	nietsdoen	–	7	–	–	moet ander station zitten
	overstappen	–	2	–	–	vader moeder zitten trein;
	staan	–	6	–	–	trein wachten
	stoppen	–	1	–	–	Kayseri zitten
	thuisblijven	–	–	6	–	jij meisje zit
	verblijven	–	2	8	–	broer zit Sahara
	wonen	1	2	–	–	in Marokko veel mensen zit samen
zijn	*zijn*	18	3	–	17	hij is weg
	gaan	–	–	–	1	Casa is bij Mohammadia
	liggen	–	–	–	1	ons tent is achter
	staan	–	–	–	1	daar El Jadida is goeje mensen
	wonen	1	–	–	1	

Zitten is acquired late by Ergün and Mohamed, whereas both Mahmut and Fatima make an early use of this verb - with a wide variety of intended meanings. Most remarkable is Ergün's strongly overgeneralized use of *blijven* for both *blijven* and *wonen*.

In Dutch, location is very often expressed by one of the verbs *liggen/ staan/zitten* instead of the more neutral or abstract verb *zijn*. The semantic conditions for selecting one of these local verbs and their causative directional counterparts *leggen/zetten/doen* respectively are extremely complex in Dutch and have hardly been described so far (see Van den Toorn 1975). Compare in Dutch:

het raam staat open	*ik zet het raam open*
het raam zit dicht	*ik doe het raam dicht*
het bord staat op tafel	*ik zet het bord op tafel*
	(bord=plate)
het bord ligt op tafel	*ik leg het bord op tafel*
	(bord=board)
de foto zit in de krant	*ik doe de foto in de krant*
de foto staat in de krant	*ik zet de foto in de krant*

This group of *liggen/staan/zitten* vs. *leggen/zetten/doen* occurs very frequently in spoken Dutch. Nevertheless, as we know from previous experience with adult L2 learners of Dutch, these verbs are extremely hard to learn.

A linguistic insecurity test was designed containing all six verbs. In this test, thirty pictures were shown twice to the informants. Together with each picture a short, simple sentence was presented (both aurally and visually). Each sentence contained one semantically wrong word, namely the verb *is* (position) or the verb *breng* (direction). The informants had to replace this wrong word with the correct one, namely *ligt/staat/zit* (pos.) or *leg/zet/doe* (dir.). Cards with these three optional verbs were on display for the informants.

The test was given to the informants during session 5 (see Table 3). For both positional and directional verbs, the same series of pictures was used. The results of Ergün, Mahmut, Fatima and Mohamed on the positional part of the test are given in Appendix 3. All informants have about the same low correct score, ranging from 10 to 13 out of 30 items. Most remarkable is Mahmut's preference for *zitten* throughout the test. This preference is consistent with his overgeneralized use of *zitten* in spontaneous L2 Dutch. Whereas both *liggen* and *staan* are almost absent in Mahmut's spontaneous L2 use (see Table 6), *zitten* is used with the intended meanings of *zitten* (12), *staan* (6), and *liggen* (3) (see Table 8).

Directional verbs

Table 9 shows the distribution of utterances with implied versus explicitly used verbs of direction, for all informants over time (sessions 1-9).

Table 9. Utterances with implied versus explicitly used verbs of direction.

		1	2	3	4	5	6	7	8	9	Ntot
ERGÜN	impl	2	7	–	5	3	–	4	24	21	66
	expl	10	7	11	23	16	16	13	38	19	154
MAHMUT	impl	8	2	5	4	2	25	1	28	25	100
	expl	–	–	2	–	3	4	–	16	12	37
FATIMA	impl	4	4	5	2	1	13	6	22	3	60
	expl	1	–	5	1	8	12	3	7	12	49
MOHAMED	impl	3	–	4	–	5	4	–	2	3	21
	expl	11	9	9	5	29	18	2	7	22	112

The same information is given in Figure 2 (in %), again with successive repetition of data at three intervals.

Fig. 2. Degree of explicitness of directional verb marking over time (in %).

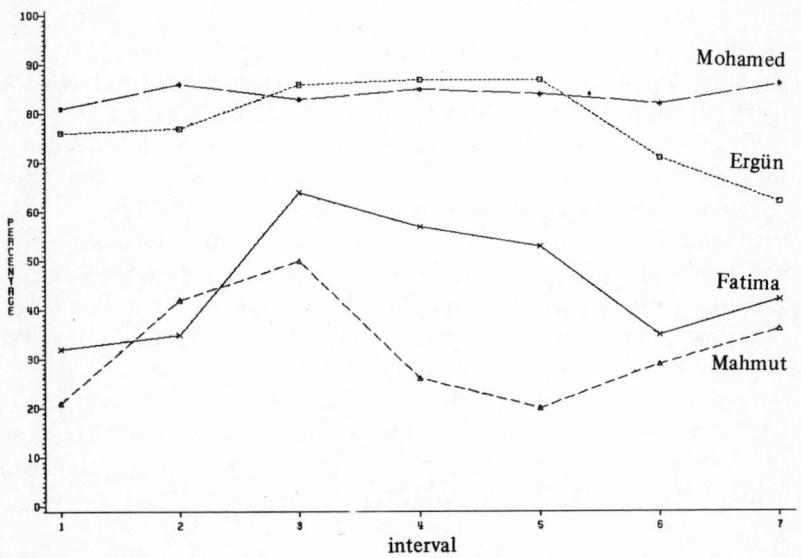

As in Figure 1, there is a more striking difference between informants than within informants over time. In both figures, Mahmut and Fatima remain at the lower end of the scale by strongly utilizing OP1 during the first cycle of data collection.

Table 10 shows the explicitly realized directional verbs (types plus tokens) which have been used by the informants during sessions 1-9.

Table 10. Directional verbs of 4 informants during sessions 1-9 (types + tokens).

		1	2	3	4	5	6	7	8	9	N tokens
ERGÜN	gaan	3	6	8	18	9	8	3	6	-	61
	komen	5	1	3	5	8	8	10	33	16	89
	lopen	-	-	-	-	-	-	-	-	1	1
	rijden	2	-	-	-	-	-	-	-	2	4
	wandelen	-	-	-	-	-	-	-	1	-	1
MAHMUT	gaan	-	-	-	-	-	2	-	-	-	2
	komen	-	-	2	-	-	2	-	16	10	30
	rijden	-	-	-	-	-	-	-	-	1	1
	wandelen	-	-	-	-	3	-	-	-	1	4
FAT.	komen	1	-	4	1	6	12	3	7	11	45
	lopen	-	-	1	-	2	-	-	-	1	4
MOHAMED	gaan	5	6	1	4	9	6	1	2	8	42
	komen	6	3	8	1	18	9	1	5	10	61
	lopen	-	-	-	-	2	3	-	-	-	5
	rijden	-	-	-	-	-	-	-	-	4	4

Even more than in the case of local verbs, the repertoire of directional verbs remains limited during these initial stages of language learning. For the whole period the following order of frequency emerges:

Table 11. Order of frequency for directional verbs (N ⩾ 2).

	Ergün	Mahmut	Fatima	Mohamed
gaan	2	3	-	2
komen	1	1	1	1
lopen	-	-	2	3
rijden	3	-	-	4
wandelen	-	2	-	-

With respect to the intended meanings of *gaan, komen, lopen* and *wandelen,* we find the evidence presented in Table 12 for OP2:

Table 12. Intended meanings of primary directional verbs.

utilized verb	intended meaning	ER	MA	FA	MO	examples
gaan	*gaan*	42	2	–	40	moet jij dit naar links gaan
	bewegen	–	–	–	1	man weg gaan naar
	lopen	2	–	–	–	de kar gaan heel langzaam
	rijden	–	–	–	1	gaan naar turkse jongens
	uitgaan(met)	2	–	–	–	misschien Duitsland weg gaan naar
	vertrekken	6	–	–	–	gister Beekse Bergen gaan naar
	geweest zijn	9	–	–	–	
komen	*komen*	84	28	35	50	3 jaar wachten en dan komen
	gaan	5	2	8	9	Turkije
	rijden	–	–	–	1	dan hij komt achteruit
	zijn	–	–	–	1	kom naar huis 6 of 8 uur
lopen	*lopen*	1	–	–	5	auto loop boven
	gaan	–	–	4	–	
wandelen	*wandelen*	1	–	–	–	auto weg; wandel achter
	rennen	–	1	–	–	auto wandelen ander dorp
	rijden	–	3	–	–	

With respect to *gaan* and *komen,* all language learners show the same acquisition pattern:

- *komen* is used more often than *gaan* (see Table 11);
- *komen* is used with the intended meanings of *gaan,* while the reverse never occurs.

Gaan is used hardly or not at all during these initial stages by Mahmut and Fatima (see Table 10), whereas only Ergün uses *gaan* with a rather wide variety of intended meanings. Fatima compensates for her lack of *gaan* by using *lopen* in this sense.

Linguistic awareness of the different meanings of *gaan* vs. *komen* is manifest in self-repairs like:

- *en dan overmorgen ik kom/uh ik ga naar garage* (Ergün, session 8);
- *misschien ko/hier gaan weg* (Ergün, session 8).

Also, Mahmut's preference for *wandelen* with the intended meaning of *rijden* is evident in self-repairs, e.g.

- *auto rij/wandelen ander dorp* (Mahmut, session 5).

Whereas the deictic verb *come* is target-oriented, *go* is origin-oriented. Target and origin are defined by the position of the speaker at time of utterance (the origo), or correspond to a perspective which he is taking. It has also been shown in other L2 studies (see Heidelberger Forschungs-projekt "Pidgin-Deutsch" 1978) that *come* is strongly overgeneralized in initial learner varieties – a fact which could possibly be explained by the assumption that the target is positively and the origin negatively marked (see Perdue 1982: 191). However, contradictory results on both order and age of acquisition of *come/go* have been observed in L1 studies, mostly based on experimental comprehension tasks (Tanz 1980; Clark & Garnica 1974), and only occasionally on elicited production tasks (Richards 1976).

4.2. *Spatial adverbs*

Spatial adverbs in Dutch are morphologically unmarked in case of location and morphologically marked in case of direction: directional adverbs are marked by a grammatical morpheme, which is a preposed function word (cf. *naar, uit*) or a bound suffix (cf. *-heen, -af*) (see Table 1).

With respect to directional adverbs, we hypothesize the following order of acquisition:

OP1: refer to direction by using *unmarked* adverbs
OP2: refer to direction by using *marked* adverbs

First, we will discuss the utilization of locally intended spatial adverbs.

Local adverbs

In Table 13 we present the locally intended adverbs (types plus tokens) which have been used by each of the informants during sessions 1-9.

Table 13. Locally intended adverbs during sessions 1-9 (types + tokens).

group	realized	intended	1	2	3	4	5	6	7	8	9	Ntot
ERGÜN	achter									1		1
	binnen										1	1
	boven										1	1
	buiten			1	4	3	3	4	3	28	5	51
	daar									1		1
	daarbij									1		1
	hier		1		5	15	5	1		28	12	67
	thuis						2	2	3	3		10
FATIMA	achter	achterin									1	1
	beneden								3		1	4
	binnen	beneden						1	1			1
	binnen								2	1		2
	boven							1	2	1	4	8
	buiten								1			1
	daar	daar						1	2			3
	hier		1		17	13	1	6	7	24	19	87
	hier	thuis						1		1		1
	hiernaast		2						1			2
	huis	thuis						1	1			2
	in	erin								2		2
	links						1	2				2
	naast	ernaast						2		2		2
	onder	beneden			2					2		2
	rechts					3	4	1	6	4	1	18
	thuis										1	2
	voor	voorin							1		2	2
MAHMUT	hier		1	1	1		3	1		6	9	21
	huis	thuis		1						5	1	
	thuis			1					4		1	11
MOHAMED	*en haut*	boven										1
	binnen					2	7	3	1	16		3
	daar		1		5		7	2	2	17	4	28
	hier					1	1	1	2			37
	hier	daar										2

The two Turkish informants gradually expand their repertoire of local adverbs over time, whereas the two Moroccan informants maintain a restricted inventory of these spatial means during the first nine sessions. If this first cycle of initial learning is taken as a whole, the following order of frequency emerges:

Ergün		Mahmut		Fatima		Mohamed	
hier	67	*hier*	87	*hier*	21	*hier*	37
daar	51	*(t)huis*	20	*(t)huis*	12	*daar*	28
thuis	10	*boven*	8				

With respect to *hier* and *daar,* all language learners show the same acquisition pattern:
● *hier* is used before *daar*;
● *hier* is used more often than *daar*.
Moreover, two informants occasionally use *hier* with the intended meaning of *daar*, while the reverse never occurs, cf. *hier tot hier* (=from here to there; Mohamed, session 5). The same preferential patterns have been found for other target languages, and for first language learners (see Tanz 1980: 70-107 for an overview).

Lyons (1968: 275) defines *here* as "in the vicinity of the speaker" and *there* as "not in the vicinity of the speaker". The basic reference point of deictic expressions is the "here" and "now" of the speaker. Deictic expressions turn out to be defined with respect to this so-called "origo". Therefore, it might be hypothesized that expressions with the feature /+/ proximity-to-the-origo will be acquired early (see Tanz 1980: 107). Tanz explains in this way that *here* is acquired before *there* in L1 acquisition. Yet it is unclear whether a *similar* order in L2 acquisition *by adults* can be based on *similar* explanatory principles. Moreover, explanations of L1 acquisition order have again mostly been based on experimental comprehension tasks, and not on spontaneous speech.

Directional adverbs
In Table 14 we present the directionally intended adverbs (types and tokens) which have been used by the informants during the first cycle of nine sessions.

Table 14. Survey of directionally intended adverbs (types + tokens).

realized	intended	ER	MA	FA	MO
Adv −spat.morpheme					
achter	achteraan/achteruit/ naar achteren	2	6	-	3
beneden	naar beneden	-	-	1	-
binnen	naar binnen	1	1	1	2
boven	naar boven	1	1	1	1
daar	daarheen	-	1	-	2
links	naar links/linksaf	-	2	-	3
rechts	naar rechts/rechtsaf	-	3	-	-
voor	naar voren/vooruit/rechtdoor	-	6	-	-
door	vooruit	-	-	-	2
Adv +spat.morpheme					
achterin	achterna	-	3	-	-
achterop	achterna	1	-	-	-
achteruit		-	-	-	2
linksaf	linksaf/naar links	4	-	-	1
metachter	naar achteren	-	-	-	1
naar hier	hierheen	-	-	-	1
rechtsaf	rechtsaf/naar rechts	4	-	-	-
rechtdoor		1	1	-	-
N tokens: Adv. −SM		4	20	3	13
Adv. +SM		10	4	1	5

The OP1 mentioned earlier predicts zero-marking of directional adverbs. This prediction is borne out by the data. Three out of our four language learners mostly apply OP1, whereas Ergün prefers OP2 and must be considered more advanced in this respect.

With respect to spatial adverbs, two types of evidence emerge in favour of the "primary" character of position vs. direction in language:
- local reference is less complex than directional reference from a linguistic point of view (–/+ additional grammatical morpheme);
- local means are initially used for both local and directional reference by the language learner.

Linguistic awareness of the differences between local vs. directional adverbs is manifest in self-repairs, e.g.:

hij achter uh achterop (=hij loopt erachteraan) (Ergün, session 9)
maar hij gaat uh achter/achteruit (Mohamed, session 9)

Finally, the adverbs/particles *weg* and *terug* appear to be used by all informants.

Table 15. Utilization of *weg* and *terug.*

		1	2	3	4	5	6	7	8	9	Ntot
TERUG	Ergün	2	3	2	3	–	8	–	7	9	34
	Mahmut	3	1	2	1	–	20	8	1	6	42
	Fatima	–	1	–	–	–	5	2	1	2	11
	Mohamed	2	–	1	–	–	2	–	–	2	7
WEG	Ergün	–	1	1	–	4	–	3	3	3	15
	Mahmut	–	–	1	1	4	7	1	6	–	20
	Fatima	1	1	1	–	1	1	–	3	–	8
	Mohamed	1	1	2	–	4	1	–	–	–	9

As was said before, their local vs. directional meaning completely depends on the spatial intention of the explicitly realized – or implied – verb (see also Table 4), e.g.

location	direction
hij terug	hij terug
hij is terug	hij gaat/komt terug
hij weg	hij weg
hij is weg	hij gaat weg

4.3. *Spatial prepositional phrases*

Few lexical domains have been studied so extensively as local prepositions. This holds for both adult and child language. For the domain of
local prepositions, Talmy (1983) gives a recent account of "how language
structures space". Weissenborn (1981) reasons about the preoccupation
for this domain in L1 acquisition studies and gives a critical overview of
observed L1 acquisition orders of local prepositions, mostly derived from
experimental comprehension tasks.

When referring to space (both location and direction) by means of prepositional phrases (henceforward PPs), native speakers of Dutch take into
account specific operating principles with respect to both *form* and
position of specific spatial morphemes. Learners of Dutch will acquire
these operating principles along specific developmental lines. We will
discuss L2 related hypotheses and data with respect to the utilization of
local and directional PPs respectively.

Local PPs
We hypothesize the following order of acquisition:

OP1: refer to location by using *unmarked* PPs
OP2: refer to location by using a limited set of locally intended
       morphemes
OP3: refer to location by expanding this set of morphemes

OP1 will result in *zero-marking* of PPs, whereas OP2 will result in an
overgeneralized use of "primary" locally intended morphemes. Although
local morphemes precede NPs in Dutch, learners of Dutch may show different characteristics, resulting in postposition of local morphemes (LM),
or even in a discontinuous position with respect to the NP.

Table 16 shows the distribution of unmarked and marked local PPs for
each of the informants during sessions 1-9.

Table 16. Local reference by NP +/– spatial morpheme.

		1	2	3	4	5	6	7	8	9	Ntot
ER	NP	4	–	6	6	12	2	3	12	3	48
	NP + morpheme	–	1	3	–	–	–	–	6	–	10
MA	NP	–	–	6	6	5	2	3	13	6	41
	NP + morpheme	–	–	–	1	–	4	–	6	2	13
FA	NP	–	–	–	–	4	4	3	1	–	12
	NP + morpheme	2	–	–	–	2	3	7	5	7	26
MO	NP	–	–	1	–	1	–	–	3	–	5
	NP + morpheme	5	1	4	8	10	6	4	13	9	60

All language learners show variability in their patterns of local reference. Ergün and Mahmut use OP1 during all/most of the sessions, Fatima goes from OP1 to OP2 in the course of her learning process, whereas Mohamed applies OP2 right from the start.

Table 17 shows the locally intended morphemes (types plus tokens) which have been used by the informants during sessions 1-9. Their position with respect to the NP is indicated as well, i.e. preposition (LM + NP) or postposition (NP + LM):

Table 17. Locally intended morphemes during sessions 1-9 (types+ tokens).

	realized	intended	1	2	3	4	5	6	7	8	9	Ntokens
ERGÜN LM	bij		–	–	1	–	–	–	–	–	–	1
+	in		–	–	1	–	–	–	–	4	–	5
NP	in	op	–	–	–	–	–	–	–	2	–	2
MAHMUT NP	achteren		–	–	1	–	–	–	–	–	–	1
+LM	buiten		–	1	–	–	–	–	–	–	–	1
LM	bij		–	–	–	1	–	1	–	–	1	1
+	in		–	–	–	1	–	3	–	1	1	3
NP	naast		–	–	–	–	–	1	–	1	1	4
	onder		–	–	–	–	–	–	–	–	1	1
FATIMA NP	in	tussen	–	–	–	–	2	–	–	2	–	2
+LM	naast		–	–	–	–	–	–	–	2	–	2
LM	*fe*	in	–	–	–	–	–	2	1	–	–	1
+	met	bij	–	–	–	3	–	2	5	1	3	11
NP	met	in	–	–	–	5	–	1	–	4	2	6
	met	voor	–	–	–	–	–	1	1	1	1	1
	van	in	2	–	–	–	2	1	1	–	1	6
	voor	bij	–	–	–	–	–	–	–	–	1	1
MOHAMED LM	*andna*	bij	1	–	1	–	–	–	–	1	–	1
	dans	op(school)	–	–	1	–	1	–	–	–	1	1
NP	achter		1	–	–	–	2	3	–	3	7	2
+	bij		1	–	–	3	2	1	–	9	1	19
	bij	in/op	1	–	2	5	1	1	4	1	1	2
NP	in	op	2	–	1	–	1	1	–	–	–	24
	met	bij	–	1	1	–	2	–	–	–	–	2
	naar	bij/in/ op/voor	–	–	–	–	–	–	–	–	–	1
	naast		–	–	–	–	1	–	–	1	1	4
	op		–	–	–	–	1	1	–	1	1	1
	voor		–	–	–	–	–	–	–	–	–	2

The L2 repertoire of locally intended morphemes is very limited for three of the informants: Ergün, Mahmut and Fatima use 3 locally intended morphemes each, whereas only Mohamed uses 8 of these morphemes. An important finding is that both *overgeneralization* (one morpheme having several intended meanings) and *underrepresentation* (several morphemes having one meaning) show up in the informants' use of locally intended morphemes:

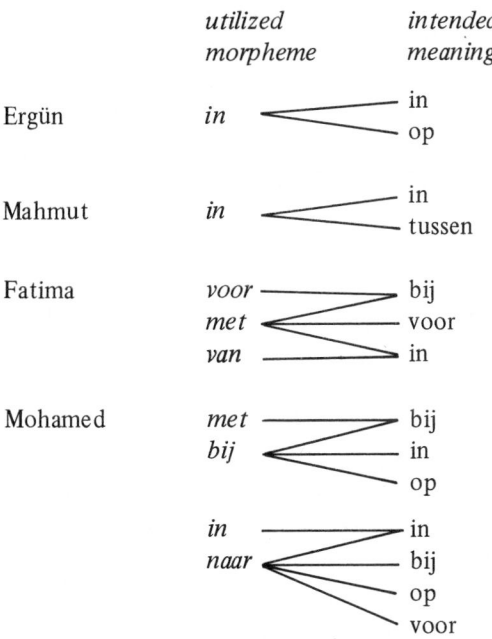

	utilized morpheme	*intended meaning*
Ergün	*in*	in / op
Mahmut	*in*	in / tussen
Fatima	*voor* / *met* / *van*	bij / voor / in
Mohamed	*met* / *bij*	bij / in / op
	in / *naar*	in / bij / op / voor

In is the most frequently used local morpheme in the L2 use of Ergün, Mahmut (except for *naast*) and Mohamed. However, Fatima does not use this morpheme at all: for her, *met* and *van* (both of which do *not* refer to space in standard Dutch) fulfil the referential function of location. Finally, Fatima and Mohamed occasionally compensate for their lack of local means by recurring to L1 and L1/French respectively (see Table 17).

Also in L1 acquisition studies, *in* has been identified as one of the first, often even the very first local preposition which learners use; *in* can be taken as the least marked preposition, only expressing "interiority", whereas all other local prepositions can be taken to be more specific.

In order to gain more insight into how our informants *interpret* spatial relation terms (especially local prepositions) we constructed a test called the "money game". Informants were shown a square piece of blank paper, a paper with a picture of a bus and some small change (1 guilder, 2 five-cent pieces). The test was administered during session 2 (see Table 3). After the terms *papier/geld/gulden/stuiver/bus* had been explained, the informants were asked to carry out specific verbal instructions in a non-verbal manner. The verbal prompts and non-verbal results are given in Appendix 4. The highest and lowest scores of Mohamed and Fatima respectively correspond with similar patterns in their spontaneous productive data (see Table 17): whereas Mohamed has the widest repertoire of locally intended morphemes, Fatima has the smallest. Although the spatial morpheme *in* is among the earliest local prepositions in most L1 acquisition studies, it is neither produced nor understood by Fatima.

Directional PPs
We hypothesize the following order of acquisition:

OP4: refer to direction by using *unmarked* PPs
OP5: refer to direction by using directionally intended morphemes

---

Generally speaking, directional morphemes precede NPs in Dutch, although the reverse may also occur, e.g. *naar het station, uit de trein* versus *het café in, de berg op*. Postposition of "prepositions" generally adds directionality to verbs of motion (see Geerts et al. 1984), e.g. *hij loopt op de weg* (non-dir.) vs. *hij loopt de weg op* (dir.).

As in the case of local reference, L2 learners of Dutch may show different characteristics, resulting in postposition of other directional morphemes (*station naar*), or even in a discontinuous position with respect to the NP (*hij school gaan naar*).

Table 18 shows the distribution of /-/ or /+/ marked directional PPs for each of the informants during sessions 1-9.

Table 18. Directional reference by NP +/- spatial morpheme.

		1	2	3	4	5	6	7	8	9	Ntot
ER	NP	5	5	1	6	3	1	5	14	2	42
	NP + morpheme	-	6	6	12	7	2	2	20	2	57
MA	NP	5	1	5	2	7	8	-	32	4	64
	NP + morpheme	-	-	1	-	-	-	-	1	2	4
FA	NP	-	-	-	1	3	1	-	2	-	7
	NP + morpheme	3	3	7	2	1	7	3	19	3	48
MO	NP	1	-	1	1	-	1	-	1	-	5
	NP + morpheme	8	7	3	3	22	10	1	3	4	61

Ergün shows variability with respect to OP4 and OP5 during these first nine sessions, although he mostly applies OP5. Mahmut almost exclusively applies OP4 throughout the sessions, whereas both Fatima and Mohamed use OP5 in all/most of the sessions.

Table 19 shows the directionally intended morphemes (types plus tokens) which have been used by the informants during sessions 1-9. Their position with respect to the NP is indicated as well, i.e. DM + NP, NP + DM, or DM *without* NP.

Table 19. Directionally intended morphemes during sessions 1-9 (types + tokens).

		realized	intended	1	2	3	4	5	6	7	8	9	Ntokens
ERGÜN	DM	in	naar	–	–	–	–	–	–	–	1	–	1
	+ NP	naar		–	3	1	4	1	–	2	11	–	22
	NP	binnen	in	–	–	–	–	–	–	–	–	2	2
	+ DM	naar		–	3	5	8	6	2	–	8	–	32
	DM	naar		–	–	–	4	1	6	–	2	–	13
MAHMUT	DM	naar		–	–	1	–	–	–	–	–	–	1
	+ NP		in/binnen										
	NP	binnen	in/binnen	–	–	–	–	–	–	–	1	1	2
	+ DM	in		–	–	–	–	–	–	–	–	1	1
	DM	in	naar binnen	–	–	–	–	–	1	–	–	–	1
FATIMA	DM	met	in	–	–	–	–	–	1	–	–	1	1
	+	met	naar	–	–	1	–	–	1	–	5	1	8
	NP	naar		–	3	5	2	–	4	1	7	1	23
		naarmet	naar	–	–	–	–	–	1	2	4	–	7
		naarvan	naar	2	–	–	–	–	–	–	2	–	4
		op		–	–	–	–	–	1	–	–	–	1
		van	naar	1	–	1	–	1	–	–	–	–	3

Table 19 continued. Directionally intended morphemes during sessions 1-9 (types + tokens).

Learner	Construction	realized	intended	1	2	3	4	5	6	7	8	9	Ntokens
FATIMA	NP + DM	naar		–	–	–	–	–	–	–	1	–	1
FATIMA	DM	naar		–	–	–	–	–	–	–	1	–	1
FATIMA	DM	naarmet	naar	–	–	–	–	–	–	–	1	–	1
MOHAMED	DM + NP	achter	achter..aan	–	–	–	–	–	1	–	–	1	2
MOHAMED	DM + NP	met	door..heen	–	–	–	–	–	4	–	–	–	4
MOHAMED	DM + NP	met	naar	2	–	–	–	3	–	–	–	–	5
MOHAMED	DM + NP	met	uit	–	–	–	–	5	–	–	–	–	5
MOHAMED	DM + NP	metachter	achter ..aan/om	–	–	–	–	2	–	–	–	–	2
MOHAMED	NP	in	door..heen	–	–	–	–	–	1	–	–	–	1
MOHAMED	NP	in	naar	2	–	–	–	–	–	–	–	–	2
MOHAMED	NP	naar		4	7	2	3	12	4	1	2	2	37
MOHAMED	NP	op		–	–	–	–	–	–	–	–	1	1
MOHAMED	NP	uit		–	–	1	–	–	–	–	1	–	2
MOHAMED	DM	uit		–	–	–	–	–	1	–	–	–	1

Ergün has a strong preference for *naar* (in preposition, in postposition, or in isolation). Mahmut hardly makes use of directional morphemes at all, whereas both Fatima and Mohamed utilize a wider repertoire in which again both overgeneralization and underrepresentation show up:

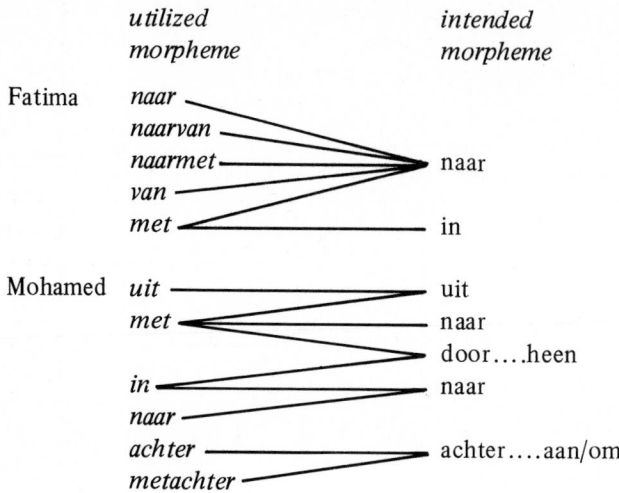

Naarvan, naarmet and *metachter* are examples of morphological innovation in learner language.

When we compare the individual use of OPs 1-2 and OPs 4-5 during the first cycle of data collection, the following picture emerges.

Table 20. Operating principles for spatial reference during cycle 1.

		Ergün	Mahmut	Fatima	Mohamed
location	OP1	(48)	(41)	12	5
	OP2	10	13	(26)	(60)
direction	OP4	42	(64)	7	5
	OP5	(57)	4	(48)	(61)

Except for Ergün's reference to direction, there is a clear symmetry in the utilized OPs: the two Turkish informants prefer *unmarked* local/directional reference, whereas the two Moroccan informants prefer *marked* local/ directional reference. Similar patterns for Turkish vs. Moroccan adult learners of Dutch have been observed by Jansen et al. (1981: 324), who interpret the "avoidance" of prepositions by Turkish L2 learners as interference phenomena. Furthermore, Appel (1984) refers to the same phenomena in L2 Dutch of Turkish vs Moroccan *children*.

Roughly the same picture emerges, when we compare the word order patterns in utilizing local/directional morphemes:

Table 21. Word order patterns in utilizing local/directional morphemes.

	Ergün	Mahmut	Fatima	Mohamed
local morpheme + NP	8	9	26	60
NP + local morpheme	2	4	0	0
direct. morpheme + NP	23	1	47	61
NP + direct. morpheme	34	3	1	0
isolated direct. morpheme	13	1	2	1

For both locational and directional reference, in most cases the following operating principle is used:

OP6: *prepose* local/directional morphemes

The two Moroccan informants make an almost exclusive use of this OP6, whereas the two Turkish informants show a more variable pattern.

A comparison of linguistic means for spatial reference in Turkish, Moroccan-Arabic and Dutch with respect to *type* and *position* of spatial NP markers gives the following results:

	Turkish	Moroccan-Arabic	Dutch
type of spatial NP marker	morpheme (suffix)	morpheme (function word)	morpheme (function word)
position of spatial NP marker	always in postposition	always in preposition	mostly in preposition

Both Moroccan-Arabic and Dutch make use of *obligatory* local/directional morphemes in preposed position with respect to the NP (whereas postposition may occur in Dutch, it never occurs in Moroccan-Arabic). As might be expected, there is no equivalence between Moroccan-Arabic and Dutch prepositional morphemes. Harrell (1962: 208) states that "no Moroccan preposition is exactly equivalent to any given English pre-position. Each one has its own range of meaning, and the translation of a given Moroccan preposition into English differs widely from context to context".

In Turkish, local/directional NPs are never marked by prepositions. Instead, three different case-suffixes are used for expressing three different spatial orientations (see Lewis 1967: 85ff.):

- /-dA/, expressing being at/in/on X, e.g.
  araba-da oturuyorum (I am sitting in the car);
- /-yA/, expressing going to X, e.g.
  araba-ya biniyorum (I get into the car);
- /-dAn/, expressing coming from X, e.g.
  araba-dan iniyorum (I get out the car).

For more specified spatial orientations, a special class of postpositional phrases is used in Turkish. Such constructions consist of a NP, linked with a genitive to a postposition that contains three morphological elements:

- a noun, specifying the type of location, e.g. *iç* (inside), *yan* (side), *arka* (back);
- an anaphoric element (the possessive suffix of the third person), which is obligatory because the postposition is linked to the noun with a genitive;
- one of the three case-suffixes mentioned before and indicating location or direction towards/from X, e.g.
  araba-nın içinde
    GEN inside-POSS3-LOC   (inside the car)
  araba-nın üst-ün-de
    GEN top-POSS3-LOC   (on top of the car)
  araba-nın alt-ın-a
    GEN bottom-POSS3-DIR   (under the car)

Both the observed *non-use* of spatial morphemes in our Turkish informants' L2 Dutch, their *utilization* of *postponed* spatial morphemes, and the *absence* of these two phenomena in our Moroccan informants' L2 Dutch may indicate *source language* transfer. On the other hand, the non-use of spatial morphemes in the L2 utterances of *all* informants may also indicate a selective intake of *target language* input: function words in Dutch are generally *non-stressed* and *minimal* (one-syllabic) units in the speech stream, and may therefore have a low saliency. Further analysis of additional data and other informants' L2 use is needed for a better inter-lingual or intralingual understanding of these particular phenomena.

Fatima and Mohamed make a strongly overgeneralized use of *met* for both local and directional reference (whereas this morpheme does not refer to spatial entities at all in standard Dutch):

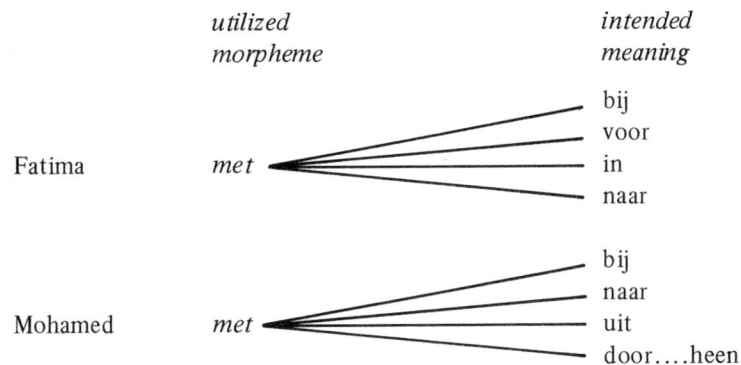

	utilized morpheme		intended meaning

Finally and again, Ergün is a special case. Table 22 provides a more detailed view of his way of referring to direction, and especially of his utilization of *gaan-naar* and *naar*.

Table 22. Ergün's utilization of *gaan-naar* and *naar* (....refers to discontinuity).

	1	2	3	4	5	6	7	8	9
(1) gaan-naar + NP	–	2	1	4	2	–	1	2	–
(2) NP...gaan-naar	–	2	5	8	6	4	–	1	–
(3) gaan- naar + ∅	–	1	–	4	–	3	–	1	–
(4) naar + NP	–	–	–	–	–	–	1	6	–
(5) NP...naar	–	–	–	–	–	–	–	8	–

Whereas in standard Dutch there is an unbreakable adjacency between *naar* + *NP*, Ergün initially assumes such a relationship between *gaan* + *naar*. His invariant use of this basic frame is a clear indication of formulaic speech (see Perdue 1982: 160-162). Notwithstanding an obligatory *naar+NP* in standard Dutch (1), Ergün's frame leads to a variable position of *naar*. It may occur in preposition (1), in postposition (2), or in isolation (3), e.g.
- *en dan broer vader moeder allemaal gaan naar Turkije* (1)
- *uh ziekenhuis gaan naar* (2)
- *ik een dag beetje gaan naar* (3)

Gradually, the formula *gaan+naar* is broken down: in sessions 7 and 8 *naar* is freed from its frozen relationship with *gaan*. Still, *naar* may remain postponed to NP, e.g.

- *een jaar streekcentrum niet naar* (5).

Linguistic awareness of sequential principles of *naar+NP* in standard Dutch emerges in self-repairs, e.g.

- *hier blijven en dan Istanbul naar/naar Istanbul* (session 8).

5. CONCLUSIONS

Having discussed different linguistic means in initial learner language for referring to space, we finally want to compare our informants on their degree of *explicitness* in referring to space and on the degree of *extensiveness/variation* of their lexicon in doing so.

Mohamed and Ergün make the most explicit use of both local and directional verb marking (see Figures 1 and 2). With respect to spatial morpheme marking in directional adverbs, Ergün is far ahead of the other informants (see Table 14). Finally, the two Turkish informants prefer *unmarked* local/directional reference in using prepositional phrases, whereas the two Moroccan informants in this case have a preference for *marked* reference (see Table 20).

Tables 23 and 24 show the degree of extensiveness (tokens) and variation (types) of the spatial lexicon respectively, taking into account 6 spatial categories during the first cycle of data collection as a whole.

Table 23. Degree of extensiveness of the spatial lexicon (N of tokens for 6 spatial categories during cycle 1).

	local verbs	direct. verbs	local adverbs	direct. adverbs	local preps	direct. preps	N tokens
Ergün	94	154	133	14	58	99	552
Mahmut	45	37	132	24	54	68	360
Fatima	36	49	34	3	38	55	225
Mohamed	56	112	71	18	65	66	388

Table 24. Degree of variation of the spatial lexicon (N of types for 6 spatial categories during cycle 1).

	local verbs	direct. verbs	local adverbs	direct. adverbs	local preps	direct. preps	N tokens
Ergün	5	5	8	7	4	3	32
Mahmut	4	4	16	9	4	3	40
Fatima	4	2	3	3	3	6	21
Mohamed	5	4	3	10	8	7	37

The position of Ergün and Mahmut within Tables 23 and 24 makes it clear that an *extended* lexicon need not coincide with a *varied* lexicon.

We have found evidence for zero-marking of spatial entities in the domains of spatial verbs (implied local/directional verbs), spatial adverbs (unmarked directional adverbs) and spatial PPs (unmarked local/directional PPs). In all cases, the same *principle of redundancy avoidance* (Perdue 1982: 188) applies. Given their limited resources, learners construe their utterances as economically as possible: information which can be derived from situational context or can be assumed to be available for some other reason is not made explicit and intended meaning is expressed by a minimal numbers of lexemes.

At the same time, we have found evidence for overgeneralization within the domains of spatial verbs, adverbs and PPs. In Perdue (1982: 189) this phenomenon is referred to as the principle of *semantic generalization*.
Initially, the learner's lexicon is sparse. To fill the gaps, he takes related lexical items and neglects some of their semantic features. He may be fully aware of the fact that the item in question is not fully appropriate, but it may also be that he does not have the full target language meaning.

In the domain of spatial prepositions underrepresentation of lexical items has also been observed. This co-occurrence of overgeneralization and underrepresentation may be traced back to the learner's uncertainty about the specific meaning of prepositions in the target language. In order to cope with this uncertainty and avoid errors, the learner seems to vary his choice out of a restricted set of alternative forms. A crucial question is whether this co-occurrence of overgeneralization and underrepresentation is more typical for L2 acquisition by adult learners than for L2/L1 acquisition by children.

With respect to spatial verbs, it looks most worthwhile to explore more thoroughly the utilization of particular *contrasts* of directional subclasses (see also Perdue 1982: 190-191). Especially the following source/target oriented pairs should be taken into account: *gaan/komen* (go/come), *geven/krijgen* (give/get) and *brengen/halen* (bring/take).

With respect to *order* of acquisition, we have found some evidence for similar phenomena within the processes of L1 acquisition by children and L2 acquisition by adults (e.g. the "primary" use of *come* vs. *go, here* vs. *there,* or the primary use of the local preposition *in*). Such similarities in order of L1/L2 acquisition are striking. Their explanation is less obvious, however. Whereas linguistic and cognitive development go hand in hand within the process of L1 acquisition, the same cannot be said for L2 acquisition by adults. Hence, the explanation of striking L1/L2 order similarities cannot unquestionable be derived from the vast literature on L1 acquisition.

The computer has been and will be a valuable tool in the processes of coding, selecting and analyzing data. The procedures applied are based upon the point of view that the researcher is an indispensable link between the raw transcripts of any session and the creation of a particular data base. Inspection, interpretation and coding of the raw transcripts are especially needed in the following two cases:

- *zero-marking* of spatial entities (as our analysis has shown, this is an important device in initial learner language);
- *direct imitations* of native speaker's utterances (which should be distinguished from spontaneous second language use).

In the Introduction we mentioned two purposes of this report:

- to describe procedures that can be used for analyzing spontaneous L2 data referring to space in a longitudinal perspective;
- to present and discuss first results, taken from selected informants and data.

Our analysis of spatial reference will be expanded to all longitudinal informants (4 Turks, 4 Moroccans) and to additional data (spontaneous and experimental data, taken from all cycles).

Appendix 1. Dutch/English word list of realized/intended spatial expressions in L2 Dutch

---

VERBS		ADVERBS	
blijven	stay	achter	behind
gaan	go	achterin	at the back
geweest zijn	have been	achteraan	(to be) at the back
komen	come	achterna	(to go) after
liggen	lie	achterom	(to go) round the back
logeren	stay with		
lopen	walk	achterop	(to ride) on the back
overstappen	change (trains)		
rennen	run	achteruit	backwards
rijden	ride	beneden	below
staan	stand	binnen	inside
stoppen	stop	boven	above
thuisblijven	stay at home	buiten	outside
uitgaan	go out	daar	there
verblijven	stay at	daarbij	near it
vertrekken	leave	daarheen	thither
wandelen	walk	door	through
wonen	live (in a house)	doorheen	through
zitten	sit	erin	in it
zijn	be	ernaast	next to it
		hier	here
		hierheen	hither
PREPOSITIONS		hiernaast	next to this
		huis	at home
achter	behind	in	in
achter...aan	(to go) after	links	left
achter...om	round the back of	linksaf	to the left
bij	by/with	*metachter	with + behind
binnen	inside	naast	beside
buiten	outside	onder	under
door...heen	through	rechts	right
in	in	rechtsaf	to the right
met	with	rechtdoor	straight on
*metachter	with + behind	terug	back
naar	to	thuis	at home
*naarmet	to + with	voor	in front
*naarvan	to + of	voorin	in front
naast	next to	vooruit	forward
onder	under	weg	away
op	on		
tussen	between		
uit	out		
van	of		
voor	in front of	* = morphological innovation
**andna	=A= at	** =A= Arabic
**fe	=A= in	

Appendix 2. Computerized records of Ergün (1-38).

	1	2	3	4	5	6	7	8	9	10	11	12
1	1	1	1	1	060	1	4	40	gaan		Edah	naar de Edah
2	1	1	1	1	069	1	4	40	gaan		Eindhoven…'s Hertogenbosch	naar E. … naar 's Hertogenbosch
3	1	1	1	1	069	2	4	50	gaan		weg	
4	1	1	1	1	192	1	2	20	blijven	wonen	Duitsland	in Duitsland
5	1	1	1	1	194	1	3	40			Nederlands	naar Nederland
6	1	1	1	1	208	1	2	10	blijven	wonen	hier	
7	1	1	1	1	222	1	1	20			Turkije	in Turkije
8	1	1	1	1	222	1	4	20	komen		hier	
9	1	1	1	1	240	1	4	40	rijden		Turkije	naar Turkije
10	1	1	1	1	242	1	4	00	komen			
11	1	1	1	1	270	2	4	20	komen		vader en moeder	bij vader en moeder
12	1	1	1	1	272	1	4	42	rijden		huis …. Tilburg	naar huis …./in Tilburg
13	1	1	1	1	289	2	4	00	komen			
14	1	1	1	1	302	2	4	00	komen			
15	1	1	1	1	317	1	3	50			weg	
16	1	1	2	1	016	2	4	40	gaan		naar Turkije	
17	1	1	2	1	028	2	1	00				
18	1	1	2	1	044	1	3	40			huis	naar huis
19	1	1	2	1	048	1	4	50	komen		terug	

Appendix 2 continued. Computerized records of Ergün (1-38).

	1	2	3	4	5	6	7	8	9	10	11	12
20	1	1	2	1	050	1	4	40	gaan		discotheek .... naar	naar de discotheek
21	1	1	2	1	062	1	2	10	blijven		daar	naar huis
22	1	1	2	1	064	1	3	40			huis	
23	1	1	2	1	068	0	2	00	zitten			
24	1	1	2	1	090	1	3	40			discotheek	naar de discotheek
25	1	1	2	1	118	1	1	50			weg	uit
26	1	1	2	1	136	1	4	40	gaan		Beekse Bergen .... naar	naar de Beekse Bergen
27	1	1	2	1	138	1	4	40	gaan	uitgaan		
28	1	1	2	1	140	1	3	40			naar die show	
29	1	1	2	1	150	2	4	40	gaan		naar die andere kant	
30	1	1	2	1	182	1	3	50			weg	
31	1	1	2	1	194	0	0	20			Tilburg buiten	buiten Tilburg
32	1	1	2	1	194	1	3	40			Hilvarenbeek	naar Hilvarenbeek
33	1	1	2	1	196	1	3	40			die kant toe	die kant op
34	1	1	2	1	224	2	4	40	gaan		Beekse Bergen .... naar	naar de Beekse Bergen
35	1	1	2	1	230	2	3	50			weg	
36	1	1	3	1	203	2	4	50	gaan		weg	
37	1	1	3	1	205	1	4	40	gaan		Rotterdam .... naar	naar Rotterdam
38	1	1	3	1	206	1	2	10	blijven		daar	

etc.

Appendix 3. Linguistic insecurity test (positional items plus results).

Item nr	Stimulus	Correct verb	ER	MA	FA	MO
01	de bal *is* op de grond (the ball is on the ground)	L	Z	Z	S	S
06	de boot *is* in het water (the boat is in the water)	L	*L*	Z	S	S
11	het kleed *is* op tafel (the cover is on the table)	L	S	Z	Z	*L*
16	het papier *is* op de grond (the paper is on the ground)	L	Z	Z	*L*	*L*
21	de vijver *is* voor het huis (the pond is in front of the house)	L	*L*	Z	*L*	S
26	die straat *is* in het centrum (that street is in the center)	L	S	*L*	*L*	*L*
02	het boek *is* in de kast (the book is in the cupboard)	S	*S*	Z	Z	*S*
04	het bord *is* op tafel (the plate is on the table)	S	Z	Z	Z	L
07	de klok *is* stil (the clock has stopped)	S	Z	Z	*S*	*S*
09	het water *is* op (the kettle is on)	S	L	Z	L	*S*
12	het nummer *is* op de telefoon (the number is on the phone)	S	L	Z	*S*	*S*
14	mijn geld *is* op de bank (my money is in the bank)	S	*S*	Z	*S*	Z
17	de auto *is* in de garage) (the car is in the garage)	S	*S*	Z	L	L
19	de deur *is* open (the door is open)	S	Z	Z	L	*S*
22	de motor van de auto *is* aan (the motor of the car is on)	S	Z	?	*S*	L
24	het stoplicht *is* op groen (the light is green)	S	L	Z	L	*S*
27	er *is* een foto in de krant (there is a picture in the paper)	S	L	Z	*S*	L
29	er *is* een tekening op het papier (there is a drawing on the paper)	S	*S*	Z	Z	L
03	de vogel *is* op de tak (the bird is on the bough)	Z	L	*Z*	*Z*	L
05	het geld *is* in de beurs (the money is in the purse)	Z	L	*Z*	*Z*	*Z*
08	die jongen *is* in de gevangenis (that boy is in jail)	Z	S	S	L	L
10	het ijs *is* in het glas (the ice is in the glass)	Z	*Z*	*Z*	*Z*	L

Appendix 3 continued. Linguistic insecurity test (positional items plus results).

Item nr	Stimulus	Correct verb	ER	MA	FA	MO
13	de riem *is* vast (the belt is fastened)	Z	Z	Z	L	L
15	de broek *is* vol vlekken (the trousers are full of spots)	Z	L	Z	L	L
18	er *is* zout op de aardappelen (there is salt on the potatoes)	Z	L	Z	S	Z
20	er *is* jam op het brood (there is jam on the bread)	Z	S	Z	S	L
23	er *is* suiker in de thee (there is sugar in the tea)	Z	S	Z	Z	Z
25	de bel *is* naast de deur (the bell is next to the door)	Z	Z	Z	S	Z
28	de deur *is* dicht (the door is closed)	Z	Z	Z	L	S
30	mijn haar *is* goed (my hair is allright)	Z	L	Z	L	S
N correctly executed tasks			10	12	12	13

L = ligt, S = staat, Z = zit

Appendix 4. The money game.

Item nr	verbal prompt	ER	MA	FA	MO
01	Leg een stuiver op het papier (Put a stiver on the paper)	+	+	+	+
02	Leg de stuiver midden op het papier (Put the stiver on the middle of the paper)	–	–	–	–
03	Leg de stuiver bovenaan op het papier (Put the stiver at the top of the paper)	–	–	–	–
04	Leg de stuiver onderaan op het papier (Put the stiver at the bottom of the paper)	–	–	–	–
05	Leg de stuiver rechts op het papier) (Put the stiver on the right of the paper)	–	–	–	–
06	Leg de stuiver links op het papier (Put the stiver on the left of the paper)	–	–	–	+
07	Leg de stuiver links bovenaan op het papier (Put the stiver on the upper left of the paper)	–	–	–	–
08	Leg de stuiver rechts bovenaan op het papier (Put the stiver on the upper right of the paper)	–	–	–	–
09	Leg de stuiver links onderaan op het papier (Put the stiver on the bottom left of the paper)	–	–	–	–
10	Leg de stuiver rechts onderaan op het papier (Put the stiver on the bottom right of the paper)	–	–	–	–
11	Leg de gulden naast de stuiver (Put the guilder next to the stiver)	+	–	–	+
12	Leg de gulden rechts naast de stuiver (Put the guilder on the right of the stiver)	–	–	–	+
13	Leg de gulden links naast de stuiver (Put the guilder on the left of the stiver)	–	–	–	+
14	Leg de gulden bovenop de stuiver (Put the guilder on top of the stiver)	+	+	+	+
15	Leg de gulden onder de stuiver (Put the guilder under the stiver)	–	+	–	+
16	Leg alle geld op een rij (Put all the money in a row)	–	–	–	–
17	Leg de gulden tussen de twee stuivers (Put the guilder between the two stivers)	–	–	–	+
18	Draai de gulden andersom (Put the guilder the other way round)	+	–	–	–
19	Pak de gulden van het papier af (Take the guilder from the paper)	–	+	–	+
20	Leg de gulden vóór de bus (Put the guilder in front of the bus)	+	+	–	–
21	Leg de gulden achter de bus (Put the guilder behind the bus)	+	+	+	–
22	Leg de gulden in de bus (Put the guilder in the bus)	+	+	–	+
23	Leg de gulden bovenop de bus (Put the guilder on top of the bus)	+	+	+	+
24	Leg de gulden onder de bus (Put the guilder under the bus)	+	+	–	+
N correctly understood instructions (+)		9	9	4	12

References

ACOM (Adviescommissie Onderzoek Minderheden) (1984), *Overzicht van lopend onderzoek naar de positie van etnische minderheden in de Nederlandse samenleving.* (Vademecumreeks 4). Leiden.

Adams, M. (1978). Methodology for examining second language acquisition. In: E. Hatch (ed.), *Second Language Acquisition.* A book of readings. Rowley, Mass., 277-296.

Akinnaso, F. (1982), On the differences between spoken and written language. In: *Language and Speech* 25 (2), 97-125.

Alderson, J. (1983), The cloze procedure and proficiency in English as a foreign language. In: J. Oller (ed.), *Issues in language testing research.* Rowley, Mass., 205-217.

Andersen, R. (1978), An Implicational Model for Second Language Research. In: *Language Learning* 28, 221-283.

Appel, R. (1984), *Immigrant children learning Dutch.* Sociolinguistic and psycholinguistic aspects of second-language acquisition. Dordrecht.

Augst, G., A. Bauer & A. Stein (1977), *Grundwortschatz und Idiolekt.* Empirische Untersuchungen zur semantischen und lexikalischen Struktur des kindlichen Wortschatzes. Tübingen.

Bakker, J. et al. (1983),*Interactie tussen Nederlandse en Turkse kinderen. Amsterdam.*

Baten, L. (1981), *Text comprehension*: The Parameters of Difficulty in Narrative and Expository Prose Texts: A Redefinition of Readability, Urbana, Ill.

Baten, L. et al. (1984), *A methodology for rendering conscious the reading process in foreign language*: can the computer serve as a teaching aid? Paper AILA-Congres Brussels 1984.

Bereiter, C. & S. Engelmann (1966), *Teaching disadvantaged children in the Preschool.* Englewood Cliffs, N.J.

Bernstein, B. (1959), A public language: some sociological implications of a linguistic form. In: *British Journal of Sociology* 10, 311-326. Also in B. Bernstein (ed.) (1971). 42-60.

Bernstein, B. (1962), Social class, linguistic codes and grammatical elements. In: *Language and Speech* 5, 221-240. Also in B. Bernstein (ed.) (1971), 95-117.

Bernstein, B. (ed.) (1971), *Class, codes and control*: Vol 1. London.

Bernstein, B. (1971), A critique of the concept of compensatory education. In: B. Bernstein (ed.) *Class, codes and control*: Vol 1. London, 190-201.

Bernstein, B. (ed.) (1973), *Class, codes and control*: Vol 2. London/Boston.

Bleichroth, N. et al. (1984), *Revisie van de Amsterdamse Kinder Intelligentie Test*: instructie, normen en enkele psychometrische gegevens. Lisse.

Bol, E. (1980), Leren lezen en kognitieve ontwikkeling. In: *Tijdschrift voor Taalbeheersing* 2 (3), 220-231.

Bon, W. van (1982), *Taaltests voor kinderen*: handleiding. Lisse.

Borel-Maisonny, S. (1960), *Langage oral et écrit.* Neuchâtel.

Bormuth, J. et al. (1970), Children's comprehension of between- and within- sentence syntactic structures. In: *Journal of Educational Psychology* 61, 349-357.

Bouwmeester, G. (1979), *De Internationale Schakelklas*: een brug tot integratie van buitenlandse leerlingen in het Nederlandse Voortgezet Onderwijs. Amsterdam.

Bowen, J. (1978), The identification of irrelevant lexical distraction; an editing-task. In: *TESL Reporter* 12, 1-3.

Brière, E. (1973), Cross-cultural biases in language testing. In: J. Oller & J. Richards (eds.), *Focus on the learner.* Rowley, Mass., 214-227.

Bruni, D., *Complesso per l'esame dello sviluppo psicolinguistico in età evolutiva* (CESPEE). Padova.

Buster, A. (1981), *Onderwijs Nederlands als tweede taal voor Turkse en Marokkaanse leerlingen.* Herziene subsidie aanvraag SVO-project 0587. Nijmegen.

Buster, A., A. Janssen-van Dieten & K. de Bot (1984), *Eindverslag SVO-project 0587.* Nijmegen.

Cancino, H., E. Rosansky & J. Schumann (1978), The acquisition of English negatives and interrogatives by native Spanish speakers. In: E. Hatch (ed.) *Second Language Acquisition.* A Book of Readings. Rowley, Mass., 207-231.

Carr, T. (1981), Building theories of reading ability: On the relation between individual differences in cognitive skills and reading comprehension. In: *Cognition* 9, 73-114.

Carrell, P. (1977), Empirical investigations of indirectly conveyed meaning: assertion versus presupposition in first and second language acquisition. In: *Language Learning* 27 (2), 353-369.

Carroll, J. (1979), What does the Pennsylvania foreign language research project tell us? In: *Foreign Language Annals* 3 (2), 214-236.

CBS (1984), *Leerlingen en studenten van buitenlandse nationaliteit in het schooljaar 1982/'83* (incl. enige gegevens m.b.t. culturele minderheden) (Mededelingen 7814). Voorburg/Heerlen.

CBS (1984), *Leerlingen met buitenlandse nationaliteit bij het kleuteronderwijs, het gewoon lager onderwijs en het buitengewoon lager onderwijs in het schooljaar 1982/1983* (Mededelingen 7809). Voorburg/Heerlen.

CBS (1984), *Statistisch zakboek 1984.* Den Haag.

Chafe, W. (1974), Giveness, contrastiveness, definiteness, subject, topic and point of view. In: C. Li (ed.) (1976), *Speaker and topic.* New York, 25-56.

Clark, E. (1978), From gesture to word: on the natural history of deixis in language acquisition. In: J. Bruner & A. Garton (eds.), *Human growth and development.* Oxford, 85-120.

Clark, E. & O. Garnica (1974), Is he coming or going? On the acquisition of deictic verbs. In: *Journal of Verbal Learning and Verbal Behavior* 13, 559-572.

Cohen, A. (ed.) (1974), *Urban etnicity.* London.

Collins, J. & S. Michaels (1980), The importance of conversational strategies in the acquisition of literacy. In: *Proceedings of the 6th Annual Meeting of the Berkeley Linguistics Society,* 143-156.

Connor, U. (1981), The application of reading miscue analysis to diagnosis of English as a second language learners' reading skills. In: C. Twyford, W. Diehl & K. Feathers (eds.), *Reading English as a second language*: moving from theory. Indiana University, 47-55.

Connor, U. (1983), Predictors of second language reading performance. In: *Journal of Multilingual and Multicultural Development* 4 (4), 271-288.

Cook-Gumperz, J. & J. Gumperz (1981), From oral to written culture: the transition to literacy. In: N. Whitehead (ed.), *Writing: the nature, development and teaching of written communication.* Vol 1: Variation in writing: Functional and linguistic-cultural differences. Hillsdale, N.J., 89-109.

Cummins, J. (1978), Educational implications of mothertongue maintenance in minority language groups. In: *The Canadian Modern Language Review* 34 (5), 395-416.

Cummins, J. (1979), Linguistic Interdependence and the Educational Development of Bilingual Children. In: *Review of Educational Research* 49 (2), 221-251.

Cummins, J. (1980), The language and culture issue in the education of minority language children. In: *Interchange* 10, 72-88.

Cummins, J. (1980), The cross-lingual dimensions of language proficiency: Implications for immigrant language learning and bilingual education. In: *TESOL Quarterly* 14 (2), 175-187.

Cummins, J. (1981), *The role of primary language development in promoting educational success for language minority students.* Paper Ontario Institute for Studies in Education.

Cummins, J. (1982), *Interdependence and bicultural ambivalence*: regarding the pedagogical rational for bilingual education. Rosslyn, Va.

Curfs, J. et al. (1980), *Nederlands van Turkse kinderen,* een meervoudige case-studie naar syntactische differentiatie. Nijmegen.

Cziko, G. (1978), Differences in first and second language reading: The use of syntactic, semantic and discourse constraints. In: *The Canadian Modern Language Review* 34, 473-489.

Cziko, G. (1980), Language competence and reading strategies: a comparison of first and second language oral reading errors. In: *Language Learning* 30, 101-116.

Damme, L. van (1982), Bessells kringgesprek. In: *Pedagogisch Tijdschrift* 7 (2), 72-76.

Davies, A. (1975), Two tests of speeded reading. In: R. Jones & B. Spolsky (eds.), *Testing language proficiency.* Arlington, Va. 119-130.

Day, R. (1983), Children's attitudes towards language. In: E. Bouchard-Ryan & H. Giles (eds.), *Attitudes towards language variation.* London, 116-131.

Dervillez-Bastuji, J. (1982), *Structure des relations spatiales dans quelques langages naturelles*: introduction à une théorie sémantique. Genève/Paris.

Descoeudres, A. (1948), *Education des enfants arrières.* Application à tous les enfants. Paris.

Despres, L. (ed.) (1975), *Ethnicity and resource competition in plural societies.* The Hague.

Dijk, T. van (1983), *Minderheden in de Media.* Een analyse van de berichtgeving over etnische minderheden in de dagbladpers. Amsterdam.

Dore, J. (1975), Holophrases, speech acts and language universals. In: *Journal of Child Language* 2, 21-40.

Dulay, H. & M. Burt (1974). Natural Sequences in Child Language Acquisition. In: *Language Learning* 24, 37-54.

Dulay, H. & M. Burt (1974), A New Perspective in the Creative Construction Process in Child Second Language Acquisition. In: *Language Learning* 24, 253-278.

Edwards, A. (1976), *Language in culture and class.* London.

Ekstrand, L. (1984), *Scaling and measuring foreign language teaching techniques.* Paper AILA-congres Brussels.

Ellemers, J. & J. Vermeulen (1980), Geselecteerde bibliografie van sociaal-wetenschappelijke publicaties over etnische minderheden in Nederland. In: *Intermediair* 1/2.

Els, T. van et al. (1984), *Applied Linguistics and the Learning and Teaching of Foreign Languages.* London.

Epstein, A. (1978), *Ethos and identity*. London.

Esch, W. van (1982), *Etnische groepen en het onderwijs*; een verkennende studie. Harlingen.

Esch, W. van (1983), *Toetsprestaties en doorstroomadviezen van allochtone leerlingen in de zesde klas van lagere scholen*. Nijmegen.

Extra, G. (1978), *Eerste- en tweede-taalverwerving*. De ontwikkeling van morfologische vaardigheden. Muiderberg.

Extra, G. (1982), Nederlands en toch geen moedertaal. In: *Tilburg Studies in Language and Literature* 3, 35-61.

Extra, G. & M. Mittner (eds.) (1984), *Studies in second language acquisition by adult immigrants*. (Tilburg Studies in Language and Literature 6) Tilburg.

Extra, G. & A. Vermeer (1984), Minderheidstalen in het basisonderwijs. In: W. van Peer & A. Verhagen (eds.), *Forces in European Mother Tongue Education*. Tilburg, 197-219.

Farhady, H. (1979), The disjunctive fallacy between discrete-point and integrative tests. In: *TESOL Quarterly* 13, 347-358.

Farhady, H. (1983), New directions for ESL proficiency testing. In: J. Oller (ed.), *Issues in language testing research*. Rowley, Mass., 253-269.

Felix, S. (1977), Repetitive order of acquisition in child language. In: *Lingua* 41, 25-52.

Felix, S. (1978), *Linguistische Untersuchungen zum natürlichen Zweitsprachenerwerb*. München.

Felix, S. (1981), The effect of formal instruction on second language acquisition. In: *Language Learning* 31, 87-112.

Ferguson, Ch. (1971), *Language Structure and Language Use*. Stanford.

Ferguson, G. (1981), *Statistical Analysis in Psychology and Education*. New York.

Foyer-stuurgroep: Bicultureel (eds.) (1983), Twee jaar Foyer-Bicultureel te Brussel. Een Evaluatie-rapport. Brussel.

Fraser, C., U. Bellugi & R. Brown (1963), Control of grammar in imitation, comprehension and production. In: *Journal of Verbal Learning and Verbal Behaviour* 21, 121-135.

French, P. (1981), Processing strategies in language and reading. In: P. Dale & D. Ingram (eds.), *Child language: an international perspective*. Baltimore, 287-291.

Gardner, R. & W. Lambert (1972), *Attitudes and motivation in second-language learning*. Rowley, Mass.

Garnica, O. & R. Herbert (1979), Some phonological errors in second language learning: interference doesn't tell it all. In: *International Journal of Psycholinguistics* 14, 5-19.

Geert, P. van (1975), *Grammaticale Analyse Test: Experimentele versie*. Groningen.

Geerts, G. (1978), Sociolinguïstische variatie en lexicon. In: B. Al & P. van Sterkenburg (eds.), *Wetenschap en woordenschat*. Muiderberg, 59-72.

Geerts, G. et al. (1984), *Algemene Nederlandse Spraakkunst*. Groningen.

Genesee, F. & E. Hamayan (1980), Individual differences in second-language learning. In: *Applied Psycholinguistics* 1, 95-110.

Glazer, N. & D. Moynihan (eds.) (1983), *Beyond the melting pot*. Cambridge, Mass.

Golinkoff, R. (1975), *A comparison of reading comprehension processes in good and poor comprehenders*. Pittsburgh.

Goodman, K. (1970), Behind the eye; what happens in reading. In: K. Goodman & O. Niles (eds.), *Reading process and program*. Urbana Ill., 3-38.

Goodman, K. & Y. Goodman (1978), *Reading of American children whose language is a stable rural dialect or a language other than English*. ERIC ED 173-754.

Graetz, N. & E. Kozminsky (1984), *Summarizing first and second language texts*. Paper AILA-Congres Brussels 1984.

Gray, T., H. Convery & K. Fox (1981), *The current status of bilingual education legislation.* (Bilingual Education Series 9). Washington, D.C.

Greene, J. & P. Zirkel (1973), *The validation of an instrument to assess attitudes toward the Puerto Rican, Black-American and Anglo-American cultures.* Microfiche ED 093970.

Grice, H. (1975), Logic and conversation. In: P. Cole & J. Morgan (eds.), *Syntax and Semantics 3: Speech acts.* New York/London, 41-58.

Guiora, A. (1984), The dialectic of language acquisition. In: *Language Learning* 33 (5), 3-12.

Gumperz, J. (1982), *Discourse strategies.* (Studies in interactional sociolinguistics 1). Cambridge.

Haddad, F. (1981), First language illiteracy – second language reading: A case study. In: S. Lopez (ed.), *Learning to read in different languages.* Washington, D.C., 32-44.

Hagen, A. (1981), *Standaardtaal en dialectsprekende kinderen.* Muiderberg.

Hagen, T. (1984), Monitoring en taalbeschouwing. In: H. Lammers, L. Lentz & H. van Tuyl (eds.), *Taalbeschouwing ter discussie.* Enschede, 88-94.

Hakuta, K. (1973), *Some aspects of the development of a second language.* Harvard Univ. (unpublished).

Halliday, M. & R. Hasan (1976), *Cohesion in English.* London.

Harrell, R. (1962), *A short reference grammar of Moroccan-Arabic.* Washington.

Hatch, E., (1974), Research on reading a second language. In: *Journal of Reading Behavior* 6, 53-61.

Hatch, E. (ed.) (1978), *Second language acquisition.* A book of readings. Rowley Mass.

Hauptman, Ph. (1971), A structural approach vs. a situational approach to foreign-language teaching. In: *Language Learning* 21 (2), 235-244.

Hawkins, P. (1973), Social class, the nominal group and reference. In: B. Bernstein (ed.), *Class, codes and control:* Vol 2. London/Boston, 81-92.

Heidelberger Forschungsprojekt "Pidgin-Deutsch" (1978), *Zur Erlernung des Deutschen durch ausländische Arbeiter*: Wortstellung und ausgewählte, lexikalisch-semantische Aspekte. (Arbeitsbericht IV) Heidelberg.

Heller, K. et al. (eds.) (1982), *Placing children in special education*: a strategy for equity. Washington, D.C.

Hinofotis, F. (1980), Cloze as an Alternative Method of ESL Placement and Proficiency Testing. In: J. Oller & L. Perkins (eds.), *Research in Language Testing.* Rowley, Mass., 121-128.

Huls, E. (1982), *Taalgebruik in het gezin en sociale ongelijkheid.* Een interactioneel sociolinguïstisch onderzoek. Ooy/Nijmegen.

Ierland, M. van (1979), Tussen 4 en 8: ontwikkelingen in taalgebruik. In: *Toegepaste Taalwetenschap in Artikelen* 7, 85-101.

Jansen, B., J. Lalleman & P. Muysken (1981), The alternation hypothesis of Dutch word order by Turkish and Moroccan foreign workers. In: *Language Learning* 31, 315-336.

Jansen, F. (1981), *Syntactische constructies in gesproken taal.* Amsterdam.

Janssen-van Dieten, A. & T. Van der Linden (1983), *Instaptoets Anderstaligen.* Onderzoek naar de niveau-indicator. (Specialistisch Bulletin CITO nr. 23). Arnhem.

Jarvella, R. & W. Klein (eds.) (1982), *Speech, place and action*: studies in deixis and related topics. Chicester, N.Y.

Jennrich, R. & P. Sampson (1981), P7M Stepwise discriminant analysis. In: W. Dixon (ed.), *BMDP Statistical software 1981.* Berkeley, Cal.

Johnson, P. (1981), Effects on Reading Comprehension of Language Complexity and Cultural Background of a Text. In: *TESOL Quarterly* 15 (2), 169-181.

Katz, J. (1979), Foreigner-talk Input in Child Second Language Acquisition: its Form and Function over time. In: C. Henning (ed.), *Proceedings of the Los Angeles Second Language Research Forum.* Los Angeles, 61-75.

Klein-Braley, Chr. (1983), A cloze is a cloze is a question. In: J. Oller (ed.), *Issues in language testing research.* Rowley, Mass., 218-228.

Kohnstamm, G. et al. (1971), *Utrechtse Taalniveautest* (UTANT). Lisse.

Kohnstamm, G. et al. (1981), *Nieuwe streeflijst woordenschat voor 6-jarigen.* Lisse.

Kok, W., C. Boonman & G. Beukhof (1980), Studievaardigheden voor de basisschool: Leren omgaan met teksten (I). In: *Pedagogische Studiën* 57, 417-432.

Kool, C. & C. van Praag (1982), *Bevolkingsprognose allochtonen in Nederland.* Deel 2: Surinamers en Antillianen. Rijswijk (SCP-cahier 28).

Kroon, S., T. Vallen & S. Stijnen (1982), Intelligentie-controle in sociolinguïstisch onderzoek; Een discussie-aanzet. In: P. v.d. Craen & R. Willemyns (eds.), *Sociolinguïstiek en Ideologie.* Brussel, 263-282.

Kusters, T. & H. Bonset (1980), Vaktaal op school: Een literatuuronderzoek met konsekwenties. In: *Toegepaste Taalwetenschap in artikelen* 8, 231-245.

Laberge, D. & S. Samuels (1974), Toward a theory of automatic information processing in reading. In: *Cognitive Psychology* 6, 293-323.

Labov, W. (1969), The logic of Nonstandard English. In: J. Alatis (ed.), *Report of the 20th annual round table meeting on linguistics and language studies.* (Monograph Series on Language and Linguistics, Vol. 22). Washington, D.C., 1-43.

Lalleman, J. (1983), The relationship between formal and content properties of speech differences between first and second language learners. In: S. Dik (ed.), *Advances in Functional Grammar.* Dordrecht, 343-366.

Lapkin, S. & M. Swain (1977), The Use of English and French cloze tests in a bilingual education program evaluation: validity and error analysis. In: *Language Learning* 27 (2), 279-314.

Leemann, E.M. (1981). Evaluating Language Assessment Tests, some practical considerations. In: J. Erickson & D. Omark (eds.), *Communication Assessment of the Bilingual Bicultural Child.* Baltimore, 115-128.

Leijenhorst, G. van (1983), *Notitie Onderwijs in de Eigen Taal en Cultuur.* Den Haag.

Leman, J. (1979), La deuxième génération des travailleurs migrants: fragmentés et non destructurés. In: *Recherches Sociologiques* 10 (2), 247-270.

Leman, J. (1980), La seconde génération: deux migrations et une seule vie. In: *La Revue Nouvelle* 9, 213-217.

Leman, J. (1982), *Van Caltanissetta naar Brussel en Genk.* Leuven.

Lesgold, A. (1974), Variability in children's comprehension of syntactic structures. In: *Journal of Educational Psychology* 66, 333-338.

Levelt, W. & G. Kempen (1976), Taal. In: J. Michon, E. Eykman & L. de Klerk (eds.), *Handboek der psychonomie.* Deventer, 492-523.

Levelt, W., R. Schreuder & E. Hoenkamp (1977), Structure and the use of verbs of motion. In: R. Campbell & P. Smith (eds.), *Proceedings of the psychology of language conference.* New York, 137-162.

Levin, L. (1972), *Comparative studies in foreign-language teaching.* Stockholm.

Lewis, S. (1967), *Turkish grammar.* Oxford (reprinted edition 1975).

Lyons, J. (1968), *Introduction to theoretical linguistics.* Cambridge.

Lyons, J. (1977), *Semantics.* Cambridge.

MacNamara, J., E. Baker & C. Olson (1976), Four-year-old's understanding of pretend, forget and know: Evidence for propositional operations. In: *Child Development* 47, 62-70.

Matluck, J. & B. Mace-Matluck (1977), *The MAT-SEA-CAL instruments for assessing language proficiency.* ED 129 877.

Matluck, J. & W. Tummer (1979), *The relationship of oral language proficiency to reading achievement.* Paper presented at the 8th Annual International Bilingual-Bicultural Education Conference Seattle.

McKay, J. & F. Lewins (1978), Ethnicity and the ethnic group: a conceptual analysis and reformulation. In: *Ethnic and Racial Studies* 1 (4), 412-427.

McLaughlin, B. (1978), *Second Language Acquisition in Childhood.* Hillsdale, N.J.

Migchielsen, M. (1983), *Attitudes van Turkse en Marokkaanse ISK-leerlingen in relatie tot de taalvaardigheid en enkele persoonskenmerken.* M.A.-thesis Nijmegen.

Miller, G. & P. Johnson-Laird (1976), *Language and perception.* Cambridge, Mass.

Moerman-Coetsier, L. & F. van Besien (1982), *Taalonderzoek via analyse van gesproken taal*: dl. 1 (TOAST). Gent.

Molony, C. (1982), Errors in Moluccan vs. Dutch elementary school children's Dutch speech: do they diverge over time? In: R. Stuip & W. Zwanenburg (eds.), *Handelingen van het zeven en dertigste Nederlands Filologencongres.* Amsterdam/Maarssen, 107-111.

Mommers, M. & D. van Dongen (1984), Het voorspellen van lees- en spellingprestaties in het eerste leerjaar. In: *Pedagogische Studiën* 61 (41) 153-164.

Mullen, K. (1979), An alternative to the cloze test. In: C. Yorio, K. Perkins & J. Schachter (eds.), *On TESOL '79.* The Learner in Focus. Washington, 187-192.

Naiman, N. (1974), The use of elicited imitation in second language acquisition research. In: *Working papers on Bilingualism* 2, 1-37.

Nation, J. (1972), A Vocabulary Usage Test. In: *Journal of Psycholinguistic Research* 1 (3), 221-231.

Noordman, L. & W. Vonk (1981), Lezen: het begrijpen van tekst. In: *Nederlands Tijdschrift voor Psychologie* 36, 385-408.

Nunally, J. (1967), *Psychometric Theory.* New York.

O'Rourke, J. (1974), *Towards a science of Vocabulary development.* The Hague (Janua Linguarum Series Minor 183).

Ochs, E. (1979), Planned and unplanned discourse. In: T. Giron (ed.), *Discourse and Syntax/Syntax and Semantics 12.* New York, 51-80.

Oller J. et al. (1972), Cloze tests in English, Thai and Vietnamese: native and non-native performance. In: *Language Learning* 22 (1), 1-16.

Oller, J. (1979), *Language tests at school.* London.

Olson, D. (1977), From utterance to text: The bias of language in speech and writing. In: *Harvard Educational Review* 47, 257-281.

Olson, D. (1977), Oral and written language and the cognitive processes of children. In: *Journal of Communication* 27, 10-26.

Onderwijsverslag (1983), *Verslag van de staat van het onderwijs in Nederland over het jaar 1982.* Den Haag.

Paris, S. & B. Lindauer (1976), The role of inference in children's comprehension and memory for sentences. In: *Cognitive Psychology* 8, 217-227.

Penninx, R. (1984), Een bibliografie van publikaties over onderzoek minderheden, uitgevoerd in opdracht van of (mede) gesubsidieerd door de Rijksoverheid: 1978-1984. In: *Onderzoek Minderheden in opdracht van de Rijksoverheid.* Den Haag, 73-98.

Penninx, R. (1984), Naschrift Rinus Penninx (bij Van Praag 1984). In: *Intermediair* 20 (29/30), 43.

Penninx, R. (1984), *Onderzoek en onderzoeksbeleid m.b.t. migratie en etnische bevolkingsgroepen in Nederland: 1945-1984.* Paper presented at NSAV-Conference: Sociologendagen, 25/26 april 1984.

Perdue, C. (ed.) (1982), *Second language acquisition by adult immigrants*: a field manual. Strasbourg (also Rowley, Mass. 1984).

Perera, K. (1984), *Children's writing and reading*; analysing classroom language. Oxford.

Perfetti, C. & A. Lesgold (1979), Discourse comprehension and sources of individual differences. In: P. Just & P. Carpenter (eds.), *Cognitive processes in comprehension*. Hillsdale, N.J., 141-180.

Perfetti, C. & A. Lesgold (1979), Coding and comprehension in skilled reading and implications for reading instruction. In: L. Resnick & P. Weaver (eds.), *Theory and practice of early reading*. Hillsdale, N.J., 57-84.

Pfaff, C. (1981), Sociolinguistic problems of immigrants: foreign workers and their children in Germany. In: *Language in Society* 10, 155-188.

Pienemann, M. (1981), *Der Zweitsprachenerwerb ausländischer Arbeiterkinder*. Bonn.

Praag, C. van (1984), Regelmatige bijstelling minderhedenbeleid gewenst. In: *Intermediair* 20 (29/30), 39-43.

Praag, C. van & C. Kool (1982), *Bevolkingsprognose allochtonen in Nederland*. Turken en Marokkanen. Rijswijk (SCP-cahier 35; herziene versie).

Rauh, G. (ed.) (1983), *Essays on Deixis*. Tübingen.

Raven, J. (1938), *Progressive Matrices*. London.

Rex, J. (1973), *Race, colonialism and the city*. London.

Richards, M. (1976), Come and go reconsidered: children's use of deictic verbs in contrived situations. In: *Journal of Verbal Learning and Verbal Behavior* 15, 655-665.

Richek, M. (1976-1977), Reading comprehension of anaphoric forms in varying linguistic contexts. In: *Reading Research Quarterly* 12, 145-165.

Rigg, P. (1977), The miscue-ESL project. In: H. Brown, C. Yorio & R. Crymes (eds.), *On TESOL '77*. Washington, D.C., 106-118.

Romatowski, J. (1973), A psycholinguistic description of miscues generated by selected bilingual subjects during the oral reading of instructional reading material as presented in Polish readers and in English basal readers. In: *Dissertation Abstracts Intern.* 33, 6073A-6074A.

Roosens, E. (1979), *Cultuurverschillen en etnische identiteit*. Brussel.

Sachs, J. & J. Devin (1976), Young children's use of age-appropriate speech style in social interaction and role-playing. In: *Journal of Child Language* 3, 81-98.

Schakel (1984), Bulletin voor het voortgezet onderwijs in een multiculturele samenleving 5 (1983-1984), 13, 20-22.

Schakel (1985), Bulletin voor het voortgezet onderwijs in een multiculturele samenleving 6 (1984-1985), 15, 32-38.

Schröder, U. (1981), Sonderschüler und 'Schulversager'; statistische Daten aus den Jahren 1977–1979. In: *Zeitschrift fur Heilpädagogik* 12, 830-850.

Scribner, S. & M. Cole (1981), *The psychology of literacy*. Cambridge, Mass.

Sharp, R. (1980), *Knowledge, ideology and the politics of schooling*. London.

Skutnabb-Kangas, T. & P. Toukomaa (1976), *Teaching migrant children their mother tongue and learning the language of the host country in the context of the sociocultural situation of the migrant family*. Tampere.

Slembek, E. (1981), Über einem Fall graphonemisher Irritation beim Zweisprachenerwerb bei Türkischen Gastarbeiterkindern. In: P. Nelde et al. (eds.) *Sprachprobleme bei Gastarbeiterkindern*. Tübingen, 157-166.

Slobin, D. (1973), Cognitive prerequisites for the development of grammar. In: C. Ferguson & D. Slobin (eds.), *Studies of child language development*. New York, 173-208.

Slobin, D. (1973), Introduction to chapter on studies of Imitation and Comprehension. In: C. Ferguson & D. Slobin (eds.), *Studies of child language development.* New York, 462-465.

Smets, P. (1981), De school doet er wel toe! In: *Meso* 7, 26-29.

Smith, P. (1970), *A comparison of the cognitive and audiolingual approaches to foreign language instruction.* Philadelphia.

Snow, C. & M. Hoefnagel-Höhle (1978), Age differences in second language acquisition. In: E. Hatch (ed.), *Second Language Acquisition.* A book of readings. Rowley, Mass., 333-344.

Spiro, R. (1980), Constructive processes in prose comprehension and recall. In: R. Spiro, B. Bruce & W. Brewer (eds.), *Theoretical issues in reading comprehension.* Hillsdale, N.J., 245-278.

Stijnen, S. & T. Vallen (1981), *Dialect als onderwijsprobleem.* Den Haag.

Swain, M. (1981), Bilingual education for majority and minority language children. In: S. Svartvik (ed.), *AILA 1981,* proceedings II. Studia Linguistica 35 (1-2), 15-32.

Swain, M., G. Dumas & N. Naiman (1975), Alternatives to spontaneous speech: elicited translation and imitations as indicators of second language competence. In: *Working Papers on Bilingualism* 3, 68-79.

Talbott, B. (1976), *The relationship between oral proficiency and achievement in a bilingual-bicultural elementary school.* Ph. D. Dissertation, Mocow Idaho.

Talmy, L. (1983), How language structures space. In: H. Pick & L. Acredolo (eds.), *Spatial orientation:* theory, research and application. New York, 225-282.

Tannen, D. (1980), Spoken/written language and the oral/literate continuum. In: *Proceedings of the 6th annual Meeting of the Berkeley Linguistics Society.* Berkeley, Cal., 207-219.

Tanz, C. (1980), *Studies in the acquisition of deictic terms.* Cambridge.

Teitelbaum, H. & R. Miller (1977), The legal perspective. In: *Bilingual Education:* Current Perspectives. Vol. 3: Law. Washington, D.C., 1-64.

Terman, L. & M. Merrill, *Terman-Merrill Intelligence Scale.* Nijmegen.

Thonis, E. (1970), *Teaching reading to non-English speakers.* New York.

Thorndike, R. (1973), *Reading comprehension education in fifteen countries.* Stockholm.

Tomlinson, S. (1981), *Educational subnormality*; a study in decision-making. London.

Toorn, M. van den (1975), Over de semantische kenmerken van staan, liggen en zitten. In: *De Nieuwe Taalgids* 68, 1982, 458-464.

Trabasso, T., C. Riley & E. Wilson (1975), The representation of linear order and spatial strategies in reasoning: a developmental study. In: R. Falmagne (ed.), *Psychological studies of logic and its development.* Hillsdale, N.J.

Traugott, E. (1978). Expression of spatio-temporal relations in language. In: J. Greenberg (ed.), *Universals of Human Language.* Volume 3: Word-structure. Stanford, 369-400.

TTT (1983), Themanummer Taal en Minderheden. In: *Tijdschrift voor Taal- en Tekstwetenschap* 3 (2), 97-102.

Uit den Boogaart, P. (ed.) (1975), *Woordfrequenties in geschreven en gesproken Nederlands.* Utrecht.

Vallen, T. & A. Kerkhoff (1984), *Beheersing van het Nederlands en doorstroming lager onderwijs/voortgezet onderwijs bij kinderen uit etnische minderheidsgroepen.* Paper presented at VIOT-Conference Tilburg.

Verhoeven, L. (1984), *Structural and temporal aspects of Turkish children's reading Dutch as a second language.* (In this Volume).

Verhoeven, L. & G. Extra (1983), Turkish children's process of learning to read Dutch as a second language. In: *Interlanguage Studies Bulletin* 7, 37-53.

Verhoeven, L. & A. Vermeer (1985), *Variation in minority children's oral proficiency of Dutch.* (In this Volume).

Vermeer, A. (1981), Survey of Linguistic Minorities in Holland. In: A. Vermeer (ed.), *Language Problems of Minority Groups.* Tilburg, 111-113.

Vollmer, H. & F. Sang (1980), Zum psycholinguistischen Konstrukt einer internalisierten Erwartungsgrammatik. In: *Linguistik und Didaktik* 42, 122-148.

Von Elek, T. & M. Oskarsson (1975), *Comparative methods experiments in foreign language teaching*: the final report of the GUME-project. Mölndal.

Vos, G. de & A. Romanucci-Ross (eds.) (1975), *Ethnic identity.* Cultural continuities and change. Los Angeles.

Vygotsky, L. (1962), *Thought and language.* Cambridge, Mass.

Walkerdine, V. (1982), From context to text: A psycho-semiotic approach to abstract thought. In: M. Beveridge (ed.), *Children thinking through language.* London, 129-155.

Webber, B. (1980), Syntax beyond the sentence: anaphora. In: R. Spiro, B. Bruce & W. Brewer (eds.), *Theoretical issues in reading comprehension.* Hillsdale N.J., 141-164.

Weissenborn, J. (1981), L'acquisition des prépositions spatiales: problèmes cognitifs et linguistiques. In: C. Schwarze (ed.), *Analyse des prépositions.* IIIme Colloque Franco-Allemand de Linguistique Théorique. Tübingen, 251-285.

Weissenborn, J. & W. Klein (eds.) (1982), *Here and there*: Cross-linguistic studies on deixis and demonstration. Amsterdam/Philadelphia.

Wells, G. (1978), Talking with children: The complementary roles of parents and teachers. In: *English in education* 12 (2), 15-38.

Wells, G. (1981), Language, Literacy and education. In: G. Wells (ed.), *Learning through interaction.* Cambridge, 240-276.

Wentholt, H. (1982), *Massamedia en buitenlandse werknemers in Nederland.* Hilversum.

Werkgroep Begrijpelijkheidsonderzoek (1982), Leesbaarheidsformules: Een overzichtsartikel van de Werkgroep Begrijpelijkheidsonderzoek. In: *Tijdschrift voor massacommunicatie* 10, 115-123.

Werkgroep Van Dongen, *Waar mensen wonen* 3, klas 5. Zeist.

Westhoff, G. (1981), *Voorspellend lezen*; Een didaktische benadering van de leesvaardigheidstraining in het moderne vreemde-talenonderwijs. Groningen.

Wijk, I. van (1984), Samenvattingen van verslagen van interdepartementale onderzoeksprojecten met betrekking tot minderheden. In: *Onderzoek Minderheden in opdracht van de Rijksoverheid.* Den Haag, 7-71.

Wijnstra, J. (1977), Het gebruik van de Cloze procedure als maat voor schriftelijke taalbeheersing. In: *Tijdschrift voor onderwijsresearch* 6, 262-269.

Williams, F. (1970), Language, attitude and social change. In: F. Williams (ed.), *Language and poverty*: Perspectives on a Theme. New York, 380-397.

Wode, H. (1981), *Learning a second language.* I: An integrated view of language acquisition. Tübingen.

Wong-Filmore, L. (1976), *The second time around.* Cognitive and social strategies in second language acquisition (diss.). Stanford.

Wong-Fillmore, L. (1982), Language minority students and school participation: what kind of English is needed? In: *Journal of Education* 164 (2), 143-156.

Ysseldyke, J. et al. (1982), Similarities and differences between low achievers and students classified learning disabled. In: *Journal of Special Education* 16, 73-85.

Zirkel, P. & J. Greene (1974), *Cultural Attitude Scales Puerto Rican, Black-American and Anglo-American*; Technical Report. Microfiche ED 102196.

Zirkel, P. & J. Greene (1976), Cultural attitude Scales: a step toward determining whether the programs are bicultural as well as bilingual. In: A. Simoes (ed.), *The bilingual child.* New York, 3-16.

Zondervan, F., P. van Steen & G. Gunneweg (1976), De leesbaarheid van basisschool-teksten. Objectieve ordeningscriteria voor instructieve teksten. In: *De Nieuwe Taalgids* 69, 426-445.

ZWO-Beleidsnota (1985), *Beleidsnota inzake wetenschappelijk onderzoek in Nederland op het terrein van de etnische minderheden.* Den Haag.

List of Authors

Kees de Bot
Nijmegen University
Department of Applied Linguistics
P.O. Box 9103
6500 HD NIJMEGEN
The Netherlands

Peter Broeder
Tilburg University
Department of Language and Literature
P.O. Box 90153
5000 LE TILBURG
The Netherlands

Alex Buster
Nijmegen University
Institute of Applied Sociology
Graafseweg 274
6532 ZV NIJMEGEN
The Netherlands

Josée Coenen
Tilburg University
as Peter Broeder

Guus Extra
Tilburg University
as Peter Broeder

Cees Galema
Groningen University
Department of Linguistics
Grote Kruisstraat 2'
9712 TS GRONINGEN
The Netherlands

Hilde Hacquebord
Groningen University
as Cees Galema

Dorian de Haan
Utrecht University
Department of Developmental Psychology
Bijlhouwerstraat 6
3511 ZC UTRECHT
The Netherlands

Korrie van Helvert
Tilburg University
Department of Language and Literature
P.O. Box 90153
5000 LE TILBURG
The Netherlands

Roeland van Hout
Tilburg University
as Peter Broeder

Anne-Mieke Janssen - van Dieten
Nijmegen University
as Kees de Bot

Anne Kerkhoff
Tilburg University
as Peter Broeder

Johan Leman
Onthaalcentrum Foyer
Werkhuizenstraat 25
1080 BRUSSELS
Belgium

Ludo Smeekens
Onthaalcentrum Foyer
as Johan Leman

Marc Spoelders
Ghent University
Department of Experimental, Social & Educational Psychology
Henri Dunantstraat 1
9000 GENT
Belgium

Ton Vallen
Tilburg University
as Peter Broeder

Ludo Verhoeven
Tilburg University
as Peter Broeder

Anne Vermeer
Tilburg University
as Peter Broeder

Johan Wijnstra
CITO National Institute for Educational Measurement
P.O. Box 65
6801 MG ARNHEM
The Netherlands

Rachid Zerrouk
Tilburg University
as Peter Broeder